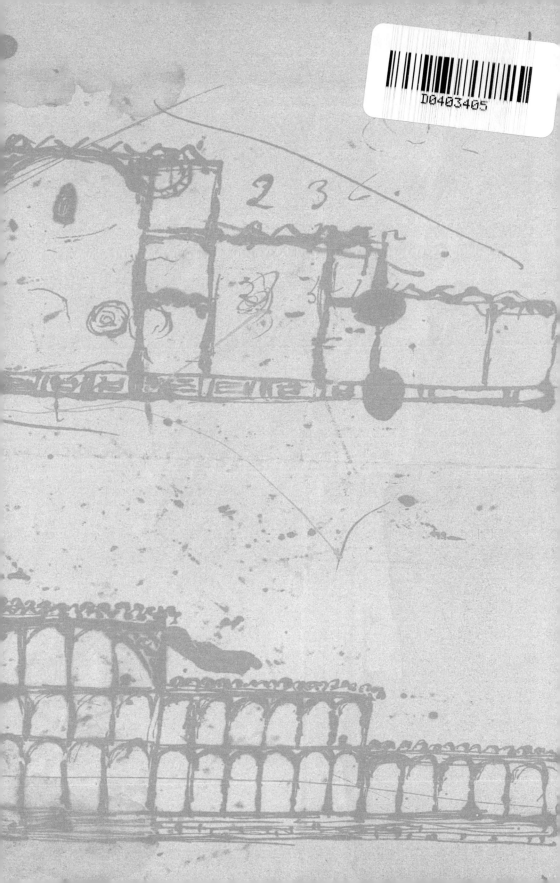

A THING IN DISGUISE

THE VISIONARY LIFE OF
JOSEPH PAXTON

A THING IN DISGUISE

〜

THE VISIONARY LIFE OF
JOSEPH PAXTON

KATE COLQUHOUN

FOURTH ESTATE • *London* and *New York*

First published in Great Britain in 2003 by
Fourth Estate
A Division of HarperCollinsPublishers
77–85 Fulham Palace Road,
London w6 8jb
www.4thestate.com

A catalogue record for this book is available from the British Library

isbn 0-00-714353-2

Designed in Stone Print by Geoff Green at Geoff Green Book Design

Typeset by Palimpsest Book Production Limited, Polmont; Stirlingshire

Printed in Great Britain by Clays Ltd, St Ives plc

She did not have to be told . . . that glass is a thing in disguise, an actor, is not solid at all, but liquid, that an old sheet of glass will not only take on a royal and purplish tinge but will reveal its true liquid nature by having grown fatter at the bottom and thinner at the top, and that even while it is as frail as the ice on a Paramatta puddle, it is stronger under compression than Sydney sandstone, that it is invisible, solid, in short, a joyous and paradoxical thing, as good a material as any to build a life from.

Peter Carey, *Oscar and Lucinda*

For David

CONTENTS

'Plan Map of Chatsworth showing Paxton's additions'

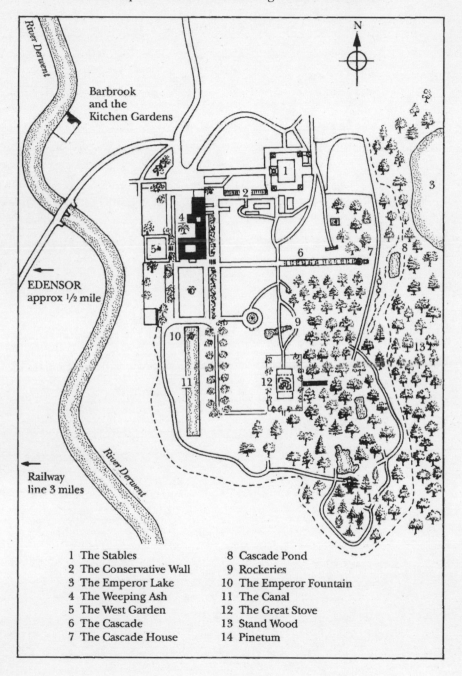

1 The Stables
2 The Conservative Wall
3 The Emperor Lake
4 The Weeping Ash
5 The West Garden
6 The Cascade
7 The Cascade House
8 Cascade Pond
9 Rockeries
10 The Emperor Fountain
11 The Canal
12 The Great Stove
13 Stand Wood
14 Pinetum

PROLOGUE

Just after 7 p.m. on Monday, 30 November 1936, a small fire started under the central transept of the Crystal Palace in south London, the greatest glasshouse ever built.

Preparations for The National Cat Show to begin the next day had just been finalised. A choir was rehearsing in the garden room, birds ruffled their feathers in the aviaries. Otherwise the Palace – with its nave of 1,608 feet and main transept larger than the dome of St Peter's in Rome – was still. Its enormous frosty surface, made up of over 1,500,000 square feet of glass, glittered and, as the moon emerged occasionally from the cloud, it struck the statues in the formal, terraced gardens spreading out below the building. In the surrounding boroughs, families prepared their evening meals and planned their Christmases.

The two Palace nightwatchmen on duty that evening were rather slow on the uptake. Their first call was made to the Penge Fire Brigade just before eight o'clock, by which time the flames could be seen clearly from outside the building and street fire alarms were being activated all over the area. At 7.45 p.m. Police Constable Parkin, passing on a bus, was one of many who also called the brigade. They arrived at 8.03 p.m. with their one, slow fire engine. Beckenham Fire Brigade followed within a couple of minutes, and soon a call went out to all the brigades in London to join them. On the great ridge, a fresh force 5 wind from the north-west fanned the fire like bellows and drove it down the giant south nave. Within 30 minutes, all the central parts of the building were ablaze – wild waves of flame battered relentlessly against the glass and leapt right up to the roof. Encouraged by the wind, the fire devoured the great stage and organ, the 20,000 chairs stored underneath and the floors themselves. It fed on the figures in a waxwork exhibition, the plants and trees, the stuffed animals and the various exhibits. It reached such an astonishing intensity of heat that the iron framework glowed white, buckled and, one by one, the vast glass panes began to explode.

As armies of fire fighters and fire engines with their bells clanging arrived from all over London, the practising choir was evacuated, the exotic birds in the aviaries freed from their cages to fly up into the smoke and take their chances. The gas company worked fast to dig a trench to cut off the main gas supply. Air forced through the organ pipes caused it to groan accompaniment. Motor pumps and turntable ladders were set up on the wide parade. Precariously balanced firemen turned scores of hoses on the fire and the new hose-lorry of the London Fire Brigade, which could reel out $1\frac{1}{2}$ miles of hose at a speed of 15 miles an hour, was used for the first time after being demonstrated only the afternoon before. However, the brigade could do little but delay the inevitable. High on the hill the water pressure was simply not strong enough. Using the five million gallons of water available in the upper reservoir, still the hoses had negligible effect. Just short of an hour after the fire began, the entire building was in flames and the firemen had to retreat to 100 feet beyond the glowing mass.

Clouds of smoke stretched for miles. An exaggerated, orange glow took over the sky. It was seen in eight counties – as far as Devil's Dyke near Brighton, about 50 miles away – causing hundreds of thousands of people to converge on the high ground of the South Downs at Epsom and on Hampstead Heath across the Thames. Tens of thousands more swarmed by every means to the Palace itself, hampering the emergency services in their race to the hill. One newspaper later reported that a parked car, used as a grandstand by hordes of onlookers, collapsed and was found the following day with its tyres burst and its wheels splayed at each corner. Many hundreds of bicycles were deserted as it became impossible to ride or push them through the dense crowds.

Throughout the 82 years it stood on Penge Hill, the Palace and its gardens had become London's most famous resort, renowned above all for its music and for the great organ with its 3,714 speaking pipes. Over one million people visited each year to attend the Saturday festivals,

wander through the historical courts or gaze at Benjamin Waterhouse
Hawkins' giant dinosaur replicas. Here they enjoyed the firework displays,
tightrope walkers and wild animals and cheered at cricket matches and
dirt-track motorbike races. It had become a national monument for old
and young well before it became national property in 1913.

Even the Duke of Kent joined the crowds to watch the fire. From
every window, every tree and every available railing, people were mes-
merised by the destruction of their poor old palace. One enterprising
man in Hillside Road, Streatham, hired out field glasses for twopence
a look. In Parliament, MPs and Lords packed the upstairs committee
rooms and terraces for a view of the angry sky.

The ferocity of the fire was awe-inspiring. By 8.35, the ribs of the
vast central transept roof had become a stark black skeleton against
the white blaze, visibly bent and twisted. With a roar and an explosion of sparks that carried for miles, they collapsed. Just before nine
o'clock, the modular arched girders of the south transept began to fall
like hoops, one by one in a macabre reversal of their construction. The
halls, the great organ, the immense library of Handel Festival music
were gone. The vast stone steps to the terraces were shattered by the
falling face of the transept, molten glass dropped from the great
girders. The firemen were dwarfed against the great bowl of flame, as
streams of molten glass poured down outside the building, forcing
them back. Explosions rocked the neighbourhood as the fire reached
the boilers in the basement, frightening a carpet of rats that streamed
out across the park. The water in the central fountain inside the
building boiled and the fish perished.

At either end of the Palace stood Brunel's magnificent towers, each
282 feet high, built to house the water tanks that fed the elaborate
fountains in the park. As the fire sped south down the building, the
alarm was raised that the south tower was under threat and a great
race was on to save it. The tower was close to the houses on Anerley
Hill and contained 1,200 tons of water and material used by the Baird
Company in their television researches; if it collapsed, it would take
many hundreds of lives with it. Locals were evacuated from their homes
– one newspaper reported that a woman was not allowed to get her
coat but was told to wrap herself in newspaper to keep warm.

By 10.30, the buildings near the south tower had burst into flames
but the tower appeared safe. The fire meantime worked against the
wind and attention now turned to the north tower. By 11.40, flames
were breaking through the roof of the northern end of the building

but, luckily, a large section of the north wing had been lost after the gales of 1861, creating some distance between it and the tower. By midnight the fire was burning itself out with no further threat to Brunel's great engineering achievements. Only the two towers, the south wing and a portion of the north wing's roof still stood, all enveloped in flame, white-hot. By three in the morning, though small fires continued to burn, the firemen packed up – over five hundred of them, more than a third of the city's brigade.

The following day, hoarding was erected to keep out the crowds, though sightseers continued to stream to the hill. The *Daily Sketch* estimated that there had been over a million visitors to the site within the first two days – the number of visitors to the Palace in a normal year. One family travelled overnight from Yorkshire. In the City, shares in Madame Tussaud's, Olympia and White City soared.

The biggest blaze in living memory, caused perhaps by a cigarette stub, perhaps by a broken flue pipe from the boiler in the office at the front of the Palace, had left only a tangled wreck of buckled iron and molten glass, with here and there the broken arm, head or leg of a statue, lodged at fantastic angles. Amazingly, not a single life had been lost. The Christmas shows were cancelled and the booking agents were in chaos. There was concern that a major venue for the May Coronation celebrations for Edward VIII had been lost.

The general manager of the Crystal Palace Company, Sir Henry Buckland, made it clear that he did not believe the Palace would be rebuilt unless the government stepped forward with at least £5 million. He dispelled reports suggesting that the building was fully insured, and confirmed that insurance was only purchased to the value of £110,000. Eighty-four years before, it had cost £1,350,000 to build.

With blind optimism, three days after the disaster, the first sod was cut for a new road-racing circuit on the lower terraces as the burnt-out hulk of the Palace loured in the background. But national and international events were to take precedence that week. As the fire had raged on that Monday night, Madrid had been severely bombed, fuelling concern about the escalating civil war in Spain. On Thursday that week, Edward VIII sparked a constitutional crisis by asking Baldwin to sanction a morganatic marriage to Mrs Simpson. A week later the King had abdicated and Mrs Simpson, the most talked-about woman in the world, was fleeing across France, chased by the world's press.

The weekend after the fire saw the first snows of winter. *The*

Observer called the site 'the very genius of December'. The naked, straggling trees were mimicked by the curious masses of twisted metal, odd twigs of ironwork and fantastic growths of remnant glass. 'The vitrified palace had become a petrified forest.'

Two months later, in *The Architectural Review*, Le Corbusier articulated the essential attraction of the glass building which, by some miracle, had remained as a last witness to an era of faith and daring: he wrote 'one could go there and see it, and feel there how far we have still to go before we can hope to recover that sense of scale which animated our predecessors in all they wrought'. Before the fire, like many millions before him, he had not been able to tear his eyes from 'the spectacle of its triumphant harmony'. His definition of architecture as a way of thinking, of achieving order and of expressing contemporary problems in terms of materials, was epitomised by the achievement of Paxton's miraculous building — the first in the world to be constructed of mass-produced standardised parts and the first to use glass and iron on such a scale. *The Architectural Review* carried its own obituary to the building, describing this 'colossal crinolined birdcage' as no fossilised museum piece, but instead a precept as 'inspiring as the Parthenon . . . as important as Stonehenge'. The building, it said, had liberalised architecture and provided the 'first structural renaissance of architecture since the middle ages'.

↩

Outliving all prophecies of structural disaster, the Victorian Valhalla, Thackeray's 'blazing arch of lucid glass', one of the greatest memorials to Victorian engineering, architectural achievement and popular amusement, had sunk to her knees, all but taking the memory of her creator, Joseph Paxton, with her. Paxton was a gardener first and last but, as a pioneer among Victorian self-made men, he was part of a generation who thought of their own time as one of transition from past to future and who embraced the innovations of the day. His character sprang from the spirit of the age – determined by imagination, unremitting energy, motivation, and enthusiasm – a coupling of enterprise and ambition. Like many of his contemporaries, he appeared to be able to turn his hand to almost any task: an untrained engineer and architect, half-amateur and half-professional, he not only built the most perfect greenhouses in history but became the greatest horticulturist of his day. He was a revolutionary – the Crystal Palace was

one of the most astonishing design and engineering feats of the nineteenth century. With his dogged single-mindedness, Paxton typified
the bold new men with abundant creative energy who grew out of
and formed the age of unparalleled industrial expansion, a quintessentially persevering pragmatist.

Yet, in 1936 a jarring, prophetic note was struck by George Bernard
Shaw. Asked by the *Daily Sketch* what he thought should replace the
Palace, he replied, 'I have no wish to see the Crystal Palace rebuilt.
Queen Victoria is dead at last.' Without its *raison d'être*, the garden's
magnificent terraces and blaze of flowers languished and fell to ruin.
The site has still to be redeveloped. The broken stone steps, one lonely
damaged statue and several sad sphinxes witness only the creep of the
brambles. A television transmitter towers starkly on the ridge. The
sculptured bust of Joseph Paxton, erected in 1869 four years after his
death, turns its back to the forlorn, now empty hill, looking away from
the vanished glory of his intoxicating pleasure dome.

PART 1

❦

EARTH

CHAPTER ONE

No.1.

Milton Bryant is a small and pretty rural village some 50 miles from London, raised slightly above the Bedfordshire plain, modestly protected from change now, as it most certainly was in the early 1800s, by its position on the edge of the Duke of Bedford's Woburn Estate. At that time the village formed part of the collected farms of the Woburn Estate, containing a manor house as well as a public house, a collection of cottages and gravel pits, a village pond and a Saxon church. Half a mile away is the site of a now vanished mansion, Battlesden Park, and a further 2 miles away is the market town of Woburn and its abbey.

On 17 May 1810, aged 50, Joseph Paxton's father William, a farm labourer, was buried there three months before Paxton's seventh birthday. The boy's family were now poorer than ever. Later in life, when he was wealthy and enjoying a fine dinner, he is said to have remarked, 'you never know how much nourishment there is in a turnip until you have had to live on it'.

There are few documents relating to the early years of Paxton's life. It has been suggested that his father was a tenant farmer, rather than a labourer – the disparity in incomes of the two positions was not slight – but his name does not appear in any of the rent books for the Woburn Estates, nor is there any mention of him in the land tax records for the area. William may have farmed his brother's land or he may have laboured at Battlesden Park, where two of his sons subsequently became bailiffs. Whether he farmed or laboured, he worked on land in a county famed for market gardening, where small-holders cropped wheat, barley and some oats.

Joseph Paxton had been born on 3 August 1803, the seventh son and last of the nine children of William and Anne, who had moved to the village by the time their fourth child was baptised. His parents had been married for about 22 years, and both were in their early forties. By 1803, their eldest child – also William – was twenty and soon to be married and it is likely that five or six of the other children still lived at home. They were John (16 when Paxton was born), Henry (14), James (11), Thomas (9), Mary Ann (7) and Sarah (about 3) – all packed into a small labourer's cottage.

It was an auspicious year for a future gardener to be born. In 1803 the Liverpool Botanical Gardens opened and the Horticultural Society was conceived; Joseph Banks sent William Kerr to collect plants in China and Humphry Repton was about to publish his *Observations on the Theory and Practice of Landscape Gardening*. In the wider context of their lives, England stood on the threshold of great political and social upheaval. On the one hand, the French Revolution of 1789 had heralded democracy; on the other, Georgian aristocracy were still pursuing their lives of privilege. The demand for universal suffrage would grow in fervour right up to and beyond the First Reform Act of 1832, but now the transition from a feudal and agricultural order to a democratic and industrial society was just beginning.

From the start of the Industrial Revolution in the mid-eighteenth century, towns had been growing as labourers moved from the land to work in 'manufactories' with their new power looms, the spinning jenny and, by the latter part of the century, steam power. Demand for new textiles and manufactured products was stimulated by the wars that had raged for years with France and by 1815 many of these factories had become great mills. Later, the demand for iron products for roads, bridges and railways would accelerate the migration as people packed into industrial towns like Manchester, Bradford, Liverpool, Birmingham and Sheffield, swelling them by an average of 50 per cent. The population of England doubled between 1801 and 1850.

By the time Paxton's father died, the distress of agricultural and factory workers alike was growing. The Luddite riots of 1811–12, where the workers' anger was directed not so much at the machines as at the bosses who refused to negotiate with them over pay and conditions, erupted and the perpetrators were, for the most part, deported to Australia. As veterans returned from the French war in

1815, post-war depression and its consequent poverty set in. Crucially, cheap wheat imports were banned by the new Corn Law – a measure which maintained the high price of bread and the increasingly dismal lot of the labourer. By 1816, the price of bread had risen sixteenfold over fifty years.

In the countryside these radical changes were less obvious, though its economic structure was changing, too. The French wars had raised the cost of food and in 1803 many potato crops failed. So there were more people and less food, a distress compounded by the enclosure system, which had begun at the end of the previous century, and which meant that labourers were no longer able to use common land to grow vegetables, forage for firewood or graze animals. Wages were not increased to compensate for the loss of these auxiliary resources – so that, earning only seven or eight shillings a week, most labouring families were subsisting on a diet of tea, potatoes, some cheese and bread. Yet the pace, if not the quality, of life in the country was still broadly as it had been for centuries. Nothing travelled faster than a galloping horse and rural life followed the traditional agricultural calendar of Valentine's Day, May Day, Summer Harvest, the village feast, hiring-fairs at Michaelmas, Guy Fawkes, late-November seeding and Christmas. Only rarely did events of national importance punctuate their rhythm: in 1814, when Napoleon was sent to Elba, there was mass celebration in Woburn, where houses were decorated with oak boughs and flowers and there was street feasting.

∽

There are several differing reports of Paxton's schooling. Given the death of his father and the consequent poverty of his family, it is fairly extraordinary that he made it to school at all. Education did not become a requirement by law until as late as 1880; farmers generally opposed the few free schools available, preferring their children to work in the fields for a few pennies, and conservative opinion considered popular education dangerous and undesirable. Some churches introduced Sunday Schools since this was often a child's only free day, but weekday teaching for the working classes was rare.

There was no school in Milton Bryant until 1853, but there was a free school for boys at Woburn, started by the 1st Duke of Bedford. In 1808 it was rebuilt, reorganised and run on a voluntary subscription. According to a report in 1818, it was 'large, of stone, three storey in

height, containing two large classrooms besides many other apartments'. Working-class schools like this functioned on the pretty disastrous monitor system in which apprentice teachers passed on, by rote,
what they may have rather ineffectually learned themselves, while one
master supervised the entire school. Few working-class children had
more than two or three years of desultory education, and few could do
more than write their names.

There are no records of pupils at the Woburn school but it seems
likely that Paxton attended, however intermittently, making the long
walk from his village twice a day, since he could certainly read and
write proficiently by the time he joined the Horticultural Society in
London in 1823. In 1808, the Duke of Bedford reported to his friend
the Liberal peer Samuel Whitbread that there were 104 boys enrolled
there, of whom about 80 attended regularly; the hours were 9 a.m. to
midday and 2 p.m. to 5 p.m. The school was divided into eight classes
run by monitors and assistants, with one supervising master; the first
class of boys were taught the alphabet by printing on a sand desk,
repeated twelve times in a day, and the second class – in which the
boys were streamed according to ability – wrote their alphabet on
slates and learned words and syllables as well as spelling from cards.
In subsequent years the boys learned arithmetic and were allowed to
write in copy books once they had mastered joined writing; the monitors read from the Scriptures, while the boys sat in silence with their
hands on their laps, and in the afternoon, Isaac Watts' hymns were
sung.

Paxton's first job in a garden was about to be offered. The 6th
Duke of Bedford was one of the most important patrons of horticulture (the science of the culture of plants). His garden was his
great love and had become a centre for innovation and experimental
gardening. Designed by Repton – the most fashionable landscape
designer of his day, who worked widely in Bedfordshire between
1804–9 – the Duke's garden had begun to receive some of the botanic
treasures being introduced by collectors from around the world.
More significantly for Paxton, in 1808 the immensely rich and
possibly insane* Sir Gregory Osborne Page Turner also employed
Repton to lay out his gardens at Battlesden Park. The elaborate series

* He was regularly in court to determine his state of mind. In December 1823 he
  was found to be of 'unsound mind', rather than a lunatic. The jurors heard that
  hundreds of clocks and watches were found scattered all over the house in
  Bedfordshire, in a serious state of disarray. *Morning Herald*, 13 and 20 Dec. 1823.

of watercolours of the completed garden which he commissioned from George Shepherd shows iron conservatories, luxuriant flower gardens and great groups of trees.

Paxton's eldest brother, William, had become the bailiff and super-intendent of the estates at Battlesden Park on a salary of £100 a year. In 1816, when his youngest brother was fifteen, William took on two leases there. The first, in March, was for 28 acres of meadow or pasture at a cost of £65 a year and included an understanding that he would take on a servant and a horse at his own expense, but keep all rents and profits generated on the land. The second, in December, formed an agreement to rent the entire garden ground for four years at a cost of £16 16s. This comprised 'four pieces of garden ground used as kitchen garden, fruit garden, old orchard and nursery, pond garden and house garden', about two and a half acres in total. Also a cottage, 'but not the pleasure garden nor the hot houses or plants and ponds thereon'. The fruit garden alone was enormous: filled with peach, nectarine, apricot, damson, cherry, plum, pear and apple trees as well as raspberries, currants and gooseberries.

The running of Battlesden had become something of a Paxton family business. His brother, Thomas, now ran the home farm at Potsgrove (part of the Battlesden Estate); he leased land from Sir Gregory as well as acting as his land agent, successfully occupying 415 acres and employing 21 labourers. Paxton probably went to live and work with William as a gardening boy at Battlesden from around the date of these leases when he would have been fifteen or sixteen. In gardens filled with fruit trees, flowers and, since there were hothouses, presumably exotic and tender plants as well, he was first introduced to the wonders of botany and horticulture and began to learn the rudiments of his trade. Paxton's granddaughter, Violet Markham, suggests that William treated him very severely and he ran away to Essex where he was taken in by a Quaker, who encouraged him to return to Battlesden. It is impossible to substantiate this story, though it is clear that later in life Paxton, far from hating William, remained fond of his much older brother, taking time out of hectic schedules to visit him and his family.

Aged fifteen, Paxton left his brother in order to work at the estate of Woodhall near Walton in Hertfordshire. The house had been bought by Samuel Smith in 1801 and Paxton was to work there under the charge of William Griffin. He was lucky. Here was an eighteenth-century park and woodland, with new gardens lately built around the house, run by an ardent horticulturist and reputed fruiterer. Griffin was the author of a treatise on the 'Culture of the Pine Apple' as well as a paper on the management of grapes in vineries; he was a part of the coalescing horticultural establishment and his name appears in 1824 among the first subscribers to the new Horticultural Society Gardens at Chiswick. A professional with a reputation for giving thorough and kindly instruction to the young men who worked with him, it is entirely possible that Griffin filled Paxton's head with stories of the new society in London and that he encouraged the boy to think of a time when he might apply to them for a position in one of their gardens.

After an apprenticeship of about three years, the young Paxton was attracted back to Battlesden Park and the gardens, where he found himself in charge of the excavation of a large lake called the New Fish Pond. Great amounts of earth would have been removed by hand and in wheelbarrows, relying largely on observation and reasoning rather than any engineering calculus. By 1823 Sir Gregory was already showing signs of the insanity into which he would soon collapse, and was declared bankrupt with liabilities of over £100,000 – the entire contents of his house would be sold at auction by Christie's the following year. Paxton had witnessed the sort of upper-class profligacy that would later find its echo in his patron, the 6th Duke of Devonshire. The house and gardens at Battlesden have not survived, but this new fish pond, with its island, bulrushes and the company of swans, can still be found today, surrounded only by fields. Its construction provided Paxton with experience he would later call upon as he undertook huge earthworks at Chatsworth.

On 14 April 1823, aged 62, Paxton's mother died and was buried in the village church at Milton Bryant. One month later Paxton's uncle Thomas followed her. Paxton's thoughts turned to London and the chance of advancement through the profession of gardening. He was almost 20 and, with the incarceration of the lunatic Sir Gregory, he was out of a job. Some records suggest that he obtained work first in the gardens at Wimbledon House, leased by the Duke of Somerset, and it is certain that his brother James was a gardener there. Perhaps it was here that sibling disaffection raised its head. Many years later the Duke of Devonshire wrote to his gardener that it would take only one word from Paxton to secure James a position as gardener and bailiff to Lady Dover, yet the Duke imagined that Paxton would not like to recommend his brother.

It has also been suggested that at around this point Paxton went to work in the gardens of the famous nurserymen Messrs Lee and Kennedy in London, though there are no records to support this. Whatever the case, by November 1823 Paxton had turned his attention to the new gardens of the Horticultural Society in Chiswick, and in so doing, secured the direction of his own future.

CHAPTER TWO

Side by side with the political and social revolutions sweeping Europe ran a cultural revolution most keenly associated with the growth of science. Interest in plants and gardening, which had been developing throughout the eighteenth century, leapt into a new life which some have called the fourth, garden revolution. From the Romans to John Tradescant in the 1620s, new plants had been arriving in England regularly if slowly. Tradescant himself had brought the apricot from Algiers as well as the first lilac. But from the middle of the eighteenth century plants were coming from all corners of the globe, predominantly from South America, the Cape and, later, North America. Between 1731 and 1789 the number of plants in cultivation increased over fivefold to around 5,000. The thirst for information about new plants was becoming insatiable and driving a need for new publications. Philip Miller at the Botanical Gardens in Chelsea then dominated the gardening world with his massively popular *Gardener's Dictionary* of 1731 and, at Kew, William Aiton's first full catalogue of plants, *Hortus Kewensis*, was first published in 1789.

Initially, new trees such as the tulip tree and magnolia, as well as hugely popular plants like the first American lily, *Lilium superbum* (which first flowered in 1738) were shipped back to England mainly by settlers. By the later part of the century, voyages of exploration such as Cook's three expeditions between 1768 and 1779 were unearthing unimagined botanical riches[*] set to transform the English garden and the role of the gardener in it. So many new plants were arriving in Britain, that Miller saw the species at Chelsea increase five-fold during his tenure alone. On 1 February 1787, the first periodical in England devoted to scientific horticulture, *The Botanical Magazine or Flower Garden Displayed*, edited by William Curtis, was published aimed foursquare at the rich and fashionable who had begun to cultivate exotics with passion. Designed 'for the use of such ladies, gentlemen and gardeners as wish to become scientifically acquainted with the plants they cultivate', it was expensively priced at one shilling in order to cover the costs of hand-coloured plates. It was nevertheless hugely popular and provided yet more stimulus to the culture of ornamental plants.

The improvement of estates and gardens among the wealthy classes had become an established vogue since Lancelot 'Capability' Brown started the rage in the mid-eighteenth century; garden-making and tree-planting were pursued on a scale never witnessed in England before. Expensive to create but cheap to maintain, landscaped parks were an indication of social rank and power, since the use of good farming land for a pleasure ground was, indeed, a demonstration of riches. Walls and formal flower beds were swept away, substituted by great stands of trees and, often, a 'ha-ha' so that from a house of any pretension the vista was uninterrupted and it appeared that nature itself reigned. All of this pleased Horace Walpole, who declared that 'all nature is a garden', and led Thomas Whately to announce in his book, *Observations on Modern Gardening* (1770), that ground, wood, water and rocks were the only four elements needed in any grand garden design. The fashion for visiting the great houses and gardens of England grew, with Stourhead and Longleat in Wiltshire and Chatsworth in Derbyshire the most popular.

At the end of the century, Brown's heir, Humphry Repton, began to reintroduce the 'romantic' back into the garden, with terraces in the foreground near to the house, as well as some flower beds and specialised flower gardens for roses or for the new North American plants that intrepid explorers were now sending back to England. Gardeners were becoming a more important and senior part of the household staff and professional nurserymen began to thrive.

By 1778 Kew Gardens, begun in 1759 for the Dowager Princess

---

[*] Thus 'Botany Bay' outside Sydney, Australia. Plants discovered on these journeys included the *Banksia*, *Grevillea*, *Protea*, *Acacia* and *Ficus*.

Augusta, was rapidly expanding under George III and its first unofficial president, Joseph Banks, who was also president of the august
Royal Society. He determined to send men on thrilling adventures to
collect plants from the Cape, the Azores, Spain and Portugal, China,
the West Indies and America, and he ensured that Kew became a centre
of excellence in which botanical science surged forward. The tiger lily,
Lilium tigrinum, sent back from China in 1804, became such a success
that William Aiton, Banks' successor at Kew, was soon distributing
thousands of its bulbs to eager gardeners all over the country.

The rise of horticulture in the nineteenth century paralleled the
expansion of the other natural and material sciences, on a far broader
base than the elite science of the eighteenth century, flourishing as the
middle classes expanded. Commercial nurseries also began to employ
collectors, indicating the growing commercial curiosity in these rare
plants, and, in 1804, *Exotic Botany* by Sir E. J. Smith became a standard and best-selling work as did John Cushings' *The Exotic Gardener*
published a few years later.

The creation of a horticultural society was the idea of John Wedgwood,
son of the potter, who in 1803 had invited several of his friends – including
Joseph Banks, William Forsyth from the Royal Gardens at Kensington
and St James's, William Townsend Aiton and others – to a meeting at
the house of Hatchard, the famous bookseller in Piccadilly. There,
Wedgwood presented the idea of forming a new national society for the
improvement and co-ordination of horticultural activities.

A prospectus for the society was written, classifying horticulture
as a practical science and dividing plants into the useful and the ornamental (with the useful taking priority). The necessity of good plant
selection was stressed, as was the design and construction of
glasshouses, and the society expressed its aim to standardise the
naming of plants. It would lease a room from the Linnean Society in
Regent Street, where it would meet on the first and third Tuesdays
in each month, providing a forum for the encouragement of system-
atic inquiry and an environment in which papers could be read, information shared, plants exhibited and distributed to interested Fellows
and medals presented.

It developed along increasingly organised lines. From 1807 its
Transactions were bound together and published, joining the growing
volume of literature available. In 1817, one of the finest English
nurseries, Conrad Loddiges & Sons in Hackney – which, according to
John Claudius Loudon, had the best collection of green and hothouse

exotics of any commercial garden – printed its own catalogue called *The Botanical Cabinet.* Horticulture stood at the doorstep of what has been called the great age of English periodicals but these publications were priced beyond the reach of the practical gardener and, for now, periodicals were made freely available to labourers and gardeners in the society's library in Regent Street.

With so many new varieties pouring into Britain, horticulture was under pressure to grow and mature. As early as the 1760s, Philip Miller had experimented with different methods of plant acclimatisation and found that many tender plants would thrive outside the greenhouse.* Many, however, would not, and these were often the rarest. The first free-standing glasshouses, using iron and wood instead of brick and stone, were emerging, themselves demanding further experiments designed to optimise the stability of the structures, the light they admitted, and the most efficient forms of heating. In the early decades of the nineteenth century, the horticultural journalist and revolutionary, John Claudius Loudon, invented, among many novelties, a form of roof design that he called 'ridge and furrow' – a zigzag glass construction which he noted maximised the access of light and therefore heat, particularly in the early morning and late evening when the sun was low in the sky. Loudon, however, maintained a preference for using glass in the more normal, flat construction.

Loudon's glasshouse breakthrough came in 1816, when he patented a flexible wrought-iron glazing bar which could be bent in any direction without reducing its strength, making curvilinear, even conical, glazing possible.† It was one of the first indications of the future use of iron for its strength and flexibility and sparked a new mania for building glasshouses in iron for their light and elegant appearance. Innovator though he was, Loudon's suggestions were not always quite so practical. Only a year later, he envisaged a day when animals and birds would be introduced into the different hothouse climates, along with 'examples of the human species from the different countries imitated, habited in their particular costumes . . . who may serve as gardeners or curators of the different productions'.

The new Horticultural Society involved itself energetically in the

---

*   Careful descriptions of Miller's experiments are found in his *Dictionary*, including new methods of forcing apricots and cherries by nailing the trees on to a screen of boards, glazing the south face and heating the north back with a hotbed.

†   Though the Bessemer-Siemens process of 'mild' steel manufacture which made large-scale production possible was not commercially available until the 1860s.

general debate over the design of new greenhouses, stimulating more designs from new manufacturers like Richards and Jones (Patent Metallic Hot House Manufacturers) and Thomas Clarke, who took his first orders in 1818 and soon supplied the Queen at Osborne and Frogmore. The Loddiges nursery had, by 1820, a huge hothouse 80 feet long, 60 feet wide and 40 feet high, heated by steam, and built according to Loudon's design.

These were the heady early days of 'modern' gardening and there was a pressing need for change and development – a new science was flowering and things were moving fast. The florists' clubs of the eighteenth century had proliferated, sparking the competitive cultivation and improvement of certain species, most especially tulips, pinks, auriculas from the Pyrenees, hyacinths, carnations, anemones and ranunculas, but also lilies from Turkey, fritillaries from France, marigolds from Africa, nasturtiums and pansies. Where others had failed for years, by 1812, Loddiges had began to cultivate orchids commercially. Miller mentions only two or three tropical orchids in his *Dictionary* but 1818 marked a milestone – the first orchid, *Cattleya labiata*, flowered in cultivation, sparking a fashionable mania for orchids and orchid collection by the seriously wealthy throughout the following two decades.

With no wars to finance, income tax dropped to two pence in the pound during the 1820s so that domestic gardening was encouraged in the middle classes by the availability of disposable income, and by inevitable social competition. 1822 witnessed two further horticultural milestones. The first was the publication of John Claudius Loudon's *Encyclopaedia of Gardening*, the Mrs Beeton for gardeners. Its two volumes were consulted compulsively by garden owners and their gardeners alike. It was stuffed not only with everything you might want to know about individual plants and their cultivation, greenhouses and methods of forcing, but with practical information like 'leave your work and tools in an orderly manner . . . Never perform any operation without gloves on your hands that you can do with gloves on . . .'

The second was the commencement of new experimental gardens by the Horticultural Society on 33 acres of land leased from the 6th Duke of Devonshire at Chiswick House, Turnham Green, on the outskirts of London. After the deaths of George III and of Joseph Banks, the Botanical Gardens at Kew had begun to languish under William Aiton and his son William Townsend Aiton, so with nothing of real substance to rival them – the Royal Botanic Society was not founded until 1838 – the gardens at Chiswick confirmed the Horticultural Society's position of enormous influence and prestige.

Chiswick was a suburb full of market gardens. The area north of the Thames, with its abundance of water due to the high water-table, had been in use since the late eighteenth century for intensive nursery cultivation to meet the needs of the growing population. For seven miles, land on each side of the road from Kensington through Hammersmith and Chiswick and on to Brentford and Twickenham, was dominated by fruit gardens and vegetable cultivation.

Chiswick House was built in the two years from 1727 by Lord Burlington, assisted by his protégé, the architect, painter, artist and landscape gardener William Kent, in the English Palladian style he pioneered. A small jewel, it was an exquisite temple to the arts, filled with the earl's collection of paintings and architectural drawings, and conceived as a garden with a villa rather than the other way around – a carefully considered work of both architecture and horticulture where the cult of taste was celebrated* and a new national style of gardening was born. The gardens were classically ornamental, an example of Kent's earliest experiments in the management of water and the grouping of trees. He converted a brook into a canal lake, and scattered Italian sculpture throughout the landscape of formal hedged avenues, pools, natural river banks and wide lawns. The cedars of Lebanon were reputed to be among the earliest introduced to England. Contemporaries claimed that this was the birthplace of the 'natural' style of landscaping, that this was where Kent 'leapt the fence' and saw that all nature was a garden.

When the 5th Duke of Devonshire inherited the house, he commissioned Wyatt to add two substantial wings to the building and, in 1813, the 6th Duke, wealthy enough to indulge his passion for building and for horticulture, gilded the velvet-hung staterooms and commissioned Lewis Kennedy to create a formal Italian garden. Samuel Ware – later the architect of the Burlington Arcade – built a 300-foot long conservatory in the formal garden, backed by a brick wall, with a central glass and wood dome. In time, it would be filled with the

---

* Later, in a letter to the 6th Duke on 4 June 1836 (Devonshire Collections; 6th Duke's Group No. 3512), Miss Mary Russel Mitford says she accompanied Wordsworth to the house – 'that fine poet . . . who while illustrating all that is charming in natural scenery has yet so true and cultivated a taste for painting and architecture, never surely so triumphantly conjoined as at Chiswick House'.

recently introduced camellias which, along with the exotic animals, captured the very height of Regency fashion.*

In 1820 the Duke's sister Harriet wrote to her sister Georgiana that their brother was 'improving Chiswick, opening and airing it: a few kangaroos, who if affronted will rip up anyone as soon as look at him, elks, emus, and other pretty sportive death-dealers playing about near it', and 'On Saturday we drove down to Chiswick . . . The lawn is beautifully variegated with an Indian Bull and his spouse and goats of all colours and dimensions. I own I think it a mercy that one of the kangaroos has just died in labour, [given] that they hug one to death'. Sir Walter Scott recorded in his diary that Chiswick House 'resembled a picture of Watteau . . . the scene was dignified by the presence of an immense elephant, who, under the charge of a groom, wandered up and down, giving the air of Asiatic pageantry to the entertainment'.

In mid-July 1821 a lease was agreed between the Duke of Devonshire and the Horticultural Society for the society to take on a substantial amount of land at Chiswick House, previously let to market gardeners, for 60 years at the cost of £300 a year. The agreement included provision for a private door into the gardens for the duke's use. An appeal went out to the Fellows of the society for voluntary subscriptions – the king subscribed £500 and the Duke of Devonshire £50.

As the first Garden Committee Reports show, exhibition, instruction and supply were the society's clear priorities. Fruit cultivation, then culinary vegetables, took the lead, with ornamental and hothouse plants following. All existing species and new plants would be 'subjected to various modes of treatment in order to ascertain that by which they can be made most effectively useful and productive'. An 'authentic nomenclature' was to be established, plants would be clearly tagged with their names, and catalogues of the fruit and vegetables would be produced.† Grafts and buds from fruit trees would be sent to all nurserymen in order to ensure that they were selling the true plant. It was stated of the fruits that 'at no period, nor under any circumstances, has such a collection been formed' and there were hundreds of varieties of

---

*   The Italian garden, the conservatory and many of the original camellia plants still exist at Chiswick House Gardens, London, W4. The first book on the subject of the camellia appeared in 1819, *Monograph on the genus Camellia* by Samuel Curtis, and listed 29 varieties being grown in England.

†   The catalogues were consistently delayed by other work, and the fruit tree catalogue was finally finished in 1827, listing an astonishing 3,825 varieties.

vegetables, including 435 lettuce types alone. Very quickly, the society established a collection of over 1,200 roses. In addition, there were large plantings of peonies, phlox and iris and 27 different lilacs in all colours. Dahlias, geraniums and clematis were particularly prized and pansies were beginning to thrive in cultivation.

One of the society's objectives was the liberal distribution of its plants and knowledge at home and abroad. It saw one of its roles as increasing demand on nurseries by awarding medals to plants of outstanding merit. At the start of the following year, a young man who would become the first Professor of Botany at the new University College of London, a pioneer orchidologist and botanist and whose own fortunes would later be linked with those of Paxton, joined the Society as Assistant Secretary to the garden, at £120 a year. John Lindley was the son of a Norfolk farmer. At 23 he was only four years older than Paxton.

From the outset, the society clearly saw itself as providing a national school for young, unmarried men to learn the craft of horticulture. In its first report of 1823 it laid down that 'the head gardeners will be permanent servants of the Society, but the under gardeners and labourers employed, will be young men, who, having acquired some previous knowledge of the first rudiments of the art, will be received into the establishment, and having been duly instructed in the various practices of each department, will become entitled to recommendation from the Officers of the Society to fill the situations of Gardeners in private or other establishments'.

The society became the hub of horticultural activity. From 1823 the gardens were open to its expanding membership and their guests in the afternoons; all had to sign a visitors' book and be escorted by under-gardeners who were required to answer any questions about the plants. It was expressly forbidden to take cuttings or any other specimens, or to tip the gardeners.

⁓

On 13 November 1823, Paxton entered the Horticultural Society's gardens as a labourer. He had been quick off the mark. The first time that his name appears in any authentic surviving document is in *Handwriting Book for Undergardeners and Labourers* for 1822–9 as only the fifth entrant. In his neat hand he falsified his birthdate and there-fore his age, writing 'at the time of my entering in the Gardens of the

Horticultural Society, my father was dead – he was formerly a farmer at Milton Bryant in Bedfordshire where I was born in the year 1801. At the age of fifteen my attention was turned to gardening . . .'

Always being the youngest in a large family, perhaps he thought twenty-two a more convincing and responsible age than twenty. He does seem to have gone out of his way to make it appear that he started work at the age of fifteen, with the implied benefit of a further two years' schooling. This lie, in the context of his life taken as a whole, was out of character. Yet, he was driven by an extraordinary new opportunity and the minor detail of the year of his birth was not going to stand in his way. So he took his place alongside Thomas McCann from Ireland, the first entrant in January 1822, Patrick Daly, who had joined on 6 October, and the various sons of shoemakers, seedsmen, stone-cutters and farmers. All were paid around fourteen shillings a week.*

It is not entirely clear in which part of the gardens Paxton was initially employed, but with the library at his disposal he set about a rigorous regime of self-education, unaware that his future lay on the other side of the fence, with the owner of the camellias and kangaroos. From November, a prodigious amount of work was needed on the arboretum, a walled area of about seven and a half acres intended to have a specimen of every kind of hardy tree and shrub capable of enduring the English climate. This was a priority for the society and necessitated the employment of many temporary labourers in the gardens. The Council Meeting Notebooks show that Patrick Daly was, in fact, taken on as only a temporary labourer, probably in the arboretum, that he later showed promise and was retained despite there being no obvious vacancies for him. Was Paxton, too, employed initially only temporarily? Did he hold his breath for those first few months in the tense hope of a permanent position?

During his first year at the gardens there was much to do: the kitchen garden walls were built, along with a pit ground for melons and pines (pineapples). The number of imported plants increased

---

*   In the second issue of Loudon's *Gardener's Magazine*, he compares these wages to those of an illiterate bricklayer who would earn around five to seven shillings a day, whereas 'a journeyman gardener who has gone through a course of practical geometry and land surveying, has a scientific knowledge of botany, and has spent his days and his nights in reading books connected to his profession, gets no more than two shillings or two and sixpence a day.' While the Horticultural Society, he said, was humanely paying fourteen to eighteen shillings a week, an average London nursery was paying only ten shillings. Loudon regularly lobbied for increased wages for garden labourers and gardeners.

dramatically, partly because of the development of better methods of plant transportation – put simply, many more specimens arrived in England alive. This was, most certainly for a gardener, the only place to be. Paxton was surrounded by the rare and curious specimens sent by the society's own collectors as well as others – the value in rarity and beauty of the collection was considered greater than any other garden in the world.

Within six months, he had moved to a position as labourer under the management of Mr Donald Munro, the Ornamental Gardener, who was in charge of the new plants. That year, the aspidistra was introduced from China, the fuchsia from Mexico and verbena, petunia and salvia from South America. In 1825 one of the greatest of all the society's plant-hunters, David Douglas, was in the midst of his expedition to the north Pacific coast of America. During the 1820s Douglas introduced over two hundred new plants including mimulus and lupins; he sent *Orchidaceae* which mingled with the exquisite new plants donated by the directors of the East India Company and consuls abroad.

All this hunting created an even greater need for better greenhouses and stoves in which to nurture and cultivate successfully the treasured tropical and subtropical plants. An increasingly technical and complex conversation was being joined by an expanding number of voices. Skill in methods to improve and force fruit and vegetables had been growing in England since the seventeenth century at least – hotbeds for salad vegetables, heated walls to ripen fruit trees, pineapple pits and the like were commonplace. Greenhouses, however, were expensive. Glass was heavily taxed by weight, so that manufacturers made efforts to make it thinner and it became increasingly fragile. There was new experimentation with cast iron and curved frameworks, and the invention of pliable putty had helped reduce the instances of glass fracturing in extreme temperatures. By the 1820s, these new, sophisticated greenhouses were classed into four categories: 'cold' greenhouses; conservatories heated in winter; 'dry stoves' where the temperature would be controlled to a maximum of 85°F during the day and 70°F at night; and the orchid house or 'bark stove' where the temperature was never allowed to drop below 70°F and might rise to 90°F on a summer's day.

John Loudon remarked that the conservatory at Chiswick was beautifully ornamental but extremely gloomy inside. He probably hated the thick wooden sash bars, always preferring iron. The results of his own experiments with glasshouse design were published in 1824 in

The Greenhouse Companion hard on the heels of his *Encyclopaedia.* Previously he had been an advocate of heating glasshouses with fires and smoke flues, but now he was experimenting with high-pressure steam, while others, recognising that steam could too easily wound precious plants, were considering heating systems which consisted of the circulation of hot water through pipes. During the 1820s and long into the 1830s periodicals would be inundated with articles and advice on new kinds of greenhouses and heating methods.

A year after joining the society, Paxton was offered the chance to apply for promotion as an under-gardener back in the arboretum and by the end of March 1825 his three-month trial period was completed satisfactorily and his wages increased to eighteen shillings a week.

It was an auspicious time to work in the arboretum. Only a handful of evergreens were cultivated in England – including the yew, silver fir, Norway spruce and the cedar of Lebanon planted widely in the eighteenth century by Capability Brown – but now the collection of conifers sent by Douglas from North America was ensuring his place in garden history. Among his many discoveries, he sent back seeds of the Sitka spruce – beginning a passion for these huge evergreen novelties – the Monterey pine and, of course, the eponymous Douglas fir (*Picea sitchensis*) which could grow to over 300 feet. Another of the society's collectors, James Macrae, sent seeds of the monkey puzzle tree[*] – the favourite of the later Victorians – from his travels in Brazil, Chile, Galapagos and Peru in the two years from 1824. Loudon calculated that 89 species of tree and shrub were introduced to England in the sixteenth century, about 130 in the seventeenth, by the eighteenth century over 440, whereas in the first 30 years alone of the nineteenth century around 700 species were brought to England. Put in perspective, in 1500 perhaps 200 kinds of plants were actively cultivated in England, whereas by 1839 that figure had risen to over 18,000. Of those plants, evergreens were to transform the English garden and landscape, until now dominated by deciduous native trees.

There was progress elsewhere in the gardens, too. During 1825 Paxton would have witnessed a tank sunk in the pit to supply water to the fruit garden, as well as the building of new carpenters' sheds and many new types of glasshouse including one with double lights for the tropical plants, a five-light melon pit, a new pine house and a new vinery between the peach house and the curvilinear fruit house. Alongside his

[*]   *Araucaria araucana* or Chilean pine, like the fern and the aspidistra a great Victorian symbol, and one that Paxton and the Duke did much to popularise.

work in the arboretum, he also embarked on a complete record and description of the most notable dahlias in the society's collection.

'Dahlia mania' had swept through the English gardening community at the end of the first decade of the century. First introduced in 1789 by the Marchioness of Bute, it had been lost until rediscovered in 1804. Within ten years, it was being cultivated in most plant collections and by the 1830s, dahlia frenzy approached that for the tulip in the seventeenth century. Conceived as a paper to be presented at one of the society's meetings, Paxton's initial work marked the beginning of a passion for the fashionable, intricate and variously formed species that would culminate in his only monograph in later life.

⌒

By 1826, England was teetering on the brink of modernisation. The criminal code had been modified and a new police force created in London by Sir Robert Peel. A year earlier, Stephenson had built his three engines for the first passenger train between Stockton and Darlington; his 'Rocket' was only three years off. This was also the year in which the Society for the Diffusion of Useful Knowledge was founded, promoting adult education for workers in cities through Mechanics' Institutes – to all intents and purposes adult night schools with libraries. These establishments were at the absolute vanguard of the notion of self-improvement and self-education even though there was still little chance of moving through the ranks. By the late 1850s and 1860s, 'self-help' would become a ruling preoccupation of the working and middle classes.

In horticulture there was a further, important development. Just as the first 'modern' strawberry (rather than the small wild woodland variety) was being cultivated, that passionate reformer and obstinate workaholic, John Loudon, launched the first periodical aimed at the practical gardener. It was the first popular magazine of its kind devoted exclusively to horticultural subjects, with the stated intention 'to raise the intellect and the character of those engaged in this art'. In his first issue, he noted the transformation of taste over the previous twenty years, recognising that landscape gardening had given way 'first to war and agriculture, and since the peace, to horticulture'.

Initially a quarterly, Loudon's *Gardener's Magazine* sold 4,000 of its first number in just a handful of days despite its five shilling price. It was different, packed with general advice and, in order to hold the price down, it eschewed colour plates and copper and steel engravings in favour of cruder wood engravings. Along with several other Loudon magazines, it was to continue until his death in 1843, criticising inefficiency in horticulture, visiting and reporting in detail on public and private gardens, reviewing contemporary books and periodicals, publishing nurserymen's catalogues and price lists as well as reporting on the activities of the Horticultural Society. Every issue described the plethora of new gadgets becoming available to gardeners and was stuffed with articles on the widest range of subjects – from the use of green vegetable manure to the washing of salads or the method of setting the fruit of the granadilla. Paxton would later use many of the ideas initially published in this revolutionary magazine as a springboard for his own innovations.

Loudon used the introduction of the first issue to discuss three points closest to his heart. First, was the love of gardening he saw among all ages and all ranks of society. Secondly, he both praised the Horticultural Society for its encouragement and development of the science, and disparaged what he saw as Joseph Sabine's mismanagement of the establishment – a criticism he would maintain doggedly until the society was reformed in 1830. Thirdly and perhaps most importantly, Loudon addressed the issue of improvement in the education of gardeners, pointing out that as the status of head gardener had risen, so had the need for development in their general instruction. This was a theme that was to continue throughout the life of the publication.

Interest in the gardens and the society was flourishing. Curiosity for new plants continued to grow so fast that, in 1827, the society held its first 'fête' in the garden. Only a couple of years later, over 1,500 carriages waited in a line extending from Hyde Park Corner along Hammersmith Road for the doors to open at nine o'clock, despite torrential rain. Paxton, meanwhile, witnessed the latest architectural and engineering technologies, examined the plants and techniques in the various departments, and spent time in the society's library with the latest catalogues. He found himself in good company – the authority and distinction of the gardens were attracting labourers from some of the largest estates in England and abroad.

⌒

In 1826, Paxton was offered a position that was to settle the course of his future entirely. 'On April 22nd Joseph Paxton, under gardener in the arboretum, left, recommended a place . . .' These Council Meeting Notes of 4 May 1826 betray nothing of the fact that this was a defining moment in the young man's life. He had been offered the position of Superintendent of the Gardens at Chatsworth – to all intents and purposes head gardener at one of the grandest estates in England and for one of the richest aristocrats in the land, the 6th Duke of Devonshire. Paxton was to be paid £1 5s a week, or £65 a year, and live in a cottage in the kitchen gardens.

The immensely rich George Spencer Cavendish, 6th Duke of Devonshire, had apparently encountered Paxton as he let himself into the gardens through the gate from Chiswick House. Son of the celebrated Georgiana, the 6th Duke had inherited his title when he was 21, in the year after Paxton's father died. With it, came estates comprising nearly 200,000 acres of land and the stately houses of Chatsworth and Hardwick Hall in Derbyshire, Lismore Castle in County Wexford, Ireland, Bolton Abbey in the West Riding and three great London palaces – Chiswick House and, in Mayfair, Devonshire House and Burlington House. With an inherited income of over £70,000 Hart, as he was known to his family, had the world at his feet.

At 36 years old, the Duke was unmarried, despite being the most eligible bachelor in England. He was partially deaf, and of a 'sweet disposition'. He was, according to Prince Puckler-Muskau, attending one of his parties in 1826, 'a King of fashion and elegance . . .' No one could excel, and few could rival him, in position. He was clever and comical, sensitive, extravagant, nervous and, despite throwing many of the country's best parties, somewhat lonely.

Given his particularly Regency interest in new, valuable and exotic plants, he is likely to have sought out the labourers in the ornamental garden, where Paxton was occupied in tending the new plants and training the creepers. In Paxton he found a straightforward youth, self-effacing as well as confident, passionate about his plants, full of energy, bright and patient. He was young and unproven but the Duke was without a gardener at Chatsworth and he acted impulsively – the appointment is not even noted in the detailed daily journal he kept for many years. He was anxious to be off. On 7 April the King had approved of his replacing Wellington as Extraordinary Ambassador to the Court of St James for the coronation of Tsar Nicholas I in Russia. Wellington was needed at home and though the Duke was a liberal Whig rather than a staunch Tory like

Wellington, his wealth and position in England and his close friend-ship with Nicholas ensured that his lobbies for the role were successful.

On 8 May, two weeks after leaving the society as a Fellow – and not yet quite 23 – Paxton collected his instructions from Devonshire House and took the coach to Chatsworth. Together, in an unlikely but astonishingly fruitful pairing, he and the Duke would make the gardens at Chatsworth famous again after almost fifty years of neglect.

CHAPTER THREE

6

I left London by the Comet Coach for Chesterfield, and arrived at Chatsworth at half past four o'clock in the morning of the ninth of May 1826. As no person was to be seen at that early hour, I got over the greenhouse gate by the old covered way, explored the pleasure grounds, and looked round the outside of the house. I then went down to the kitchen gardens, scaled the outside wall and saw the whole place, set the men to work there at six o'clock; then returned to Chatsworth and got Thomas Weldon to play me the water works, and afterwards went to breakfast with poor dear Mrs Gregory and her niece. The latter fell in love with me, and I with her, and thus completed my first morning's work at Chatsworth before nine o'clock.

Chatsworth is in the heart of England, about 12 miles from Chesterfield, 26 miles from Derby and 10 miles from Matlock, below the Peaks in wild natural scenery a million miles from the soft lines of Bedfordshire or Chiswick. The park in which the Palladian mansion stands is nearly 11 miles in circumference and the setting is magically diverse – hills give way to peaks, thick woods to pasture, and through it all snakes the River Derwent.

The coach would have taken between ten and fifteen hours from London. Paxton apparently walked from Chesterfield, across the high moors through the night, arriving about three hours later at the thousand-acre estate. As the sun rose on this rural idyll and birdsong joined the ripple of the Derwent to pierce the morning silence, he would have seen for the first time the breathtaking natural grandeur of his new home. With his irresistible energy he was keen to take stock of the scope of his astonishing new job.

The old walled kitchen garden, probably conceived by Capability Brown in the 1760s, was a whole 12 acres designed to produce the finest quality fruit, vegetables and flowers, month in and month out. It lay in a quiet spot on the banks of the swiftly flowing river, a fifteen-minute walk from the house across parkland dotted with sheep.

The garden over which the young man now had control had a long and various history, constructed and planted over several hundred years according to prevailing fashion. In 1555 Bess of Hardwick, a rich and powerful local heiress, married William Cavendish and started to build the first house. The steep east slope was terraced and fish ponds, fountains and formal plots with orchards and gazebos in the Tudor style were introduced. In 1570 it provided a prison for the exiled Mary Queen of Scots.

In 1659 Bess' grandson – the 3rd Earl – modernised the gardens, adding a massive and intricate parterre with formal, geometrical beds. Between 1687 and 1707 the 4th Earl (now 1st Duke of Devonshire) rebuilt the Elizabethan house in classical, Ionic style, employing as his architect William Talman, one of the first great gardener-architects. The famous pairing of London and Wise, owners of the enormous nurseries at Brompton Park on the outskirts of London, in turn made its mark on the gardens. George London designed a new parterre to the west of the house, the planting of these elaborate embroidery designs supervised by Le Nôtre who had laid out the patterned gardens at Versailles. Henry Wise (of Hampton Court renown) later partnered London on the design of a further parterre to the south of the house. A great greenhouse, a separate masonry construction with huge south-facing windows, was erected along with a bowling green with its own classical temple.

Befitting the zenith of the formal style, these new gardens were filled with fine stone and brass works of art. The Dutch sculptor, Cibber, who worked with Wren on both St Paul's Cathedral and Hampton Court, fashioned sea horses for the fountains, the garden deity Flora, and many other works to watch over the gravel paths, shady basins, formal orchards and ornamental knots. This was formal gardening on a grand scale,

introducing architectural features to the landscape in order to comple-
ment the great classical house that was rising out of it.

Inspired by a vogue in France and Holland, waterworks were to
become the most characteristic feature of great gardens. On the steep
east slope, a grand cascade was therefore fashioned by another
Frenchman, a hydraulics engineer, Monsieur Grillet (a pupil of Le
Nôtre). In the two years from 1694, he constructed a feeder reservoir
on the top slope – earthworks on a massive scale that could only have
fired Paxton's imagination as he took it all in that morning. The elegant
cascade house was added a few years later and water poured over the
domed roof of a temple and through the mouths of its sculpted dolphins
before tumbling over steep, wide steps towards the house below.

On the south front of the house, beyond the grand parterre, the
slope was levelled and a canal dug in the last years of the seventeenth
century, a flat sheet of water reflecting the sky and the lime walk to
its west in stark contrast to the majestic River Derwent. Already in
1700, Chatsworth had become a school in which to learn gardening
on a grand architectural scale. The gardens were freely open to the
well-heeled public and the many visitors were astonished by this
display of social rank and civilisation in the midst of the wild
Derbyshire Peaks.

From the 1730s, much of this old garden, though not its architectural features, began to be erased. Kent, architect of Chiswick House,
was the leader of the new style of gardening which embraced nature
and fields over the formal designs and fountains of his predecessors.
The 1st Duke's grand masonry greenhouse at Chatsworth was now
moved, a pineapple house built and a lawn melting into park obliter-
ated the parterre. All that remained of the ornamental was swept away
in favour of the elitism of the landscaped park. Bess' terraces were
destroyed. Lancelot 'Capability' Brown removed the straight lines, the
patterned planting and most of the flowers and topiary and undertook a massive tree-planting programme with carpets of grass
stretching to distant stands of trees. Once again the gardens were
moulded by fashion and Chatsworth, rich in Walpole's perfect elements
for a romantic garden – ancient trees, massive rocks, sweeping rivers
and dashing natural waterfalls – provided an impeccable framework
for grand rural 'improvement'.

This was the park inherited by the 5th Duke and his beautiful and
wayward wife Georgiana, and by their only son, the 6th Duke. Since
Georgiana and her husband both preferred courtly and political life

in London, the gardens saw almost no activity for 50 years – a grotto was built for Georgiana but little else – and they were all but neglected.

Soon after inheriting in 1811, the new duke started to rearrange again. Embracing the latest interest in flowers and flower beds, he reintroduced a parterre in front of the greenhouse in 1812 and a few years later he planted nearly two million forest trees in the old Stand Wood, rising on a hill to the east of the house. The trees covered an area of over 550 acres. Oak, ash, beech, elm, sycamore, poplar and birch, larch and spruce firs were all planted 4 feet apart. In the early 1820s, over 30,000 more trees were planted, earning the Duke the Gold Medal of the Society for the Encouragement of Arts, Manufactures and Commerce.

The 6th Duke was a child of the Regency period and highly civilised, a patron of the arts and sciences but, unlike his parents, he was a liberal in politics and sentiment. Delayed by the weather, he had left for Russia that morning, 9 May, not to return to England for six months. In his absence, there was work in progress. He had commissioned the fashionable architect, Jeffry Wyatt,* to begin a vast remodelling of the house and parts of the garden and, when Paxton arrived that morning, the enormous new north wing extension, which would entirely change the scale of the house, was in the final stages of construction. Vast alterations in the layout of rooms and corridors were being planned; a new scullery, larder and kitchens were finished, new staterooms, an elaborate ballroom, dining room and sculpture gallery were projected. It was the height of modern aristocratic luxury, testimony to the Duke's grand conceptions and deep purse. At the time of Paxton's arrival, stirred though he must have been by the glorious gardens, this part of the house must have still been something of a building site – he describes the library as looking like 'a lumber room'.

Wyatt was also turning his attention outside, forming plans for the garden in the new Picturesque† taste practised by Repton and directing a refocusing of attention from landscape and park to a formality of design based around the house, with symmetrical arrangements of

---

*   On the Duke's suggestion, Wyatt remodelled the Royal Lodge at Windsor, and then, starting in 1824, Windsor Castle for George IV. This got him his knighthood in 1828 and the rather grander name of Wyatville by which he is now most often described.

†   The Picturesque as a landscape theory was first described by Sir Uvedale Price in the 1790s. Repton took up the idea in his own landscapes to create the sense of 'embellished neatness' where the art of horticulture prevailed over nature.

sculpture and clipped trees and new embroidery parterres. The parkland immediately surrounding the house was being transformed into
a 'pleasure ground' in which nature was once again dominated by horticulture. A new wide gravel walk nearly a third of a mile long and to
be flanked by the Duke's favourite trees, the monkey puzzle, was being
fashioned, in what the Duke was later to call Wyatt's 'first great hit
out of doors'. The west garden was to be relevelled out of Brown's
slope, with the sea-horse and tulip fountains fed by underground pipes
from water in the cascade and, ever a perfectionist, the Duke also
moved the whole cascade sideways to be in a more perfect alignment
with the new building.

As the numbers of visitors increased during the early part of the
nineteenth century, regulations concerning the visiting public were
put in place and altered only marginally each year. Before the railway
came to Rowsley, parties were limited to about a dozen; the house
and garden were freely open every day from 10 a.m. to 5 p.m, with
reduced hours often imposed on Saturdays; carriages had to depart
and return later for their passengers; dogs were expressly forbidden
and on wet and dirty days permission could be refused to visit the
principal apartments. In the gardens, the groups were accompanied
by one of the garden staff, and the waterworks were played for all
visitors on request.

In the Duke's *Handbook*, printed privately for his sisters in 1845,
the Duke wrote that when Paxton arrived he found 'at the kitchen
garden . . . 4 pine houses, bad; two vineries which contained 8 bunches
of grapes; 2 good peach houses, and a few cucumber frames. There
were no houses at all for plants, and there was nowhere a plant of
later introduction than about the year 1800. There were 8 rhododendrons and not one camellia.' Of the kitchen garden he wrote '[it] was
so low, and exposed to floods from the river, that I supposed the first
wish of the new gardener would be to remove it to some other place.'
Paxton did not move it. He made it flourish.

Whatever he thought of the state of the gardens, Paxton could not
have failed to have been dazzled by the gilding on the windows of the
south and west aspects of the house. While the story of his scaling of
the kitchen garden walls has been mythologised and succinctly demon-
strates his extraordinary vitality and thoroughness, an interesting note
in an unpublished diary suggests that in fact he particularly felt his
own youth on this morning and understood the importance of an
impressive start: 'instead of going to bed, walked round grounds and

so set men to work at 6 – being young this gave him the authority which he wanted'.

This done, the housekeeper, Mrs Hannah Gregory, and her niece, Sarah Bown, were waiting to meet him in the kitchen. Sarah was the third of a family of four daughters from Matlock, where her father owned a small mill turning parts for the cotton-weaving industry. She was three and a half years older than Paxton, with a generous private fortune of £5,000. Only one hasty sketch by William Henry Hunt exists to show her as a young woman – slender and perhaps rather plain. She was, by all accounts, educated, determined and reserved, and she was on the shelf. Her aunt, running the house and answerable only to the steward, was earning £20 a year against Paxton's £65. As the housekeeper, Hannah benefited from living in the house with her full board. As head of the gardens, however, Paxton was one of the highest paid members of the estate, answerable only to the Chatsworth steward, Thomas Knowlton, who earned £150 a year.

As Paxton describes, he and Sarah fell in love at first sight. The earliest of his letters to have been preserved is, appropriately, addressed to her, written during 1826. She is his 'lovely endearing angel . . . the adorable object of my heart. To say I love and adore thee my dear is but trifling – you are the very idol of soul . . . rest assured while I draw breath it will be my study to make myself more dear . . . I am and shall ever be yours till Death.' She had apparently asked for him to send her a copy of the lines of a popular verse called 'Fare You Well', but she could not have known the irony implicit in this leave-taking almost from the moment they first met.

Sarah and Paxton were married on 20 February 1827 and moved

into the cottage on the edge of the kitchen garden, the broad river to their right, the steep hills and woods to their left and with the windows of the great house flashing on the slope to the front.

CHAPTER FOUR

There were regulations in force in the gardens and it is likely that Paxton reviewed these when he arrived, fresh from the strict environment of Chiswick. The men were encouraged to keep diaries for their own improvement – noting new plants, weather fluctuations and daily activities. Above all else, there was to be prompt attendance, good order and sobriety, and contravention of these key rules could mean instant dismissal. The hours were 6 a.m. to 6 p.m. during the summer with a half-hour for breakfast and one hour for lunch; in the winter, working hours were decided according to the weather. Sunday hours were from 8 a.m. to 4.30 p.m. between November and March and from 7 a.m. to 5.30 p.m. for the rest of the year. Fines were imposed: sixpence for anyone arriving later than ten minutes after the lodge bell had rung, two shillings for anyone absent without permission – a rule applied to Christmas Day like any other. Sixpence would also be levied on any man found lounging or wasting time in the gardens, failing to clean and stack the tools allocated for his personal use, or if any panes of glass were broken through his inattention. The gathering of fruit, vegetables, flowers or plants without permission attracted the serious fine of five shillings, and dismissal on the second occurrence. All fines were deducted fortnightly from wages and, according to James White, one of the under gardeners, 'if anyone feales himself greaved or aney ways unfairly dealt with in the administeration of these rules I desire to have the matter explained'.

Paxton had soon roused the men to a flurry of activity. Despite the mess created by the building work, principal paths had to be maintained and smartly gravelled; there was trenching, digging of beds, raking of leaves and clearing of cuttings to be done, and pots had to be washed and stacked ready for the needs of constant transplanting. In the summer, the more tender plants were carted from their shelter and planted out into beds; hedges and grass-edges had to be clipped, trees tied back, soil or dung carted to where it was needed. Everything had to be managed carefully, lest the Duke should decide to arrive at any moment.

He did indeed return to Chatsworth from Russia in early December and he noted in his daily journal: 'Chatsworth, che gioya! I found great progress.' The next day, having looked over his property, he noted, 'I am enchanted . . . My new gardener too, Paxton, has made a great change.'

Throughout 1827 the Duke was preoccupied with his duties as Lord Chamberlain to the Royal Household – duties he cared little for but could not happily decline – and by his place in the House of Lords, where great electoral reform was being debated as a result of the wars in Europe and the growing, predominantly urban unrest at home. Socially, Devonshire House and Chiswick occupied his attention in all but the shooting season when he returned to Chatsworth, and was again delighted by the progress he saw.

That year the Duke appointed Benjamin Currey as his London solicitor and auditor with direct responsibility for all his affairs and accounts. This was indicative not only of the aristocrat's lethargy when it came to accountable expenditure, but also an increasing movement towards professionalism in the running of large estates. Currey was not a landowner himself as had always been the case in the past, but a member of the professional upper middle class. All the agents on the Duke's various estates reported to Currey.

Quietly, Paxton worked away in the gardens. Gradually all the fountains were repaired and improved, iron pipes replacing lead. In the west garden, an ornamental wall was constructed, drains were repaired or replaced and parts of the garden newly laid out, with new walks added to the pleasure grounds. With his own eye for structural detail, Paxton began to work with Wyatt to amend the architect's orangery designs. The Duke, in his own words now 'bit by gardening', conceived it as a conservatory to join the sculpture gallery to the new wing. He wanted it quickly and he purchased orange trees from the Empress Josephine's collection at Malmaison, an expensive *Rhododendron arboreum* from Knight's exotic plant nursery in the King's Road, and an *Altingia excelsa* which came to be particularly admired. Paxton must have been thrilled with the Duke's growing interest in plants and in the changes he was hurrying forth.

The following year, Paxton's attention turned to the kitchen garden. A new orchard was added to it and the wire fence around the flower garden was removed. On a modest scale, he turned his attention to glass. A number of famous glass buildings had recently been constructed in England including those at Syon House in Brentford, Hungerford Market in London, the upper terrace garden of Covent Garden Market and a surprising conical glasshouse at Bretton Hall designed by Loudon and Baileys. At Chatsworth, Paxton repaired the existing pineapple and peach houses and then started to build and experiment with the design of a number of new greenhouses and stoves in which to cultivate and force all manner of fruit and vegetables.

When later asked to describe the process of design and construction of the Crystal Palace, built for the Great Exhibition in Hyde Park in 1851, Paxton was at pains to emphasise a process of years of experimentation with glass buildings, a logical development which had led him to that point. In his first reading of a paper in public, he noted that 'in 1828 . . . I first turned my attention to the building and improvement of glass structures'. He found the various forcing houses at Chatsworth were made from coarse, thick glass and heavy woodwork, which rendered the roofs dark, gloomy and ill-suited for the purpose for which they were built. So he bevelled off the sides of the rafters and sash bars, lightening them considerably and discovering that the buildings lost no structural stability in the process. Frustrated by putty which failed to withstand the extremes of sun, rain and frost and which disintegrated and allowed water to drip constantly inside the houses in rainy weather, he also contrived a new, lighter sash bar, with a groove to hold the glass, obviating the need for putty altogether.

While Paxton thought that the popular, modern metallic glasshouses espoused by Loudon were graceful in appearance, he concluded that wooden structures were preferable. One advantage was that wood was less expensive than iron. More importantly, he understood that, as the iron in the sash bars and rafters expanded and contracted according to the outside temperature, the glass was prone to breakage. In addition, iron corroded and was far more complicated to repair, whereas a wooden roof needed only a common carpenter. As the debate was revisited in the pages of the *Gardener's Magazine*, and as his own experiments proceeded, Paxton became increasingly convinced of the superiority of treated wood over iron, experimenting with finer and finer sashes and rafters to admit the greatest amount of light into the house. Within a very short time, the new glasshouses he built yielded fruit and vegetables in perfection, and a profusion of flowers capable of filling the house.

~

Nine months after their marriage, on 5 December 1827, Paxton and Sarah's first daughter, Emily, had been born. She was baptised twelve days later in the local village of Edensor. Sarah quickly became pregnant again and their first son, William, was born in January 1829.

The Duke had spent much of 1828 away from Chatsworth, returning only in September and October and noting again the great progress there. He began to take a closer interest in his gardener, visiting the kitchen garden and asking Paxton to thin the woods – showing a confidence in his new man which no doubt put the regular woodsman's nose out of joint. In early 1829, the Duke walked out in the snow with Paxton to see the woods and sought him out on several occasions to discuss the management of his trees. He returned again in April, when an entry in his diary reveals the growing regard he held for the gardener who was transforming the park before his eyes: 'I went to woods, much pleased – poor Paxton has been very unwell.' Paxton rarely complained of illness, whereas the Duke was something of a hypochondriac, beset with hayfever, flu, inflamed eyes, stiffness and a multitude of other, often minor, afflictions which could cause him to be bedridden for weeks at a time. He had a peculiar tenderness for another man's health.

This was a particularly happy year for the Duke. His sister Georgiana's daughter, Blanche – his adored, adoring and favourite niece – announced her engagement to William Cavendish, Lord Burlington, the son of the Duke's cousin, and his appointed heir. He, meanwhile, was busy with Wyatt, with politics and with parties in London, leaving Paxton to embark on his first great landscape scheme for the park and one of the earliest of those curiously Victorian garden features – the pinetum.

Pinetum is the name given to a collection of one or more of each variety of conifer worthy of cultivation. With tens of new varieties now being introduced to Britain, the formation of one offered satisfaction of the collector's instinct on a grand scale. Here, Paxton's early experience at Chiswick combined with the Duke's own strong arboreal interests to create a startling miniature world. It is still there, a place of surprising and extraordinary tranquility, a group of trees strikingly foreign compared to the native hardwoods in the Stand Wood higher on the slope. In spring, swathes of daffodils and piercing birdsong delight in the sunlight filtered by the cool green branches.

That this was to be one of the earliest collections to be planted in England is not entirely surprising.* The creation of a pinetum required not only a serious budget but a large amount of empty ground, separate from any other garden feature. In 1829, 8 acres of the south park were given over to the plan and the ground began to be formed in the summer. Paxton carried the seeds of the Douglas fir, the pride of California and reputed to reach 200 feet high, from London wrapped in his own hat. A Norfolk pine was fetched from Ireland by Andrew Stewart, Paxton's foreman in the kitchen garden. A giant redwood, the monkey puzzle, hemlock spruces and the Japanese white pine were purchased and planted along with tall larches. In all, over 50 species of pine were mixed with cypress, juniper, Salisburia, thuja and yew, creating a collection of every kind of hardy conifer that could possibly be procured, each planted according to its botanical classification and clearly named on painted wooden tallies. According to the Duke, the pinetum was quickly admired 'but no two of a party take the same view of it; one extols the scenery, another is in raptures at the old oaks, and a third wonders and asks, why I plant the fir trees so thin'.

It must have been tremendously invigorating for the young Paxton to have control over the conception and planting of such a valuable and extensive collection, combining scientific with ornamental purpose. It is possible that even at this early stage, he conceived it as part of a much larger collection of trees, an arboretum, which in some years' time would be planted around a new 4-mile walk through the pleasure grounds since part of the new walk was already completed by the time the Duke returned to Chatsworth again in the summer. In addition, the west garden was now newly planted and Cibber's great sphinxes had been moved there.

---

*   The fashion for these odd shaped evergreen trees was fed by the publication, in 1831, of a complete listing of all known conifers in cultivation by Charles Lawson. In 1838 he followed this with the publication of *Pinetum Britannicum.* By the end of the nineteenth century, it is estimated that over 250 different species of pines were available.

So pleased was the Duke with his gardener that he took him to Bolton Abbey – his property in Yorkshire – to shoot. Paxton was 'enchanted' – quite the best reaction for a Duke proud of his castles and palaces, deeply desirous that they should be admired and provide enjoyment for his visitors. As if he needed further reason to value the gardener, the fruit ripening in the new greenhouses, particularly melons, figs, peaches and nectarines, started to win medals at the Horticultural Society shows at Chiswick House.

The Duke was becoming deeply charmed by Paxton and began to give him increasing responsibilities, including that over all the woods and forests. In three years, the gardener had shown that he was reliable, intuitive, a practical empiricist when it came to designing plant houses, thoroughly capable of achieving whatever he set his hand to, and, furthermore, a dreamer of schemes to improve the landscape of the park in keeping with the very latest horticultural fashions. As head gardener and forester he now hired and paid his own men, managed their labours and ran his own accounts. These accounts still had to be submitted to the Chatsworth agent, and to the solicitor, Benjamin Currey, but they marked Paxton's status and responsibility. Not only did the Duke sanction the building of a new office at Paxton's house in the kitchen garden, but he increased his salary threefold to reflect his seniority within the household. As 'Gardener and Woodman' Paxton was now to be paid £226 a year, which included an allowance for finding and keeping a horse.

The increasing expenditure on the gardens and pleasure grounds during these first years indicates the changes that were being wrought. It rose from £505 to almost £2,000 by 1829, much of which was spent on the numerous new glasshouses in the kitchen garden. In addition, the Duke's own private account books show that he gave a total of £400 to Paxton over several months, to be used for 'new stoves'. It must be said that in the context of the Duke's wider spending, these sums were almost insignificant. Tens of thousands of pounds were being spent on Wyatt's improvements to the house and thousands more on collections of books, sculpture, art and furniture. The Duke was happy to spend £942 during Doncaster races week alone in his efforts to outshine his neighbour the Duke of Rutland.

Just before Easter 1830, the Duke purchased a large weeping ash from a nursery garden near Derby. Around 10 years old, its roots alone were 28 feet in diameter, and its branches radiated on each side of the trunk to a distance of 37 feet. It weighed 8 tons. Paxton was dispatched to engineer its particularly problematic removal and carriage to Chatsworth. He took with him with 40 labourers, at least 6 horses and a new machine constructed to his own design by Messrs Strutt of Belper. By Good Friday, the Duke was in a lather of anticipation. 'Up at 6 in hope tree had come but it did not all day.' He went to church instead.

On the first attempt to lift the tree from the ground, the strong chain snapped and it was some time before it was ready to be moved the 28 miles to Chatsworth, just managing to squeeze through toll bars along the route, contrary to the expectations of the many doubters. Four days after they had set out to collect it, the tree arrived at the park gates which had to be lifted from their hinges, parts of the walls taken down and several branches lopped off to allow it in. Finally the Duke met the weeping ash at the new northern entrance to the house. He was delighted, declared it miraculous, and watched 450 labourers under Paxton haul it into place in its hole in the centre of the courtyard, spread out its roots, peg them down and form a mound of earth around its trunk. It remains there to this day.

It is not now uncommon to see mature trees hydraulically uprooted and transported over great distances and replanted. It was somewhat revolutionary in 1830; large crowds gathered to witness the curiosity and the local papers reported the 'experiment of a novel and extra-ordinary description', and Paxton's 'ingenious contrivance' in detail. Paxton had undoubtedly moved fairly large trees before in his respon-sibilities as the Duke's forester and in the formation of the pinetum. A voracious reader on all subjects horticultural, he would have added to his own practical knowledge the systems of others. Only a year later he would include an article in his new magazine *The Horticultural Register* recommending a method of earth excavation in order to leave a large root-ball intact. Later still, in the first volume of another of his own magazines, *The Magazine of Botany,* he would return to this favourite theme with a full description of how to remove large trees, accompa-nied by clear diagrams to illustrate root-ball preservation, the use of cross-levers in lifting, and replanting techniques. For the Duke, the weeping ash was a high point of the year and, such was the widespread interest in its removal, that he received a vexatious eight-page letter from Sir Henry Steuart, author of a treatise on practical planting. Steuart warned him that he should have taken his advice, for the tree would surely not survive transplantation so late in the year. He added an amusing postscript 'I know that gardeners are, as well as poets rather an "irritable race", I should take the liberty to advise . . . that this letter

be <u>not</u> communicated to Mr Paxton.' The Duke's reply was restrained.
'Mr Paxton, my woodman, who has long been in the habit of moving
large trees has no doubt of the success . . . of the experiment.' He could
have added that Paxton was the least 'irritable' man in his employment.

By 1830, the first lawnmower was patented,* an early indication that
gardening was to become one of the greatest of all middle-class English
hobbies. The kitchen garden at Chatsworth held 22 hothouses and
numerous forcing pits. In the pleasure ground, new flower gardens
framed the house and plants, in particular, rose to prominence. With
new glasshouses to protect them, and a man fit to cultivate them, it
became expedient to augment the collection by swapping and
purchasing plants and seeds – and these begin to be listed in the
garden accounts. At home, Sarah was pregnant again with their third
child.

Outside their enclosed world, there was revolution in France and
political unease in Britain. The word 'scientist' was coined; invention
and experimentation was creating a new world of possibility. In
September 1830, Stephenson's Rocket raced along its tracks at 16m.p.h.
from Liverpool to Manchester carrying passengers as well as freight
for the first time, promising a revolution in travel particularly for the
expanding urban populations.

Paxton was poised to burst into action in the two most fruitful and
exciting decades of his life, years where it hardly seemed possible for
him to draw breath for new ideas and experiments.

*

By Edwin Budding. Illustrated in the *Gardener's Chronicle* of that year. Uncatalogued
material in the Chatsworth Collection shows that a Ferrabee mower was purchased
in 1833. At an early stage Ferrabee shared rights in the mower with patentee
Budding and licensed Ransomes of Ipswich to make them.

CHAPTER FIVE

'I was just going to write and tell you how much pleased I was by the amount of your prizes in the Sheffield paper, when I got your dismal letter about the frost . . . I am coming to look at what is left on 1 June. Please tell Mrs Gregory.' So wrote the Duke to Paxton on 14 May 1831. The frost had also destroyed the prize dahlias at Chiswick, demolished the magnolia leaves and ruined the blossom and vegetables. If this was not the first letter from the Duke to Paxton, it is the earliest to have survived, and it points at the priority now given by the Duke to all things horticultural. From this time, his diaries become peppered with references to plants and trees seen and coveted, to visits to the famous nurseries in and around London, and to the efforts and results of other gardeners at many of England's great estates and smaller private gardens.

If the improvements at Chatsworth were intended to provide a grand display case for his passionately collected works of art, literature and sculpture, the garden and grounds soon became an equal obsession. Paxton was beginning to fashion a pattern of new walks through the woods, as well as paths and slopes between the orangery and the flower garden near the house. His enthusiasm was infectious to the beauty-loving aristocrat and the gardener's early successes and obvious ability began to fire the Duke's somewhat competitive and acquisitive nature. He started to study botanical books avidly, swept up in a rising intoxication for all things rare and ornamental.

Together, the Duke and his gardener would walk the woods and strike out on to the moors above the house, in a boyish and delightful search for new springs that could be diverted to feed the waterworks. The Duke visited gardens in Canterbury in September, noting some tulip trees which must be had for Chatsworth. When he arrived back, he visited the kitchen garden and saw all Paxton's rarities. He was in raptures. Chatsworth had become, quite simply, 'delicious', his enjoyment of it filling the pages of his diary and his letters. Lady Newburgh, a Derbyshire neighbour, wrote to Blanche that 'Chatsworth is getting every day more beautiful inside and out, you will hardly know it again, so much has been done.'

From the beginning of the year, across the country there was almost no talk but of 'the Bill'. The first reading of the Great Reform Bill – introduced by the Whigs and designed to begin a realignment of power through the abolition of rotten boroughs and the extension of the vote to the prospering middle classes and male householders – was heard in the Lords at the end of September. It had a rough ride and on 8 October it was rejected. There were riots in Derby, Bristol and in manufacturing towns across England. In December, on its second reading, it was thrown out again by a majority of 160. Like its continental cousins, Britain seemed on the verge of potential revolution and the army were put on alert.

The Liberal Duke was alarmed and distressed – and he went shopping. Then he wrote jubilantly to Paxton: 'I have bought you the Araucaria excelsa!' He fussed about the safe arrival of the monkey puzzle, dreading delay on the canals by frost. He also sent heaths, and signalled his great desire for a glorious red euphorbia, for an amaryllis, for Barringtonia and for *Eucalyptus desfoliata*, once the stoves in which they could be cultivated had been completed.

If the urban population was disaffected and angry, in the enclosed and rarefied country air of the Chatsworth estate, Paxton had different distractions. His second daughter was born in April and named after the Duke's niece, Blanche. He was also working on plans to launch a new gardening magazine, *The Horticultural Register and General Magazine*, jointly edited with Joseph Harrison, the gardener to Lord Wharncliffe at Wortley Hall near Sheffield. The first issue, published in July, thrust Paxton into the public arena. He was just short of his 28th birthday.

Plantsmen, eager for information on new plants and their cultivation, were already well served by the early *Botanical Magazine* and its rival the *Botanical Register*. The Horticultural Society issued its

Transactions and nurseries their catalogues, including Loddiges' *Botanical Cabinet*. All these contained coloured plates of foreign varieties, but they were expensive, and hardly suited to the 'practical' gardener. The most extensive horticultural journalist of his day was John Claudius Loudon. The *Gardener's Magazine* included detailed reports of the activities of the societies, of nurseries and gardens visited, of recently published books and periodicals as well as articles on all aspects of the gardener's responsibilities. Most radical were Loudon's own articles, advocating novel and revolutionary ideas such as national schooling, adult education and green belts around cities.

Many other, smaller magazines came and went during the late 1820s, stimulated by an increasingly literate reading public and by the new methods of steam printing which reduced the costs of production. What exactly drove Paxton to set up a new monthly magazine, and how he met Harrison, is unclear. It may be that part of Sarah's dowry was used to fund the project. It was a bold step, but he was never timid.

The first volume of the *Horticultural Register* stated its intention to 'embrace everything useful and valuable in horticulture, natural history and rural economy . . . It is evident that a taste for horticulture in all its branches, both of vegetable culture and propagation, also landscape and architectural gardening, has within the last twenty years very rapidly increased, and a corresponding improvement has consequently attended it; for at no time has it reached so high a state of perfection as the present.' Paxton was at pains to emphasise that the readiness of garden proprietors (like his Duke) to encourage their gardeners to experiment and develop their art was a fundamental factor in effecting this change. The editors wanted to produce an affordable magazine, directed at all classes of society, to circulate it as widely as possible and to include the broadest possible array of articles 'in so plain and intelligible a form . . . as to be within the comprehension of all its readers'.

Including articles ranging from the grandest of horticultural schemes to the botanic minutiae of particular plants, the magazine would be divided into five parts, covering gardening in all its branches. There were reviews of and extracts from articles in other horticultural and rural publications, news of discoveries and interesting accounts of natural history, reviews of books and journals published and 'miscellaneous intelligence'. Neat engravings would serve as illustration, the need for correct descriptions of all new and valuable plants would be met and it would close with a monthly horticultural calendar – a novel approach to managing the monthly practicalities of the gardener's art which has been copied up to the present day. In order to include as much as possible, without increasing its price, the magazine was printed in small type and, at the end of each year, a bound volume contained additional lists of fruit and flowers recently classified, and of the most successful fruits and vegetables already in cultivation.

Paxton's magazine provides a snapshot of the contemporary horticultural world. The first issue included remarks on new modes of glazing, on the materials to be used for hothouse roofs and on how to alter the colour of hydrangeas or retard the blooming season for common English and French roses. There is a description of how to force vines in pots by the gardener at Willersley Castle, Derbyshire, and the first reprint of an article from the *Gardener's Magazine*. Catholic in its coverage, driven partly by Paxton's own preoccupations, the magazine eclipsed its rivals and was immediately successful.

It brought Paxton head to head with Loudon who realised that his publication was, for the first time, facing serious competition. Piqued, the brilliant monomaniac set out on a tour of northern and Midland estates. The next issue of the *Gardener's Magazine* carried a stinging criticism of Chatsworth which 'has always appeared to us an unsatisfactory place'. He disapproved of the square pile of building, its situation and the scattering of its waterworks. He recommended the cascade steps should be transformed into a waterfall, railed against the gravel on the walks and offered only one morsel of praise – that the Duke allowed the waters to be played to any visitor without exception. Loudon reserved his sharpest barb for Paxton himself, lambasting the kitchen garden for including ornamental plants, ragged box edging and wooden ranges of forcing houses. He went on to say that he had 'since learned that Mr Paxton disapproves of metallic houses and of heating by hot water; and here we are not sorry that this is the case, because the public will have an opportunity of judging between his productions and those of other first-rate gardens where metallic houses and hot water alone are employed'. He was referring to Woburn, Syon and Bretton Hall in a way designed to inflame Paxton, who was not at home during the visit. It was a possibly impulsive, certainly tactless and arrogant censure from a man plagued by pain and illness and entirely devoted to the maturation of horticulture into a professional science.[*]

[*]   When his right arm broke for the second time, it was amputated. It was said that
     after the operation in the morning, Loudon was back downstairs in the afternoon
     dictating to his wife Jane.

Paxton was still a little known quantity, but his riposte showed his mettle and left Loudon in little doubt that he was not for bullying. Such public disapproval, timed just as his own patron was particularly attentive to activity in the gardens, and which also attacked the very house and grounds of which they were so proud, would have shaken a less resilient man. The sting came not from an anonymous contributor, but from the most famously trenchant of horticultural authors and journalists, the greatest garden innovator and designer of the early nineteenth century.

In the third issue of the *Horticultural Register*, Paxton was the model of restraint and measure, but his reply to Loudon was no less vigorous. 'A person might almost conjecture that Mr Loudon came with a pre-determination to find fault, if not it must be because he did not give himself the time to consider before he wrote his ideas of what he terms improvements.' He questioned Loudon's taste and he took issue with him for failing to even enter the house, from where the gardens should be viewed. He pointed out that, while at least two of the glasshouses in the kitchen garden were heated by hot water, the method was generally uneconomical in the severe winters of Derbyshire where fires warmed more consistently and needed less attention.

Paxton drew his line in the sand over Loudon's criticisms of his preference for wood over metal in glasshouse construction. They not only admitted as much light as if they were built of metal, he said, but they provided a combination of strength, durability and lightness, honed to a more perfect balance than had ever been achieved previously in wooden ranges. In addition, his wooden ranges had cost less than a third of the price of metal ones. Finally, Paxton questioned the judgement and the veracity of the older man. He reproved: 'did you not say to the young man who accompanied you round, that Chatsworth was altogether the finest place you had ever seen in your travels? How then is it that Chatsworth is so unsatisfactory a place?' It was an able and finely-judged deflection. Sharp-minded Sarah, acutely judgemental herself, would have cheered the confident rebuttals of her husband.

The *Horticultural Register* continued to prosper, gaining sales over Loudon's magazine. Occasionally, Loudon would try to prick the confidence of his young competitor who would reply with restrained sarcasm, but on the whole the magazines continued in successful parallel and later the two men would come to a rapprochement. Some time in 1832, Paxton's partner in the venture, Joseph Harrison, quit the magazine and the editorship devolved wholly on Paxton. He continued to contribute articles on a variety of subjects from the tiniest detail of plant qualities, to the characteristics of large groupings of plants and the chemistry of soil, a living embodiment of his belief that gardeners should know not only the names of plants but the detail of their structure, their habit and peculiarities in order to understand the requirements of heat, soil and nutrition. Through his own writing he began to formulate and consolidate his own aesthetic and horticultural theories.

In June 1832, the Reform Bill – perhaps the most important piece of early nineteenth century legislation – was finally passed, to great general exultation. In one strike it increased by 50 per cent the number of people eligible to vote. The changes in the wider world hardly touched Chatsworth, however, where Paxton concentrated on the conversion of the beautiful old stone greenhouse, built in 1697, into a stove. He added a new glass roof, remodelled the interior to form terraces on which plants were placed in pots, included a basin for aquatic plants, and modernised the heating equipment to include four furnaces whose flues passed into the back wall of the house. The heat from the fires circulated through iron grates in the front path and via a hot air cavity round each of the front basins. The venerable old building was reborn, and the Duke was delighted. 'My new stove is the loveliest thing I ever saw, done entirely by Paxton.'

Once the alteration was complete, Paxton worked on designs for a new parterre to be laid out in front of it, planted with bulbs and plants to give colour almost throughout the year, edged with rhodo-dendrons and box hedges. Cut out of the grass were square and semi-circular beds and two long beds in which moss roses were layered over the surface, dotted with half-standard perpetual roses rising above

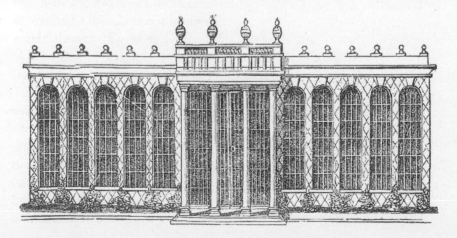

them. The transformation in the gardens was widely noted, nowhere more so than in letters to the Duke. Lady Southampton was typical in her praise, finding herself 'enchanted' and 'delighted'. The Duke's niece, Blanche, thought that it 'surpassed anything I ever saw'.

On 18 October, the Duke's recently decorated new dining room was used for the first time in rehearsal for its first royal visit. The following day, the young Princess Victoria and her mother, the Duchess of Kent, arrived as part of a tour of the great English estates. Victoria was thirteen; it was her first 'grown-up' dinner and the house was gleaming and opulent in its new finery. The future queen planted an oak, her mother a chestnut, in the west garden, and in the evening there were charades.

Paxton had been planning and his men had been arranging his first *coup de théâtre*. All the waterworks in the park were illuminated with coloured Bengal lights which were changed between each act. Even the Duke had never seen anything like it. First, the fountains glowed red, but when the group returned to the windows the gardens were bathed in blue 'moonlight'; then the cascade appeared to turn to fire, and rockets went up in every direction. The 13-year-old and all her party were enchanted. While they slept, hundreds of garden labourers worked through the cold October night to return the gardens to their immaculate perfection so that, by the morning, there was not even a trace of autumn leaves on any of the paths. When the Princess moved on the following Monday to Sheffield, fireworks again awaited her, but the Duke was adamant that they came nowhere near the effects of Paxton's illuminations of water and fire.

CHAPTER SIX

Paxton was now in his thirtieth year. He had three children, a successful magazine, a growing reputation, the confidence of his employer and the gardens at Chatsworth were organised and flourishing. Then, at the quiet beginning of the following year (1833), the Duke had one of his only disputes with Paxton, 'who was not exact in my accounts . . . He says he must have discovered his mistakes but I doubt that and it makes me very glad to have kept my accounts as perfectly as I do.' In the light of his future vast debts, the Duke was delusional over his own accounting abilities. Paxton may not have been a great deal better (though he certainly had to deal with more complicated accounts on a daily basis, ably assisted by Sarah) and it is very possible that from 1831 he was taking private maths lessons in a neighbouring village. Characteristically, all was forgotten only a fortnight later as the Duke whisked Paxton off on a tour of great country house gardens, ostensibly to further the gardener's education but, one also suspects, in order to share with him their mutual passion for all things horticultural.

They travelled together by coach, and it was the first time Paxton had been away from Sarah for an extended period. Coach travel was very soon to be overtaken and outdated by rail. During these early years of the 1830s, the great trunk lines were developing, including the London to Birmingham that very year. The days of master and man together, and of the enclosure of the coach, were nearing their end.

Their first stop, Dropmore – about thirty miles outside London in Buckinghamshire – was owned by Lady Grenville and maintained by her gardener Philip Frost. Lady Grenville was possibly the first gardener to challenge the sterility of landscape by introducing bedding, cutting into the grass to provide space for the flood of colour available from showy displays of the many new plants now widely cultivated. There, they also found glorious examples of pines and they were astonished to see the *Araucaria excelsa* planted out of doors and thriving, and American laurels arranged as if wild. They went on to Althorp, Paxton stealing ten minutes after midnight to write to Sarah, bemoaning his separation from her and his 'little family', his loneliness mitigated only by the Duke who 'pays me the greatest possible attention'. At Windsor they were depressed by the wretched state of the orange trees, but again the Duke 'took great pains to explain everything to me'. Sarah hated their being apart, and was clearly distressed not to hear from him more often, but Paxton and the Duke were on the move and letters took time to arrive. Ultimately, she did not have to wait long for her 'dearest love', the Duke sprained his knee and was forced to return to London.

When Paxton arrived back at Chatsworth he sent flowers to the Duke convalescing at Chiswick, who was so delighted with them that he sent them on to the Queen. His estimation of Paxton continued to rise as his own study of botany matured – possibly not to the appreciation of his gardener at Chiswick where the Duke said that he now saw and understood the 'bad management of my plants'. Between 1830 and 1835, Paxton spent over £2,500 on plants, trees and seeds on behalf of the Duke. Many were greenhouse plants, but purchases also included the more obvious tulips, auriculas, carnations, camellias, roses, lilies, and even primroses, obtained from local Derbyshire nurseries as well as the famous London and continental establishments.

With the Duke fit again and en route to Italy, taking with him horticultural gifts for many of his friends, Paxton continued to experiment at Chatsworth. In 1833, in contemplation of continuing his experiments by building a new range of hothouses, he revisited the possibility of erecting metal structures, drawing up plans and sending to Birmingham and Sheffield for estimates. But he was horrified by the enormous costs – both estimates were over £1,800 – and 'I at once set about calculating how much the range would cost if built of wood . . . I was able to complete the whole range including masonry (which was omitted in the metal estimates) for less than £500.' Next he considered how to design a house into which the greatest possible amount of light would be admitted in the morning and afternoon, while minimising the violence of the midday sun.

Loudon had already set out the principle of fixing glass at angles on a 'ridge and furrow' construction and it now occurred to Paxton that his wooden roofs would admit much more light if the sashes were so fixed. It was an insight that proved to be one of the most important mental leaps of his career. He reinvented and refined Loudon's nascent principle to such a perfect model that it became his signature practice in glass roofing, a revolution in glasshouse design that would last for over a generation. The principle worked on the basis that light in the mornings and evenings, when the sun was low in the sky, would enter the house without obstruction, presenting itself perpendicularly to the wide surface of the glass. Conversely, the strength of the midday sun was mitigated by the fact that it hit the glass at a more oblique angle.

Fired by his success on small buildings, Paxton was now inspired to build a new glasshouse of considerable dimensions to accommodate the Duke's growing orchid collection. The new house was to be 97 feet 6 inches long and 26 feet wide – a considerable span – made up of 15 bays, and constructed again of wood supported only by 16 slender, reeded cast-iron columns. The floor was made of slatted board, allowing earth to be swept through, wooden rafters were entirely abolished and the sash bars were made lighter than ever before. In

addition, the front columns were to be hollow, with a metal pipe inserted to act as a conduit for the water from the roof, directing it to a drain laid in the gravel walk outside. The angled panes of the roof were set fast, with the least possible unsightly and uneconomical overlap, and, since the sash bars were grooved, less putty was needed. The panes at the front and end could be easily slid aside, allowing entry to any part of the house without the need for a door and maximum possible ventilation. In this new house, Paxton arrived at a system of construction the principles of which would now underpin the design of every subsequent wood and glass structure that he built. Notwithstanding the tax on glass, he pronounced it to be economical, costing around twopence a cubic foot.

During the five years from 1830, Paxton spent the considerable amount of £3,409 on maintaining and constructing greenhouses, mushroom houses, forcing houses, a strawberry house, a large pine house, a melon and cucumber house, several vine ranges and a peach house – all of glass, wood and iron. He was not working in isolation but within a contemporary fashion for experimentation with the design and structure of glass buildings, often on a massive scale. Loudon, for example, designed a radical building with massive glass domes for the Birmingham Horticultural Gardens, which was widely publicised though never built. Demonstrating just how hard these types of building were to erect, the 'Antheum' in Hove, with its 60 foot high dome spanning 170 feet, swerved into famously serpentine lines when its scaffolding was removed, before collapsing within the month. Paxton's own experiments though were impelled by the needs of utility, stability, convenience, economy and the desire to overcome technological limitations within the constraints imposed by the glass tax, rather than aesthetics of design or the development of his own reputation. They succeeded in their aims entirely.

He grabbed at every conceivable opportunity with indefatigable energy. In February 1834 he launched another, more ambitious, monthly magazine, *The Magazine of Botany and Register of Flowering Plants*. Priced at two shillings it offered detailed study of plants and their husbandry, containing four accurate and well-coloured engravings of the most prized new plants, as well as numerous other woodcut illustrations and a range of articles. It provided a cheaper alternative to magazines like the *Botanical Register* and, like its sibling the *Horticultural Register*, it promised to break away from the elitism of most journals, by using the most plain and intelligible language possible. Aiming for the broadest appeal, it would give botanical descriptions of plants in English, the culture of plants in short paragraphs and calendars of work for each month. Unsurprisingly, it was badly reviewed by Loudon who damned it as only 'useful to the manufacturers of articles which are decorated with the figures of plants . . . To botanists it is of no use, as the plants are neither new, nor described with scientific accuracy.' But the new magazine would be steadfastly supported for a generation, augmenting not only Paxton's reputation, but his income.

The *Magazine of Botany* was, from the start, printed by Bradbury and Evans of Whitefriars, London (in 1835 they also took over the printing of the *Horticultural Register*). William Bradbury, three years Paxton's senior and a famed liberal employer, would become one of the greatest of all Paxton's friends. Along with his partner, Frederick Mullett Evans, the company printed Charles Dickens' novels, and built a reputation as one of the most efficient printing firms in England, with twenty of the most modern steam-driven presses running 24 hours a day, and a specialisation in illustrated magazines and fine-art printing.

Throughout 1834 Paxton's contributions to the *Horticultural Register* declined sharply. He chose to review *Hortus Woburnensis* – the descriptive catalogue of Woburn plants compiled by the Duke of Bedford's gardener James Forbes – on the whole favourably, while deploring its lack of concision. Bedford and Forbes had initiated similar schemes at Woburn as Paxton and the Duke and there was healthy competition between them.[*]

The journalistic battle continued to rage between Loudon and Paxton in their respective magazines. Plagiarism in the form of reprinting the abstracts of articles from rival papers was the norm, driven by commercial realities, but it was one of the key areas of contention between the two men. Although the new magazine was

[*] Paxton was often coming up against Forbes, and the two certainly met several times. The Duke of Bedford and his gardener wanted to rival Devonshire and Paxton at Chatsworth. In a letter to Sarah, 26 January 1836, Paxton wrote: 'I went to Woburn on Friday and what do you think old John Bedford has been at? Why, making an arboretum this winter in emulation to the one at Chatsworth, it will be a miserable failure. This is not all – the old codger has had Sir Jeffry Wyatville from London to design a STOVE. I suppose they are jealous of us . . .' (Devonshire Collection; Paxton Group No. 260). 'The Duke declared the hothouse 'handsome . . . but not new or original' and the gardener Forbes 'a very consequential stupid fellow – very different from my gardener I think'. (6th Duke's Diaries, 10 November 1836).

more about plants than horticulture, Paxton included short articles on the subjects about which he and the gardening world were most preoccupied, including designs for greenhouses, different methods of heating stoves and designs for ornamental labourers' cottages. Many of these were themselves reprints from the *Horticultural Register*, including those on moving large trees and designing subscription gardens, and some were taken from Loudon's magazine, which infuriated him.

At the start of April 1834, the Duke wrote to Paxton from Florence asking him to leave immediately for Paris, with a small monkey puzzle and some rhododendrons. He wanted him to see the gardens at Versailles and St-Cloud, but he gave him little more than a week to organise his journey: 'if you cannot arrive by the 20th in Paris, you had better not come'. Paxton left immediately, arriving on the 19th, his lips blistered and cracked by the speed of the journey. The following day they visited the Louvre and Palais Royal together on foot. They went on to visit St-Cloud and several private gardens, all the while collecting plants and seeds for Chatsworth. At the eighteenth-century Jardin des Plantes they saw vast, inspiring new glass ranges, unlike anything they had ever seen. When the Duke left for London, he ordered Paxton to stay a further week to purchase horses for him at the Russian horse sale, and to see the grand waterworks on display at Versailles at the start of May.

Paxton was bursting with excitement and news of his first foreign tour: 'I wish to God you were here seeing all these things with me, you would be quite delighted,' he wrote to Sarah. 'I shall not be able to contain myself until you are acquainted with the details of my journey . . . I have come so far and seen so much that it seems an age since I left home.' He was irritated by officials at French customs, by the lack of soap in the Hôtel du Rhein in the Place Vendôme and by the dirty streets. He was caught up by Ridgway, the Duke's steward, and Santi, his Russian servant, and taken to a gambling house where 'Santi was a fool enough to lose £70 . . . they wanted me to try my luck but I know better – Santi was like a madman all yesterday.' He caught cold at the horse market and was laid up for a week with only Coote, the Duke's musician, left with him. In his letters home, he complained that the hotel staff were so stupid that he could have died for all they cared – the merest trifle took them up to an hour to bring.

The waterworks at Versailles were a disappointing affair to Paxton, who found them 'not half so fine as I anticipated'. It was intolerably hot, and there were crowds of thousands. What did impress him were the immense numbers of horse soldiers gathered to be received by the King. As he set his face again for London, keen to see Sarah and the children and hoping that he would not be delayed by the Duke, he vowed that he would never forget it. In London, he found a packet of letters from Sarah awaiting him, eager to know all his news. But all at once, he was up to his eyes with things to do for the Duke and 'the hurry and confusion I am in renders it almost impossible for me to answer any of your questions', he wrote. He assured her that he would return to Chatsworth with the Duke in two days, and rescue the reins of Chatsworth management from her. In the meantime it was down to her to call all the men in from the woods, arrange for the gardens to be neat and clean, and to order the men to lay down new gravel along the east front of the house. He told her that the tiger at Kew Gardens had died – which upset him far less than the loss of a plant at Chatsworth.

By the time the Duke arrived at Chatsworth in the middle of May after an absence of nearly six months, he found the new greenhouse completed in the kitchen garden. He was delighted. Soon, the two men were plotting great improvements together, while entertaining or visiting botanists around the country. In October, the Glasgow botanist, William Hooker, came to stay at Chatsworth, and in November, Paxton and the Duke travelled to Liverpool to see the botanic gardens there. In effect, these Liverpool gardens, only ninety or so miles from Chatsworth, were the first municipal gardens in England, albeit established by private subscription at the turn of the century. They had just moved from the city centre to a more rural site, and the Duke now considered them worth going a thousand miles to see. Correspondence between both men was now filled with horticultural news: William Aiton sent plants from Kew including some trees ('generous Aiton. Treasure!' wrote the Duke), Countess Amherst sent news of wonderful new plants from Montreal, the Duke was offered a collection of American aloes by a gardener in Chesterfield, the new arboretum in the pleasure grounds at Syon was charming. The two men were inspired.

At the end of the year, as with the *Horticultural Register*, Paxton gathered up the year's parts of the *Magazine of Botany* and published them as a single volume, which he dedicated to his patron 'with the greatest respect and gratitude . . . in testimony of his . . . enthusiastic love of botany . . . and . . . as an acknowledgement of the innumerable favours conferred on his Grace's obliged and most obedient servant Joseph Paxton'. It was usual to flatter the sympathies of patrons, but it is possible that Paxton was nudged into this first dedication by William Hooker, Professor of Botany at Glasgow and future director of Kew Gardens. Recently, Hooker had written to thank the Duke for his stay in Derbyshire, adding 'I cannot tell you what delight it gives me, who has devoted at most thirty years uninterruptedly to the study of Botany, to find a nobleman of your . . . distinguished rank and fortune so zealously devoted to this delightful pursuit . . . the next volume of *The Botanical Magazine* completes the 8th volume and after the botanical and intellectual feast I have enjoyed at Chatsworth, I was irresistibly led to dedicate that volume to your Grace.'

Such dedications recognised the moneyed luminaries of the relatively small world of international horticulture – a world which was, on the whole, generously and mutually supportive. As the news of the transformations of the gardens at Chatsworth spread, many gardeners began to feed it with their own choicest offerings* and Hooker also now promised to write to his correspondents the world over requesting them to send their finest plants to Chatsworth for the growing collections there.

The arboretum in the Horticultural Society Gardens at Chiswick and that at the nursery of Loddiges in Hackney, as well as the enormous variety of new trees available for planting, all contributed to a long-term desire in Paxton and his Duke to create a far more complete collection of trees than the pinetum. Characteristically, they were always setting their sights higher. Now they wanted to form a large experimental ground filled with trees of all species. From the start of 1835, labourers were employed in clearing the ground to be used. An enormous number of trees and shrubs were removed and the ground trenched ready for planting. The collection of trees was to be laid out in about 40 acres of park and woodland, either side of the walk already designed to form a circuit of the pleasure grounds. Winding paths split off from the meandering main walk in order to admit views of the distant park.

The work involved enormous upheaval and digging. The Duke was excited and wrote to Paxton 'I don't mind in the least how dirty it

---

* In December, the horticulturist Dr Daniel Rock sent from Alton Towers, with Lord Shrewsbury's compliments, a banana (*Musa sapintum*), hearing of the Duke's interest in curious tropical fruits: 'it may be eaten raw but I should think that it would be far more pleasant when cooked in a thin silver dish, like a pudding. I think (I speak in doubt) with butter.' (Devonshire Collection, 6th Duke's Group, 2 Dec. 1834.)

may be, I shall be glad to find the pleasure ground up to my neck in mud all over.' In constant contact by letter, he also urged Paxton to allow Thomas Bailey, his gardener at Chiswick, to work in the arboretum in order to learn about the management of trees, and he reminded Paxton of the fine trees at Syon.

Progress was astonishingly rapid despite the fact that Paxton also faced the huge task of diverting a natural stream 2 miles from its original position on the east moor to form a course so apparently artless that it seemed to have been made by nature. In February, the Duke noted in his diary that it was 'a wonderful alteration' and in April Lord Burlington visited the park, writing to his wife that almost 130 types of azalea were already planted. He added that the place looked rather a mess but that Paxton had assured him that in two years it would be perfect.

By the beginning of June, only six months after the work began, the arboretum was all but complete. The Duke wrote again to Paxton from his estate at Hardwick that he had been 'enraptured with the concluded half of the arboretum road . . . I had abstained from going, having taken it into my head that it could not have been done, and there it is finished . . . I can complain of nothing.' Signalling a rapprochement, Loudon invited Paxton to write an article for the *Gardener's Magazine*, in which he set out his rules for the formation of arboreta and rejoiced 'in the idea of an arboretum on a large and comprehensive scale . . . open every day of the year and shown to all persons rich and poor without exception . . . the arboretum at Chatsworth will thus be seen by thousands'.

The arboretum, when it was finished, formed the largest collection of herbaceous plants in Europe, planted according to their scientific orders. Some 75 orders of trees were planted, including over 1,670 species and varieties, with plans to increase the number to 2,000. The smaller trees were planted nearest to the walk with the largest extending beyond them, all with room to grow into single ornamental specimens.

With some pride, Paxton claimed that the plan had been financed entirely from the sale of wood from the felled trees. Ever true to his training at the Horticultural Society and his own tidy mind, and witness that this was above all a place to be visited, to exhibit and educate, all the trees were named on wooden tallies. These were made of hearts of oak, steamed to draw out the sap, boiled in linseed oil and painted with three coats of black paint with their names in white paint, including their scientific name, country of origin, year of introduction, estimated final height and their English or common names. When the Duke saw the completed arboretum for the first time, his gardener's most ambitious plan yet, he confided to his diary: 'it is transcendent'. That Paxton had all but completed it in six months was confirmation of his singular powers of organisation and will. Four years later even Loudon, now reconciled to Paxton's true genius, was to praise it though later still, having completed the first public arboretum in England, in Derby, he tactlessly argued that Paxton's ordering and classification were unsatisfactory.

Paxton had not, however, been directing only the great arboretum undertaking – the Duke had his eye on a quite different and expensive venture. In February, James Bateman of Knypersley Hall in the Potteries wrote to the Duke about a tremendous orchid collection being offered for sale by his friend John Huntley, the Vicar of Kimbolton on the Bedfordshire–Cambridgeshire borders. Bateman, himself the owner of one of the finest collections of orchidaceous plants in England, had published *The Orchidaceae of Guatemala and Mexico* in a huge folio illustrated by the renowned Mrs Withers and Agnes Drake Huntley, he said, had been collecting for 20 years and only financial necessity would induce him to sell his collection of over two hundred species. The Duke was interested. He had bought his first exotic orchid in 1833 for £100 – *Oncidium papilio* or the butterfly orchid, a stunning plant with orange and yellow flowers and mottled leaves. The orchid was a serious status symbol and the Duke was driven to possess a collection to surpass all others.

These exotic beauties, whose cultivation frequently ended in failure, had been prized above all plant rarities since 1731 when the first tropical orchid flowered in England. By the 1760s 24 species of orchid were in cultivation in Britain, including only two from the tropics and the rest native or European. In 1782, the flowering of the serene nun orchid – *Phaius tankervilleae* introduced from China – at Kew Gardens had excited widespread attention and when, at the turn of the century, Francis Bauer completed the very first drawing of the nucleus of a plant cell, tellingly he used an orchid specimen. In 1812, Conrad Loddiges & Sons had started orchid cultivation in England on a commercial basis and in 1818 succeeded in cultivating *Cattleya labiata* for the first time, the orchid named after William Cattley, who had assembled a pioneering collection of the gorgeous plants at his London home. When *Cattleya labiata* flowered, it was an immediate sensation, heralding orchid growing as a fashionable pastime. By 1826, 154 orchid genera had been discovered and the Horticultural Society had erected their own orchid house in the gardens at Chiswick, which received increasing numbers of visitors.

The *Horticultural Register* was publishing expansive and expanding lists of *Orchidaceae* in its catalogues of rare and beautiful plants. Along with the *Magazine of Botany*, it charted Paxton's own experiences in the management of orchids and those of countless other gardeners and nurserymen. Paxton experimented with temperature and humidity with increasing success, emphasising in his articles the absolute need to know and understand the native habitat of each plant, and to assimilate it as closely as possible in the artificial environment of the greenhouse and stove.

With money at his disposal and a gardener who could foster the collection as well as any other man in Britain, the Duke now entered into a protracted correspondence with the loquacious Huntley. The whole process was, to the vicar, a broken-hearted expedient, and he insisted that his collection remain entire and that he would not sell only those varieties most prized by Chatsworth. Paxton was dispatched to Kimbolton on the thrice-weekly coach, where he worked from the moment he arrived at 3 p.m. until he had to meet the return coach at 1 a.m. He pronounced the collection, numbering almost three hundred plants, 'sumptuous', and impressed Huntley, who considered him 'far beyond his situation'. Paxton had found a collection of disappointingly small plants, yet it was an important one, rivalled only by Bateman and Loddiges, and filled with novelties which he longed to possess. However, concerned about the price, he wrote to the Duke that he had not closed the deal, 'with all my anxiety to have a collection for your Grace unsurpassable by anyone, I cannot recommend your Grace to spend so serious a sum'.

Daily letters poured from the desperate pen of Huntley, who had heard that the Duke was considering sending his own plant collector to Calcutta. He assured the Duke that he was continuing to add rare and beautiful specimens to his collection, and railed that the £100 difference between the sum Paxton had offered and the sum he required was but a trifle to the great nobleman. He threw in his collection of cacti and other stove plants. Long letters also raced between the Duke in London and Paxton at Chatsworth, the Duke exhorting Paxton to clarify whether he thought the plants of sufficient value. Uncharacteristically, Paxton dithered. On the one hand he thought the collection superb. On the other, he was overwhelmed by the price, and

felt Huntley to be mercenary. He applauded the intention behind maintaining the collection as a whole, but was equally clear that it contained
plants that were not needed, so that 'Mr Huntley may be given to
understand that we shall chop and cut his collection to make a good
one of our own and dispose of the rest for other plants.' Finally he
advised against the purchase.

This was all that was needed to help the Duke to a decision. If
Paxton wanted the plants, hang the expense. So, without further delay,
Huntley received his asking price of £500. With a mixture of concern
and competitive glee, Paxton wrote 'our collection of orchideae has
now mounted completely to the top of the tree. I am fearful some of
our neighbours will be a little jealous of our progress – the race will
lay between Lord Fitzwilliam and Mr Bateman.'

It would take nearly a week to prepare the plants for their journey
to their new home and a young gardener under Paxton, John Gibson,
was sent to complete the task. In September, the erstwhile secretary
of the Horticultural Society Gardens, John Lindley – now Professor
of Botany at University College London and in the process of claiming
his title as 'the father of orchidology' – had named an entire genus of
plants *Cavendishia*, charming the Duke completely.

∽

Since their trip to Paris together, the Duke was in the habit of summoning
Paxton to London at a moment's notice. Paxton was busier than he had
ever been and had four young children at home (Victoria, his third
daughter named in honour of the future Queen, was born some time
between April 1833 and March 1834). He had monthly editions of two
magazines to oversee, as well as their compilation into volume form at
the end of each year, quite apart from the daily business and big schemes
of Chatsworth. Unsurprisingly, his normally robust constitution
succumbed to the increasing strain of his workload and he became
bedridden with a sore throat and headache, although he managed to
maintain a regular correspondence with the Duke in London about plans
for Chatsworth and the continued planting of the arboretum.

The Duke's reaction to his incapacitation substantiates the regard in
which he held him: 'I had rather all the plants were dead than have you
ill,' he wrote. Paxton and the Duke were both rare men and the regard
in which they held each other – given the polarity of their stations –
was becoming remarkable; they had become friends. The Duke's sister,

Harriet Countess Granville, noticed it and wrote to her brother about his decision to accept neither the offer of Lord Chamberlain again, nor that of Lord Lieutenant of Ireland, under Melbourne's new Whig government. She imagined 'you and Paxton, sitting under a red Rhododendron at Chatsworth, under the shade of palms and pines in your magnificent conservatory, with . . . no thought of your country's weal and woe'.

In April 1834, Paxton finally relinquished his editorship of the *Horticultural Register,* citing extreme pressure of business which entirely deprived him of the leisure necessary to conduct the magazine along the lines to which he had been accustomed. Subscribers were assured that his advice would continue to enrich its pages, and a professional editor stepped in.

Later that year, when the Duke returned from the continent, he was again enraptured by all that Paxton was achieving, in particular with the stoves and plants in the kitchen garden. Hardly a day passed when he did not visit it, returning to note some new glory in his diary. The round of horticultural shows and visits to commercial nurseries continued and, at the end of November, Paxton was summoned to London, to visit the Chelsea Physic Garden, Knights' and Loddiges' nurseries, John Lindley and an assortment of private gardens. The Duke bought another fine orchid from a garden in Tooting and together they did what they both loved: hatched grander and grander schemes to enrich the gardens and grounds at Chatsworth.

At the beginning of December, the Duke hurried Paxton off on an impromptu garden tour, or 'norticultural tower' as Paxton called it.[*] At Dropmore the pines remained glorious, at Highclere the grounds quite beautiful. They travelled west to Stonehenge and Bath, got up in the wind and rain to see Wilton's fine cedars, the striking ruins of Fonthill Abbey and the magnificence of Longleat. It was freezing, and although Paxton was travelling on the box with the coachman, his delight in all he saw remained boyish. Of Stonehenge he wrote to Sarah 'I have never seen anything so <u>wonderful</u>'. They took in the ruins of Thornbury Castle and Berkeley Castle, 'a very curious mixture of antiquity and vulgarity', and noted Nash's perfectly beautiful cottages in Blaise Hamlet. They took

---

[*] A rare indication of Paxton's accent. Leveson-Gower noted the Bedfordshire accent which never quite left Paxton, in particular his misuse of the letter H which could cause some confusion: 'he once said that his employer had the heye of an 'awk and when it was proposed to build a church . . . in his neighbourhood he offered to 'eat it'.

the hot waters at Bath and journeyed on to Blenheim, where it was so cold that only Paxton went out into the gardens. He was exhausted by all the sights, the grand houses and their gardens and, since the Duke was travelling without entourage, further strained by arranging everything for His Grace. He wrote to his wife that he was being whisked 'hither and thither and Lord knows where', that the Duke's plans were up in the air and there was even talk of going to Paris.

Paxton's letters were torture to Sarah whose return mail was chasing him around the country, never quite reaching him before he moved off again. All was far from well at home – measles in the village had spread to the children and William, in particular, was coughing violently. Her letters are discouraged, frustrated and frantic. Longing to hear from his wife, and seeing that a letter from her was among the Duke's parcel of letters, Paxton split open the parcel and retrieved his letter, only to read of the suffering of his children. Noticing his distress, the Duke asked what was the matter, but Paxton dared not admit that he had broken a cardinal rule of the house with regard to the letter bag, that Sarah had written, and that their son was sick. He was beside himself with suspense:

> I am now most seriously afraid that it will go hard with poor William, the bodily suffering that poor child has endured makes me shudder to think of – I never wanted to do anything so much in my life as I do to come home at this time . . . don't deceive me if you think there is danger, let me know and I will start out immediately . . . all I can think of is my dear, dear children – what a melancholy thing it would be if the poor child was to die and me not see him again . . . but from the first moment I had forebodings for poor Will . . . Do all you can for our dear children, and kiss them a thousand times for me.

He suffered for two days before another letter from Sarah freed him from his torture. It was not good news. On Friday, 11 December, the Duke wrote in his diary, 'poor Paxton went off to Chatsworth, hearing of the dangerous illness of his boy'. Paxton must, therefore, have been at home when his only son, William, died five days later, just short of his sixth birthday. The Chatsworth household accounts for that week show the making of 'a lead coffin for young Paxton' and for soldering it up. Paxton only twice referred to the boy in any of his surviving letters, when as an old man, his memory was stabbed by the resemblance of two of his grandsons to his own lost boy.

CHAPTER SEVEN

Paxton and the Duke were ambitious for yet more floral prizes and they knew that orchid treasure was there for the taking. With almost 30,000 species and native to every continent except Antarctica, flourishing in the most arid desert and the densest cloud forest, orchids make up around 10 per cent of all flowering plants, exceeded in variety only by the daisy family. 'Of all tribes of plants this is the most singular, the most fragrant and the most difficult of culture,' wrote Lindley in Loudon's *Encyclopaedia of Plants*. 'The flowers are often remarkable for their grotesque configuration . . . The species are found inhabiting the mountains and meadows of the cooler parts of the globe, or adhering by their tortuous roots to the branches of the loftiest trees of the tropical forest to which their blossoms often lend a beauty not their own . . .' The most seductive tribe of plants, orchids held a unique status in the horticultural world. So, with thriving trade routes assisting botanical exploration, and with the Indian collections of William Roxburgh and Robert Wight as precedent and stimulus, it was to the tropical mountains in India that the Duke decided to send his explorer to search out prized epiphytes, the orchids found clinging to the branches of host trees.

The Duke had been interested in the progress of various plant hunting expeditions for some time – he had subscribed to an unsuccessful expedition to Mexico the previous year, from which the collector had returned early and unwell, with few new plants. Huntley had sent a man to 'the Spanish Main' in the formation of his own collection. As he sent off the cheques to Huntley, the Duke gave orders to Paxton that arrangements should be made and put into action for their very own adventure.

Lord Auckland, a friend of the Duke, had been posted to India as Governor General and was making his own preparations for departure. This was their opportunity. 'The expense of the journey to Calcutta,' wrote Paxton to the Duke in March 1835, 'if permission was given to go out with the Governor General would not exceed £100, otherwise it might cost a serious sum.' Paxton next considered *who* should be sent. He chose one of his 'intelligent' gardeners at Chatsworth, John Gibson: 'he has a good knowledge of plants, particularly orchideae, is obliging in his manner and very attentive'. Gibson had been drawn to Paxton's attention when he submitted an article to the *Horticultural Register*, published in October 1832. The following year, he had arrived to work at Chatsworth from the gardens at Eaton Hall near Congleton, where he had worked with his father. Now he was sent for a season to learn the secrets of orchid cultivation from Joseph Cooper, a specialist orchid grower for Earl Fitzwilliam at nearby Wentworth Woodhouse. In preparation for his expedition to India, he was then dispatched to trawl the nurseries in London and as many public and private gardens and herbaria as he had time to examine.

While Gibson set about accumulating as much knowledge as possible to ensure the success of his mission, the Duke approached his friend Lord Auckland, on the point of sailing. He also wrote to solicit the assistance of Dr Nathaniel Wallich, the curator of the Botanical Garden in Calcutta which had become something of a clearing house for plants from all over southern Asia. From Glasgow, William Hooker wrote letters of introduction and at Chatsworth, Paxton began a collection of double dahlias and other showy flowers that were likely to thrive in India, all to be packed up as a gift for the Calcutta gardens. He was very aware that the success of the expedition relied not only on finding new varieties, but in transporting them home alive, advising Gibson that all his plant discoveries should be established in boxes at least three months before they started their journey home, to maximise the likelihood of their surviving the voyage.

The transportation of plants by sea, their exposure to the wind and salt in particular, had been a hit-and-miss affair and it was often the case that a vast proportion of plants sent home from abroad would perish in transit. Happily, the surging numbers of new plant species

being discovered around the world now acted as an impetus to innovation. Gardening magazines, including the *Horticultural Register*, were
filled with illustrations of 'new' designs for boxes, cases or jars, all of
which promised increased success. For the Indian trip, John Lindley

One of the many new designs for plant transportation cases.

suggested that Gibson take a new kind of packing case which had
already been used with some success. Loddiges, too, recommended the
use of these air-tight boxes made of wood and plate glass into which
the plants were placed in soil and watered, before being tightly sealed.

These were the 'Wardian cases', designed by Nathaniel Ward after
a chance discovery, during which he found that a sealed jar into which
he had placed a moth cocoon had also preserved the small plants hidden
within the moss used as packing material. He had reasoned that, so
long as the plant material was watered before the jar was sealed, moisture would evaporate and condense against the glass, maintaining a
consistently moist environment, perfect for plants. For overseas collection, this was a real breakthrough and, as their success was proved,
smaller and more decorative Wardian cases also became fashionable
in the drawing rooms of many middle-class Victorians in Britain, used
particularly for the display of the ferns that so fascinated them.

Orchids were not the Duke's only obsession. In 1826 Nathaniel
Wallich had discovered an evergreen tree with velvety leaves and
glorious scarlet and yellow flowers in Burma near the town of Martaban
on the Salven River. He claimed that the tree was unsurpassed in

magnificence or elegance and his descriptions inflamed the imagination and desire of botanists and gardeners everywhere. *Amherstia nobilis*, as it was called, had never survived transportation to England. Its very rarity, quite apart from its beauty, meant that it would be the perfect prize for Chatsworth, and the Duke valued it above all else. So Gibson was also to go to Martaban to procure *Amherstia* for the glory of the Devonshires.

After numerous delays Gibson, outfitted for the most arduous journey of his life, laden with flowering and medicinal plants, fruit trees and seeds for distribution to foreign gardens, joined the *Jupiter* at Woolwich and sailed in late September on rough seas for Madeira. He recognised that this was his chance for glory and he was full of gratitude to Paxton. He was clearly excited despite the pressure to return with a valuable cargo of *Orchideae*. His only concern was with the famed air-tight cases stored on the poop deck, in which the outgoing plants were already looking rather sick.

Gibson's journey to Calcutta was to take six and a half months. During a week in Madeira he found no new plants but, abroad for the first time in his life, he was caught up in admiration and wonder at the spontaneous growth of oranges and lemons, grapes and bananas and the flowering hedgerows of mixed myrtle and fuchsia. The season was unfavourable for collecting in Rio de Janeiro and he had time during his fortnight there simply to make out a list of the plants considered worthy of transportation to Chatsworth and to set up the means of organising their shipment. He found a man in 'an English garden' willing to amass the plants and swap them with the Duke for orchids, palms and other showy plants from the English collection. By December, after heavy gales that carried off two of the *Jupiter*'s sails, he arrived at the Cape of Good Hope, where he worked hard, collecting over two hundred species of plants, including ericas and proteas, on a single journey of only 20 miles up country. This was just the beginning. Although Cape plants were not particularly valuable, they would all be new to Chatsworth and the bulbs he gathered, when resold in England, would pay for the freight of the plants.

As Gibson departed England, Paxton was considering a magnificent project – to erect an innovative jewel-box in which to house the plants they expected to be coming home. His experiments on the glasshouses at Chatsworth were propelling him towards the design of one that would be capable of holding the most gigantic of tender plants, allowed to grow to their full potential. In Paxton's imagination, 'the Great Stove' would be the apotheosis of all greenhouses, of colossal dimensions and unrivalled in Europe. A greenhouse on this scale was entirely untried – the Palm House at Kew, for example, would not be built for almost a decade. Paxton's construction would take the form of a central nave with two side aisles, cover an acre of ground, be 227 feet long, 123 feet wide and 67 feet high, and be built almost entirely of wood supported by iron columns. In a break from the pitched-roof houses he had designed and built in the kitchen garden, the form of the glass roof was to be curvilinear, made up of a series of undulating ellipses like the waves on a 'sea of glass . . . settling and smoothing down after a storm'.

A century earlier, perhaps, the Duke would have built a temple or mausoleum as a permanent memorial to his passions, but this was the age of scientific discovery, and scientific obsessions. This stove, unlike an ordinary, small greenhouse, would be composed internally of beds and borders rather than trellises to hold potted plants. The design was the natural child of his own experiments: he had already supplied designs for a large curvilinear palm house at Loddiges' nursery in Hackney constructed with wood rather than iron, though, as he said in the *Magazine of Botany*, here 'the curve is much depressed, and its breadth trifling compared with the height'. Other curved glass structures may have influenced him – most particularly the Jardin des Plantes in Paris, begun in 1834, and the new structures at the Sheffield Botanical Garden and at Hove. But this was larger even in span than contemporary railway sheds. The expense would be enormous and in London that autumn there was much discussion between Paxton and the Duke and Benjamin Currey, who both considered that Paxton should solicit further advice. In November 1835, John Marples, a foreman carpenter at Chatsworth, made a scale model of Paxton's designs. With the model in their carriage, the Duke went with Paxton to Loddiges. They also attended a meeting of the Horticultural Society, where they took several Fellows aside for the same purpose, and they visited John Lindley at his home in Turnham Green. Reaction was positive; the scheme would go ahead.

Early in 1836, with Gibson pursuing his course across the oceans, work was begun at Chatsworth to clear a broad rectangle of several acres of land in the woods at some distance above the house, and on laying out a series of roads to take away the spoil. Paxton had exclaimed regularly in his magazines that glasshouses should be conspicuous and ornamental features of a garden, standing proud rather than hidden. Nevertheless, he also felt strongly that, however beautiful glasshouses could be in themselves, they were architecturally unique and should therefore not stand in competition with any other building. Remoteness was an absolute principle to him and so the stove would be positioned some distance from the main house, out of sight of its windows.

The land chosen was high, but it was protected from the wind and screened from the house by a belt of forest trees. The first sod was cut on 6 June, and the mighty excavation for the foundations, by shovel and wheelbarrow, continued into the autumn. Under the stove, Paxton designed a basement chamber to contain the boilers, which would run a hot water rather than fire-driven heating system. These would require a large amount of coal, transported regularly across the park from the main road. To conceal the transit of carts to and from the building, a new road was cut through the trees, with a subterranean service tunnel running directly under the cascade, through which wagons loaded with coal would run on railway tracks right into the centre of the basement.

The plan was ingenious and every detail was considered. To test the efficacy of his principles on a curved roof, and in order to ensure that nothing was left to chance when the construction of the huge building began, a smaller hothouse, only 60 feet long, was built in the kitchen garden. Since the rafters for the roof were to be made of wood rather than iron, they had to be composed of several long, thin boards, bent and securely nailed together over templates of wood cut out to an exact curve. Paxton was neither a trained architect nor an engineer but his experiments often brought him to the same conclusions as experts in the field. These wooden rafters were found to be far stronger than cast iron, which had no strength in tension and Brunel's famous timber viaduct – the 'skew' bridge across the Bristol Avon – built much later in 1845, would use laminated timber in a similar way.

The crucial elements of Paxton's great design were in place. He would again set the glass on the ridge and furrow principle, utterly convinced now of its greater stability. It not only maximised the amount of light available to the plants, but withstood the rigours of wind and hail far more satisfactorily than conventional glazing. It had added advantages: glass set in this fashion was permanent rather than movable, reducing the risk of breakage, and rainwater ran off far more quickly, without dripping on the plants below. It was perhaps more expensive, since it necessarily used a greater quantity of panes than conventional pitched roofs, but, again, he was confident that the benefit to the plants and to the building, in terms of its stability, mitigated the small additional sum involved.

Since cast iron was strongest under compression, 36 slender cast-iron columns would again be used in two parallel rows to support the roof and would also function as drains for rainwater and condensation from it. But, apart from the frame, the whole of the rest of the material – aside from glass – was wood. Ventilation would be provided by means of shutters let into the low masonry pediment. The soft rain-water run-off, so beneficial to plants, was channelled through over 1,000 feet of piping to be collected in cisterns, where the hot-water pipes of the heating system warmed it to the temperature of tropical rain.

⌒

While the final details of the design were completed, John Gibson arrived in Calcutta on 8 March 1836. Wallich was away but his assistant, Masters, took Gibson to live with him and together they unpacked the boxes of plants brought from England, finding, with relief, that those in the closed cases had fared far better than the rest. Gibson was overwhelmed by what he saw in the Botanic Gardens – the *Amherstia* in flower for the first time and the rare orchids on display. Masters wrote to the Duke that he ran around 'clapping his hands like a boy who has got three runs at a cricket match'. Wrapped up in delight at the novelties before him, he waited for Wallich to return and advise him on the details of the journey ahead, occupying himself by settling the Chatsworth plants into the gardens, demonstrating how best to look after them, and preparing and packing plants to be sent back to England immediately from the Calcutta collection. He sent home various orchids and the banana *Musa superba*, one of the most showy of the plants in the garden, noting in wonder that its stem grew to a circumference of $1\frac{1}{2}$ feet.

Letters took about five months to travel the distance between England and India and Gibson could not have known quite how apposite was his choice of the *Musa* for inclusion in that first shipment. He did know that Paxton had formed an attachment to a dwarf banana plant and had become convinced that he could induce it to flower, and thereby fruit. Paxton had apparently seen an illustration of the tiny banana on some gorgeous new hand-painted Chinese wallpaper, hung at Chatsworth a few years earlier, and determined to cultivate it at all costs. Chinese in origin, it had in fact already been discovered in Mauritius in the late 1820s and was purchased by Paxton from Young's nursery in Epsom. The banana, it must be remembered, was still a curious novelty – no one was quite sure how it should be eaten.

The dwarf banana, named *Musa cavendishii* by Paxton in 1837, grows to a maximum of 5 feet and was a perfect acquisition for any stove. Of the two plants acquired by the nurserymen Messrs Young of Epsom, one was bought by the Duke of Devonshire and the other was sent abroad. Paxton's plant was kept in a pit, filled with 'plenty of water, rich loam soil and well-rotted dung', maintained at a temperature between 65 and 85°F, and flowered at Chatsworth for the first time, as Gibson set sail, in November 1835. By May 1836 over one hundred fruit were ripening, weighing between 30 and 40 pounds. Paxton exhibited it at the Horticultural Society at the start of May where it caused an immediate sensation and was awarded the coveted Knightian silver medal.

In fruiting the sweet, dwarf variety Paxton was again at the vanguard of his profession. Open to the opportunities of the press, he ensured that the news was widely circulated, penning articles for his own *Magazine of Botany* and, at Loudon's request, for the *Gardener's Magazine*. He was delighted by his success, and he wrote proudly that he intended building a small *Musa* house in order to fruit two dozen plants a year, which would be managed so that they bore fruit in circulation all year round. He described the flavour as combining that of the pineapple, the melon and the pear and insisted that there were only two other authentic dwarf banana plants in Britain, both of which came from his plant at Chatsworth. Because of the publicity surrounding the banana, Young's were now desperate to procure one for themselves. They regretted the sale of a plant destined to be such a commercial success to Paxton for only £10 and proclaimed that they should have charged him ten times that. They had missed their chance, and their churlish rancour outraged Sarah.

By 1840, Paxton had cultivated enough plants to begin distribution among the ardent horticulturalists of the day. In February that year, the Duke delivered several plants to a horticultural meeting where it was, again, 'exceedingly approved of. Mrs Lawrence pocketed some, and the rest – twenty in number – were swallowed by the company in a moment.' *Musa cavendishii* is said to be the parent of all edible bananas now grown in Britain. A plant was taken from Chatsworth to Samoa by the missionary John Williams, whence it was later spread to Tonga and Fiji in 1848 and from Tahiti to Hawaii in the 1850s. Australia and New Guinea probably received it from the same source.

◡

Wallich returned to the Botanic Gardens in Calcutta in May, as the Knightian medal was being conferred on Paxton, and advised Lord Auckland that Gibson should concentrate his energies in an orchid-rich district in the Khasi Hills in Assam, making a 250-mile trip up the Hugli River and its tributaries to Sylhet, basing himself in the hills at Cherrapunji, one of the wettest places on earth. It would be an arduous and possibly dangerous journey, navigating uncharted waters, past 'dacoit' villages to the foothills extending southwards from the Himalayas. Assuming his safe arrival, the plan was for Gibson to remain there for about a month before making a three-month journey to Martaban in search of the *Amherstia*.

Gibson kept himself busy in the gardens of Lord Auckland and his sisters, the Misses Eden, waiting for the rains that would fill the tributaries of the Brahmaputra River and mark the start of his expedition. The wind was like fire as the heat climbed close to 100°F. In need of news from home, the delay and the unnerving heat exacerbated his anxiety about the dangers ahead. He was very well aware, as he wrote to Paxton, that 'duty calls on me to exert myself to the utmost extent . . . boats on the river are upset and go down in numbers and never afterward heard of. The wind is so strong and so instantaneous that they have not time to get on shore before they are sunk.' He left Calcutta in a small boat with a handful of local guides on 6 July.

Three weeks later, having successfully battled through the powerful waters in the foothills, Gibson arrived at a small bungalow in Cherrapunji. It was teeming with rain, but he knew immediately that he had, indeed, found a botanical treasure-chest: 'I never saw nor could I believe that there was such a fertile place under the Heavens had I not the inexpressible pleasure of seeing it,' he wrote. What was better, he believed that all the plants would be entirely new to European collections. Over 520 different kinds of orchid thrived on the plateau and the rains had transformed the jungle into an endless horizon of flowers and colour. Every day he splashed out into the steaming, echoing wilderness around him, returning with the plants and shrubs that began to crowd his veranda – orchids with their roots tied in moss, and seeds which required the constant maintenance of fires to dry. Every day he found something new and he exulted in the possibility of sending such a collection home, alive, to England.

Gibson wrote a continuous stream of letters to Wallich in Calcutta, describing a new *Dendrobium* and a most beautiful *Aeschynanthus* of which he had found four species. He asked for advice on packing plants in such a climate and he rejoiced in the flavour of the local pineapples while describing leaves, flowers, pods and seeds in minute botanical detail. He wrote to Miss Eden's maid, Mrs Wright, that the air was filled with butterflies and that he was in his glory. Miss Eden forwarded the letter to the Duke in England, noting whimsically: 'there is something rather sublime in the idea of Gibson in his glory. Scene, a tent at Cherrapunji with a foreground of Palangium and bearers and Gibson in the midst crowned with an orchideous wreath, and holding a large purple Emperor by one wing.' It emerged that Gibson had been so frightened before setting off that he had entrusted Lord Auckland's gift to him of a silver goblet, knife and fork to Mrs Wright, fearing that native savages would murder him for the cup and eat him with his own knife and fork. With no experience of the hazards of his journey, he perhaps had in his mind the recent death of the intrepid collector David Douglas, who had fallen into an occupied bull pit in the Sandwich Islands in 1834.

Gibson found at least fifty new kinds of epiphytic orchids clinging to the branches of forest trees. He began to send back specimens almost immediately so that the first boatload of these and other plants was received by Wallich in Calcutta at the beginning of October, along with letters in which Gibson pleaded with Wallich not to forward them to England before the following spring, fearing that the cold winter winds would kill them. Exultant with the quality and diversity of the collection, Wallich replied that Gibson should stay in the hills, abandoning his plans for Martaban, since he now believed that a plant of the *Amherstia* could be supplied from the Calcutta gardens. In his isolation, Gibson was growing increasingly triumphant. To Paxton, he wrote in September: 'I never addressed you with so much pleasure and satisfaction . . . I do assure you that such is the extent and splendour of my collection as to make it one of the richest collections that has ever crossed the Atlantic . . . the Orchideae are splendid indeed and I don't hesitate in saying that I shall supply from 80 to 90 new species which are not in England.' He prayed fervently that they should survive the journey home.

⌇

In England, on 29 September 1836, the foundation stone of the Great Stove was laid by the lovely Blanche, Countess of Burlington, and the cutting out of the foundations continued throughout the winter. Realising that such an enormous expanse would require significant manual labour to glaze, Paxton turned his mind to the problem of abridging the process of grooving the sash bars to receive the glass. He visited workshops in London, Manchester and Birmingham hoping to find new inventions that would answer his need. He found only a manual grooving machine, but when he attached this to a steam engine – all the time reassuring himself that the odd rumbling noises could be overcome – and improved the detail of its features by making repeated small modifications, he found that it would answer perfectly.

Letters carrying word of Gibson's treasures were still at sea when, in January 1837, he left the Assam hills, many of his discoveries preceding him, already laden into cases and chests and embarked on ships returning to England. He arrived in Calcutta at the start of February, 'almost wild from being too long in the woods and jungle', with further boatloads of orchids, rhododendrons and primulas. On 3 March, Gibson left Calcutta on the *Zenobia*, returning with his princely cargo of thousands of tender exotics of which at least 300 were new and around 100 were previously undiscovered varieties of orchid. Some 45 plant cases had been packed on different ships; the richest living collection ever to be brought to England. Gibson had still not received one word from home – his joyous letters written in the autumn were only beginning to arrive in England as he left India. He sat in his cabin nursing his orchids, many of which were still attached to their host branches suspended from the roof. Two plants of *Amherstia nobilis* were at his side day and night – 'depend on having Amherstia dead or alive,' he wrote to Paxton.

One hundred and forty days after leaving Calcutta, the *Zenobia* entered the English Channel bound for St Katharine's Docks. Gibson was 'filled with joy at the sight of my native shores from which I hope I shall never again take my departure. 'Tis a feeling inexpressible.' Plant losses were inconsequential in all but one respect. One of the two *Amherstias* had perished. It was the plant addressed to the Duke. The survivor was clearly addressed to the Directors of the East India Company. Gibson wrote to the Duke exhorting him to make a claim for the plant, before it entered customs and was 'lost to us but also quickly lost to England'. He wrote also to Paxton urging him to press his suit with the Duke, who indeed supplicated for the plant within a couple of days.

Paxton was in a stew. From the moment he heard of Gibson's imminent arrival, he could apply himself to nothing else, writing to the Duke in London: 'I am in such a state of excitement . . . particularly to what relates to the Amherstia, that I shall worry myself to death if I am to stay at Chatsworth until all this is settled in London. If I ever put my hands on Amherstia, all the Directors in the world shall never make me let go of it till it reaches Chatsworth.' He left for London immediately, travelling straight to the docks only to find that Gibson and his cargo had already left for Devonshire House. He followed.

As his carriage pulled up, just before nine o'clock in the morning on Saturday, 22 July, the Duke's valet, Meynell, put his head out of the window and called Paxton to come immediately to the Duke. He flew up the grand stairs in a whirl of excitement and then, as he wrote to Sarah that evening, 'came the solemn introduction . . . to my long cherished love the Amherstia. I cannot detail how this important introduction took place – suffice it to say the Duke ordered his breakfast to be brought to the Painted Hall, where the plant stands, and he desired me to sit down and lavish my love on the tree.' Gibson, looking well, introduced him to the remainder of the beauties. The Duke and Paxton held court for the rest of the day, Lindley and Messrs Loddiges being among the first to arrive to worship at the horticultural shrine.

East India House kept the men on tenterhooks for almost a fortnight before sending its reply at the end of July – the Duke was to accept the *Amherstia* as a gift, along with the honour of introducing the plant to Britain.* Gibson's amassed collection included over 1,000 tender exotics, *Gloriosa superba*, *Melastoma*, *Impatiens*, *Hoya* and *Bignonia* and over 100 hundred species of orchid, including 50 new varieties of *Dendrobium*.

Paxton then ordered a ducal narrow boat to race the cargo of botanical riches along the 200-mile canal from London to Cromford, some 12 miles from Chatsworth, where they were loaded on to sprung wagons and arrived in record time. Gibson was promoted to foreman of the exotic plant department.

Many of these treasures would be figured in the pages of the *Magazine of Botany* over the next months and years, including his prized *Aeschynanthus* and the *Dendrobium paxtonii*, named in his honour by John Lindley. Most would flower for the first time in Britain, at Chatsworth. Inspired partly by Gibson's success and the sheer number of new plants he brought home, that same year Lindley began *Sertum Orchidaceum, or a Wreath of the Most Beautiful Orchidaceous Flowers*, an expensive folio for the tables of wealthy collectors. The first illustration was of *Stanhopea devoniensis*, newly named in recognition of the Duke.

The Indian expedition, given the enormous quantity of cases to be sent back to England, incurred for the Duke very great expense – it was possibly the most costly expedition ever mounted at that time – but the intrinsic value of the plants returned ensured the Duke, Paxton and Gibson their place in horticultural history. Along with the enormous work still underway on the Great Stove, it was clear that the Duke, with Paxton, was getting into his spending stride. Money was flying out of his accounts. In his usual diary summary of the year, he noted, without undue concern, a complete failure to keep a rein on his expenses. He was having fun.

* Presumably Gibson could have simply substituted the labels on the plants to avoid the emotional upheaval of the weeks spent waiting for this reply. We can only assume that his own kind of Victorian morality precluded his doing so. In the light of his own fever over the tree, I doubt whether Paxton would have hesitated.

CHAPTER EIGHT

Over the next two years, the content of Paxton's magazines moved away from the detail of subjects like propagation and cultivation, to concentrate on the more general pleasures of the garden and of gardening. Pages were filled with designs for flower gardens, articles on garden ornament and discussions on various aspects of the kitchen garden in particular. Underpinning everything, plants were the thing – and especially 'celestial orchideae'. While Gibson was collecting and Paxton was writing and experimenting with his glasshouses, the Duke boasted to his diary that 'no one could come up to him about plants'. He was drunk with Chatsworth.

With the *Magazine of Botany* now taking precedence in Paxton's affairs, the last volume of the *Horticultural Register* went to press at the end of 1836. One of the last articles was filled with advice for young gardeners and set out a code of principles which formed the basis of an ideal horticultural education. The gardener intent on profession-alism and promotion, the article advised, should know something of geology – the strata, clays, loams and sands which make up the earth. He should have a basic understanding of chemistry in order to be able to test the soil for the metallic oxides injurious to plants, and he should be proficient in geometry in order to form designs, present improve-ments on paper or map landscapes. Gardeners, like shepherds and sailors, should be observers of the face of the sky, habituating them-selves to notice the atmospheric changes that herald alterations in the weather. A practical knowledge of botany was, of course, imperative in order to understand the care and culture of exotic and curious plants, and so a young gardener should learn botanical names, while taking care to be conversant with the natural habitats and nature of plants and their propagation. The botanical classification systems of Linnaeus and Jussieu were useful in describing the physical differences in the structure of plants and an understanding of the physiology of plants would in turn recommend the methods for healing wounds, grafting stocks or making roots grow. The young gardener should read poetry in order to learn the rules of composition and keep a diary to record the year's operations. Propriety of conduct, moral worth and faithfulness were stressed above all. Paxton was setting out his creed.

As Gibson's orchids swayed in the beams of his cabin, the Duke did something entirely unexpected. From London, Paxton wrote to Sarah, 'when I had been out with the Duke all day he desired the coachman to drive to Mr Briggs, Middlesex Hospital, and arriving there the Duke asked Mr Briggs if he had time to paint an individual. The Duke then turned round and said "this is the person I wish you to make a portrait of". You may imagine how I felt . . . I have sat twice . . . he is considered a first rate artist. The Duke will have to pay £60 for it . . . I am fearful every body will be jealous. I dare not tell anyone and it must come out.'

Sarah was deeply thrilled at the news, at the same time moved by what she saw as the Duke's unbounded kindness. She worried that Briggs would make Paxton's face too white, fashionably erasing the ruddy health of his complexion. She wanted a true likeness of the man she adored. She was also concerned that such an honour was likely to inspire great envy among the Duke's senior staff though, despite the Duke's favouritism, Paxton's very straightforwardness and affability appear always to have deflected criticism from his peers. Briggs' portrait shows a man on the edge of his seat, as if an open door to the garden beckoned and he were holding his breath to keep himself still, trapped into an uncomfortable and unfamiliar stasis.

In London, Paxton now pursued his own interests as much as those of the Duke. He visited nurseries, advised the Duke's friends on gardeners for their estates, met regularly with Bradbury over unsold volumes of the *Magazine of Botany* and pleaded with Sarah to join him to assist him in his many tasks. But Sarah was hard to prise away from

Derbyshire, her children, or her newly-hatched goslings. In any case, she was several months pregnant. On 21 November 1836, their fifth baby was born – the first since William's death. It was a boy, George.

Quietly, Sarah and Paxton began to invest in railway shares. The 1830s were the earliest heyday of the railway revolution – new companies and new lines were springing up all over England. In 1834 Robert Stephenson's main Birmingham to London line had just begun and the great trunk routes were mapped, including Brunel's Great Western Railway between London and Bristol and the lines of the Great Eastern. Three years later, there were 700 miles of track in the country; within ten years there would be 2,000. The first railway terminus hotel would be opened at Euston in the late 1830s, just as Brunel's steamship the *Great Western* cut the Atlantic journey to an astonishing 15 days and 5 hours. Confidence was secured in Britain's growing industrial prominence, and private savings began to be invested as never before by the prospering middle classes. Within a decade, speculation would become the rage.

Just before Gibson arrived home in that summer of 1837, when William IV died and all England became Victorians, Paxton again accompanied the Duke in his coach from Chatsworth to London. The aristocrat was an altered man. Finding himself near the end of a long love affair with his mistress, Eliza Warwick, doubts about his faith had brought him under the influence of an evangelical clergyman, Mr Beamish of Trinity Chapel and, feeling himself to be lost, he had begun to immerse himself in scripture and sacrament. Paxton was horrified. The Duke, he told Sarah, had become 'a ranting, canting saint' who 'battled about religion almost all the way from Chatsworth to London'. Paxton himself had a no-nonsense attitude towards religion; his was a down-to-earth disposition and he feared the loss of his Duke to a kind of spiritual insanity. In the carriage, they were locked in discussion for over ten hours and he employed robust argument to return the Duke to a more realistic sense of himself, engaging him with a frankness he later partially regretted, writing to his wife that he was afraid that the Duke would 'not relish what I have said to him, though he took it all in good part'. The following day, the Duke went to church twice and to the chapel 'with all the rag tag and bob tail' in the evening. From Devonshire House, Paxton poured out his frustrations to his wife: 'all this nearly breaks my heart. My attachment to the Duke is so great that nothing could make me dislike him, but my love for him is now mixed up with some gall and wormwood.' Sarah was a Unitarian who held no truck with evangelists, considering them to be canting hypocrites. She feared the Duke was lost and that Paxton would have to build a chapel instead of a stove.

On Gibson's return, orchidomania broke out. Now with the finest collection of orchids in Britain at his command, Paxton experimented and practised with the plants at Chatsworth, concentrating on perfecting his methods of cultivation. He began to formulate a set of rules that he considered standard for their care, advocating the provision of separate houses for plants from different climates, the benefits of a far lower average temperature than had been considered crucial, more efficient ventilation – in particular during the growing season – the occasional watering of the paths to maintain a moist atmosphere, and improved methods of potting, drainage and root-development. To his delight, he found that the orchids thrived in the loamy soil of the Chatsworth woods, high in fibrous matter.

He also worked throughout 1837 on his only published book, a monograph on the cultivation of the dahlia, the flower that Empress Josephine had collected obsessively in her garden at Malmaison, and which had arrived in Britain at the close of the Napoleonic wars. Particularly expensive, the dahlia had become hugely fashionable throughout the 1820s and 1830s and a movement developed to establish it as a new 'florists' flower'. Its astonishing range of colour and form made it a favourite for exhibitions and it was cultivated for coveted prizes and medals. Filling the pages of his monograph with his observations on dahlia structure and habits and his experience of their nurture and supervision, even in the bleak north of England, Paxton showed himself to be an educated and unselfconscious writer. The book was immediately translated into French, German and Swedish.

The mania for new plants, and Gibson's particular success, emboldened others to finance expeditions in search of new rarities for the stoves and greenhouses of England. The Duke was invited to subscribe to a journey to the unexplored regions of Panama and Guatemala, which he declined that summer. He and Paxton were more interested in extending the work of David Douglas and they discussed the possibility of sending men to the north-west shores of America in search of hardy and gigantic firs as well as ornamental shrubs. Examples of these kinds of trees were still rare and inestimably expensive in England, broadly unobtainable from nurseries and even then only as grafts and cuts rather than in their more prized seed form. This time, they decided that a number of subscribers should finance the expedition, sharing equally in any treasures returned to England.

To that end, Paxton wrote in early November to any member of the nobility or gentry who might be considered a potential patron. He proposed that each should take a £50 share, with the appointment of four gardeners to meet the seeds and plants on their arrival in England to divide them fairly. Two men would be sent together, as had been advocated by Douglas before his death, since they would be able to offer each other protection against personal danger and would stimulate and spur each other forward. Soon, Paxton had 24 subscribers and the leading nurseries of Loddiges, Knights, Rollison, Young and others were invited to join. Then he began to plan a route, writing to William Hooker in Glasgow and to John Lindley in London for their advice. While he was tempted by the sea journey to Guatemala, collecting South American orchids along the way, he was alive to the potential criticism that this was his personal, unbounded particularity, as he wrote to Hooker, and a distraction from their primary purpose. Paxton therefore proposed that the men travel overland with the Columbian expedition of the Hudson's Bay Company to York Factory, traversing the Rocky Mountains and the head waters of the Columbia River and from there turning south along the Pacific coast to California and Mexico.[*]

The Hudson's Bay Company emphasised the hazards of an over-land route from the east coast of America to its Pacific seaboard. Hooker and Lindley also advised against it. Since the Hudson's Bay Company had a ship leaving England in October, which could deliver the men to Fort Vancouver by the following summer, in a season perfect for plant collecting, Paxton abandoned his preference for the overland route and postponed the trip until the autumn.

At the same time, and at the instigation of his friend John Lindley, Paxton became involved in his first public appointment. The Queen's accession had led, as usual, to a parliamentary examination of royal expenditure and, at the end of January 1838, the Treasury appointed a commission to inquire into the management and expenditure of the royal gardens. The chairman was Edward Ellice, MP for Coventry, known as 'the bear' less for his ferocity than for his own connection with the Hudson's Bay Company's fur trades. The now-noted botanist and professor, John Lindley, assisted by two practical gardeners, was asked to make a survey of and report on the condition of the gardens. Lindley's two assistants were Paxton and the Earl of Surrey's gardener,

[*]   California was at this date part of Mexico.

Battlesden Park & Gardens, by George Shepherd, 1818.

At the time of my entering in the Garden of the Horticultural Society my Father was dead – he was formerly A Farmer at Milton Bryant in Bedfordshire where I was born in the year 1801 – at the age of 15 My attention was turned to Gardening, and I was 2 years employed in the Garden of Sir G. O. P. Turner Bart at Battlesden, from there I went to the Garden of Saml Smith Esq at Woodhall under Mr Wm Griffin where I continued 3 years. and then returned to be Gardener to Sir G. O. P. Turner at Battlesden I remained there 2 Years after which I came to the Garden of the Society being then 22 Years of Age and unmarried

Joseph Paxton

Paxton's entry in *The Book of Handwriting of under gardeners and labourers,*
Horticultural Society, November 13, 1823.

William Cavendish, 6th Duke of Devonshire, by Sir Thomas Lawrence.(1811).

Amherstia nobilis

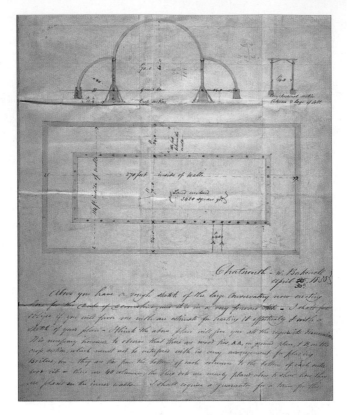

Sketch of the Great Stove, April 1838, with letter requesting an estimate for heating.
This letter is written by Paxton's secretary, Samuel Hereman.

Photo of the Great Stove before its destruction in May 1920.

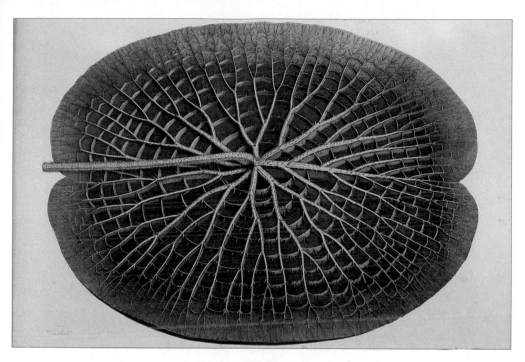

Underside of lily leaf.

The Emperor Fountain, 1844.

Handpainted Chinese wallpaper showing the dwarf banana *Musa cavendishii*.

not be able to leave Malta before the first of
May owing to the 21 days quarantine which
we shall have to pass there — You will think I
shall never return again by these protracted delays but
I believe you have no cause in the end to regret my
long journey for my health is so well established
that I hardly feel the same person — My dear
children would not know me if they were to see me
now I wear a Greek Cap and Italian Cloak
something like this   with long flowing hair
but I will moderanize   myself before I come
home I hope the dear   little creatures a
ill will I long   know any thing
to hear all their   little prattles as of
and to see you   all placed round
happy table   it will be of no
you writing   after leaving this
as I am   some to be on
the way home before another letter could reach me
what a time it seems since I was at home
from the number of events that have crowded
upon each
appears almost six years — I have how little
news to tell   you here as our
own hearts are the only ones in this part of the
world that you either know or care about
may remember me kindly to yours one

Letter to Sarah from Paxton in Constantinople, March 1839.

The portrait of Paxton by Henry Perronet Briggs, commissioned by the 6th Duke and painted May 1836.

John Wilson. They were to examine Buckingham Palace, Kensington and St James's gardens, Hampton Court, the gardens at Windsor and the Pavilion garden at Brighton, with a particular view to the feasibility of their continuing to supply foods and flowers that could be as readily procured at markets elsewhere. Separately, they were to examine the Royal Botanic Garden at Kew, evaluating not only its ability to provide flowers for all the palaces, but its efficiency in extending botanical knowledge through the cultivation of new and rare plants. They were to assess the gardeners, minutely inspect their salaries, accounts, records and management practices. This would involve examination of the venerable Aitons – John Townsend, who had served at Kensington and St James's for 46 years, and his older brother William Townsend, the 71-year-old director of Kew, appointed by George III.

On a cold Monday in early February, the three men assembled at Lindley's house in Turnham Green to formulate their schedule. The following day they inspected the Palace, Cumberland Lodge, Frogmore House, Cranbourne and Maestricht gardens at Windsor. On Wednesday they left for Hampton Court and in the following days examined Buckingham Palace gardens, the royal kitchen garden at Kew and the royal forcing gardens at Kensington, where the ground was covered with snow and it was impossible to see which crops were being grown. The following Monday they went to the Botanic Gardens at Kew, spending the rest of the week examining accounts, forming estimates and considering their report. At Kew, they found the elderly William Townsend Aiton particularly obstructive and reluctant to help.

Letters came back to Sarah from Paxton.

We have been engaged up to this time, half past eleven on Wednesday night inspecting the gardens . . . we found all the gardens in *excellent* wretchedness, the most miserable places that were ever beheld. Dr Lindley tells me . . . that Mr Aiton is about to resign, his salary is 1000 per annum. I know I could get the place with the least exertion, if the Duke would part with me, but I shall not attempt it as I am sure the Duke would be miserable, and may justly think me ungrateful. I am sure Dr Lindley is dying for me to get it – he thinks I should make something of their majesties' gardens if I was at the Head.

One thousand pounds a year was a very great deal of money and, while she loved Chatsworth, Sarah questioned her husband's wisdom in dismissing the idea out of hand. Paxton, though, did not have to think twice. He loved Chatsworth and was strongly attached to the Duke and the plans they hatched together. He knew that to move to Windsor would be a great mistake – he would have to start from scratch there, with years of anxiety and worry. He had also made a faithful promise to stay with the Duke, but he was canny enough to know that a single mention to his employer that he had refused to entertain the idea would increase his stock with him still further. No doubt he found a time to do so – at some point in the year the Duke increased his salary by £50 to £276, extending his responsibilities to cover all the roads on the estate. His house at Chatsworth, of course, formed part of his salary and the latitude of the Duke allowed him far wider scope in Derbyshire than he would have enjoyed at Windsor. Nevertheless he had passed up a significant opportunity.

In forming their final report, the men worked typically from nine in the morning to eleven at night. It was completed within a fortnight and was scathing.

> We are irresistibly drawn to the conclusion that the Royal Gardens have been badly managed . . . we do not think that the value is equal to the cost . . . the crown possesses nearly 900 yards of . . . forcing houses of all descriptions and yet they did not in the year 1837 furnish a strawberry or a grape in the months of January or February and scarcely even in March . . . Notwithstanding the large expenditure of more than £10,000 a year, the Royal household is not better supplied with fresh fruit than that of most private gardens.

They noted that as schools of horticulture each garden failed dismally – discipline was lax, there was no effort to educate or instruct the gardeners, fruit trees were not labelled, the salaries were too low and the gardens generally exhausted. Lindley, Paxton and Wilson recommended a complete reformation of the whole system, with higher salaries and grants to enable the gardens to form libraries for their men, based on the practice of the Horticultural Society. They were appalled that Windsor appeared to be the only palace in Europe without a garden of any quality. Wyatville's flower garden there was already in an appalling condition because of forceful westerly winds and badly prepared beds. It was recommended that only two kitchen gardens remain, including a new one to be built for Windsor at Frogmore. The pleasure ground at Buckingham Palace and the ornamental flower garden at Windsor should be maintained on the civil list, but all other gardens should be abandoned.

The Botanic Gardens at Kew, and William Aiton in particular, bore the brunt of their displeasure. He was credited with allowing public access to the gardens, but they could see no reason why anyone would want to go there, since they appeared worse than useless. There was no attempt to name the plants, no communication with the colonies for plant collection and distribution, and no classification observed in the gardens. Aiton was found wanting and derelict in his duty, the gardens were a dead weight on the civil list. They recommended that they should be relinquished by the royal household and taken for the public, expanded and made worthy of the country as a powerful means of promoting the science of botany. Alternatively, they should be abandoned.

The royal gardens had cost £10,000 to maintain over each of the previous three years, not including the necessary purchases of flowers, fruit and vegetables from elsewhere. Now Lindley and his gardeners estimated that the new garden at Frogmore would cost £30,000 to create, the enlargement of the Kew kitchen garden a further £7,000, and to bring the Botanic Gardens up to scratch £20,000 was needed. To finance the various schemes, they suggested that a small portion of the gardens at Kensington should be maintained in order to force flowers for Buckingham Palace, but that the larger part of it should be used to form a new road linking Bayswater to Kensington. Plots of land on either side of the new road would be sold off for private housing.

When the report was presented to the Treasury, Lord Melbourne was surprised by the costly recommendations and the Queen recorded in her diary that 'they asked £28,000 for making an entirely new garden at Windsor . . . a Dr somebody of the Horticultural Gardens, and the gardener of the Duke of Devonshire's at Chatsworth, who never thought of what was economy, were on the committee . . . [Melbourne] never quite approved of it from the beginning'. It was not considered politic to introduce such extravagant expenses for parliamentary consideration and, for a while, the report languished.

That year, the Botanic Society was founded by James de Carle Sowerby and the Duke of Norfolk as a rival to the Horticultural Society and for the promotion of botany in its application to medicine, the arts and manufactures. The new society created their gardens on land leased from the Crown in Regent's Park and felt that this could, perhaps, form an alternative to the Royal Botanic Gardens at Kew. The Horticultural Society disagreed, and petitioned the government for the retention of a national botanic garden. A campaign was launched, reported regularly in the pages of *The Times*. Two years later, the government finally proposed the complete abolition of the gardens at Kew, offering the plants to the Horticultural Society on the understanding that they would allow public access to their gardens on two days of each week, but the society refused. Public opinion concentrated, and later that summer the botanic gardens were officially transferred from Crown property to the Commissioners for Woods and Forests, and national ownership. Aiton had retired in March and John Lindley and William Hooker were both proposed as the new director. Petitioning the government and claiming that he was cheaper than Lindley, Hooker was successful, and he moved down from Glasgow to take over. He was paid £300 a year plus £200 in place of a house, and he was instrumental in turning the Botanic Gardens at Kew into the world's foremost botanic institution.

Finally, the government accepted all Lindley's recommendations, though a further two years passed before groundwork began on the new kitchen gardens at Frogmore, Windsor, in December 1841. When completed, with 25 vast glass forcing houses,[*] it was roundly praised as perhaps the most perfect garden of its kind in Europe. The kitchen garden land sold in Kensington Gardens to finance Frogmore resulted in the formation of Kensington Palace Gardens (originally called Queen's Road) – still a private road on the edge of the park where the grand houses are now used primarily as foreign embassies.

As Paxton's role in the Royal Gardens Inquiry drew to a close at the end of February 1838, the Hudson's Bay Company suddenly decided to send an overland dispatch to the north-west coast of America the following month. With the means now available to send plant collectors earlier than had been expected, two men from Chatsworth – Robert Wallace and Peter Banks – were quickly chosen and equipped. One could speak French and the other Latin, both were bidden to learn Spanish. Paxton's secretary, Samuel Hereman, drafted an agreement signed by all three men – Wallace and Banks would be absent for three years, each to be paid £1 4s a week. They were enjoined to

[*]   Now demolished.

conduct themselves civilly, keep accounts of their expenses, and beware
of bears and women. They sailed to New York on 20 March 1838 and
from there embarked on a steamboat up the Hudson, which made the
400 mile journey to Montreal in just four days. Within a month they
were encamped at Lachine in Lower Canada, preparing birch-bark
canoes for the journey across the inland rivers to the Columbia.

Soon after Wallace and Banks left England, on the death of Thomas
Knight and at the insistence of Dr Lindley, the Duke became president of the Horticultural Society, confirming his now extraordinary
status in horticultural circles. Paxton remained at Chatsworth where
500 workers were permanently occupied with the construction of the
Great Stove. Employed on site, his steam-powered cutting engine was
now honed to perfection, churning out the required 40 miles of sash
bars which would otherwise have been cut by hand. The heating system
would be underground, set within the outside walls of the building,
and Paxton supervised all the excavation, earth moving and the setting
of masonry himself. There were to be 8 boilers linked by 7 miles of
4-inch iron pipe, each fed by coal brought along the tunnels beneath
the building. As the structure rose, excitement in the gardening world
climbed with it and gardeners began to offer the choicest plants from
the pick of their private collections once it was completed. James
Bateman offered the largest of his tropical trees and, on the death of
Lady Tankerville, her collection of enormous palms were promised to
the Duke.

Paxton's reputation widened and his advice was occasionally sought
not only in judging competitions but also in the formation of new
buildings. At around this time he designed and built a large conservatory some 150 feet long as an extension to the house of Edward
Davies – a friend of the Cavendishes – at Capesthorne Hall in Cheshire.
The house had been recently remodelled and the conservatory would
provide a link from it to the chapel. Formed of laminated wooden
arches, cast-iron pillars and vertical glass sides, the conservatory had
a pitched ridge and furrow roof. He did not, perhaps, see this architectural sideline as particularly significant as there are no references
to it in his correspondence with Sarah. But it added to his increasing
workload at Chatsworth – a workload that would continue to expand
partly because he was particularly well liked. A letter to the Duke that
spring, from his friend the Countess Mulgrave following a visit of two
days to Chatsworth, is worth noting as much as an indication of his
popularity as of the transformation of the grounds. She wrote, 'I never

particularly raved about Chatsworth before but really now there is a glow of . . . beauty about it that is only like a poet's or painter's dreams. I think the way the old garden is now connected with the house is so well done.' She talked of a delightful new stove (not the Great Stove, which was still being constructed), of all the tropical plants doing so well, of the blaze of flowers and the beautiful roses. 'And now I must say a word about Mr Paxton who is the most delightful person I ever met with, he pours whole floods of knowledge into me. He has no affectation but a delightful enthusiasm for his art, for art it is.' She, too, wanted to make a greenhouse on Paxton's plan.

⌇

As the Great Stove rose, ideas had coalesced separately for another project of similar scope, if not innovation. Throughout the early 1830s, the design of labourers' cottages had become a popular theme in horti-cultural magazines, backed by a tradition of at least fifty years of 'pattern-book' publications – books in which a wide range of archi-tectural styles were illustrated. Since his visit to Nash's Blaise Hamlet several years earlier, the Duke had been warming to the idea of his very own modern model village, a grand scheme which would also respond to a practical need for improved housing.

First, in 1836, Decimus Burton, a contemporary of Paxton's, and a student of Nash, was asked to design a new farmhouse and stables on a new site some distance from the mostly derelict existing village of Edensor. The following year, the Duke commissioned Wyatville to design and build two ornate lodges at the entrance to what would be the new village, one Tudor and one Italianate in style, as well as a new gate for the park. Then, in early 1838, ten designs for cottages were bought from John Robertson, Loudon's draughtsman, several of whose drawings had been published in the hugely successful *Encyclopaedia of Cottage, Farm and Villa Architecture* published by Loudon in 1835. Robertson's designs for the new buildings embraced almost every character, including Norman, Italianate, Tudor, Jacobean, Swiss and English cottage styles, the Gothic and the Castellated. All the houses were to be made of solid local sandstone and enriched with gables or other ornament, scattered in true Picturesque manner up a hillside rising from the opposite side of the road from where the village originally sat.

Tenants were rehoused in the nearby villages of Beeley and Pilsley.

By the spring, templates were being made for setting out the new cottages and the foundations for Wyatville's eastern lodge and drainage and excavation for the cottages continued throughout the summer. With all this in train, the Duke left England for an extended tour of Europe, accompanied by his spaniel, Bony, his new doctor, Condell, Meynell and his second valet, the cook Cornelius, Theodore the courier and Robert the second footman.

In the autumn, as the work progressed, Paxton visited London to find a letter from the Duke ordering him to leave immediately for Switzerland. With no time to collect his thoughts, or much luggage, he wrote breezily to Sarah that he was off – 'God bless you all, be quite easy on my account . . . you will hear from me again in a few days.' He would not return for more than nine months.

CHAPTER NINE

Paxton left Devonshire House at five o'clock on the morning of 23 September, fought his way through the London traffic, battled with customs at Boulogne, and arrived in Paris that evening having eaten nothing since breakfast. From Paris he travelled in a diligence, non-stop for four days until he arrived in Geneva, where he found the Duke grumpy with his courier who had turned out to be a dreadful liar, and keen for the calming presence and organisational skills of his friend. The Duke was amazed at how quickly Paxton had arrived, and told him that no one else he knew could have managed it. Paxton wrote to Sarah: 'His Grace has been in a terrible stew for want of me for some time . . . I am to be the grand leader of the band, until all the grand sights are exhausted.' He was already so full of the wonders he had seen that he felt like 'a steam boiler with the safety valve . . . ready to burst'.

The Duke had saved the great sights of Switzerland for his arrival. Together they travelled in a carriage, venturing 6,000 feet up the glacier of Mont Blanc to the perpetual snow, taking in 'wonders on wonders'; it was the first time Paxton had seen the majestic Alps. They swept across the Simplon Pass and down into Milan and Lake Como, talking non-stop and all the while dreaming up new plans for the embellishment of Chatsworth. The Duke, while occasionally irritated that Paxton slept when he wished to talk, wrote in his diary that 'he is everything for me'. With Paxton there, his temper abated and he was in great spirits, much to the relief of all his entourage.

If Sarah, on the verge of giving birth to their fifth child, was hanging her hopes on the fact that her husband would be home for Christmas, she was to be disappointed. While she lumbered through the last month of her pregnancy in an England lashed by winter gales, her husband was full of excitement on the other side of Europe, writing with enthusiasm that they might eat their Christmas dinner in Greece. He might have imagined her reaction as she read his letter, for he enjoined her not to laugh or cry at his news, 'only think what an opportunity it is for me to see all these fine and wonderful things'. Despite her condition, her place was to 'keep a sharp look out about the Great Stove and let everything be in readiness for a grand move in the spring . . . I have promised the Duke it shall be done.'

The Duke would always win the war for Paxton's attention. Paxton adored his wife and small children, but he not only felt bound by a deep sense of duty to his employer, he was also enlivened by his company and their shared passion. He had become the Duke's anchor – a gardener, a practical organiser and a buoy to the spirits. By the end of October, the courier had abandoned them and Paxton had taken over. But this was no ordinary position. Like a father, the Duke went out of his way to be particularly kind – as Paxton wrote to Sarah: 'he don't think half so much of pleasing himself as he does of gratifying me whatever sights I want to see'. The Duke read all his letters from home, taught him Italian ('full of music and sweetness') as they travelled together in the carriage, took him to the fish markets and teased him with the prospect of eating frog's legs (Paxton declined). They smoked together, the Duke eight cigars a day to Paxton's two, and the Duke gave him (and only him among his staff, enjoining Paxton's discretion) a £5 lottery ticket with the prize of a grand palace in Milan. Paxton was tempted to buy another to increase his chances. Cautiously, he did not.

Together, they travelled on to Brescia, Lake Garda, Verona, Vicenze and Padua, arriving in Venice at the start of November. Paxton marvelled at the quiet of the gliding gondolas and the constant ringing of the bells from 102 churches, but he despaired of the vast amount of starch used in his collars, which consequently cut into his neck. He bought a new frock coat and cloak in order to keep up appearances, commenting that his hand was always in his pocket so much was he tempted by souvenirs for Sarah and the children. In Venice, he dreamed that he had a new son.

Paxton's correspondence with Sarah was a promise they kept

throughout their marriage when apart, and if either lapsed there were sharp words on either side. Letters took about two weeks to travel between them, so that Sarah read the news of her husband's great pursuits, and his questions about progress at Chatsworth, as she recovered from the birth of her fourth daughter, Laura.[*] She was wistful for him to see her 'pretty smiling face . . . beautiful dark blue eyes [and] profusion of very light hair'; she longed to see Rome and the remains of the once great city – 'so bring me something from there, if only a pebble'. In her letters to him, she reported the daily details of their Derbyshire life, of progress on the Stove and the building of its chimney high up in the woods so that the smoke from the boilers would not pollute the air around it. She wrote of the delivery of the boilers, which would be installed underneath the stove in corridors high enough for men to walk in, and told him how the older girls, Emily, Victoria and Blanche, flew home from school in nearby Ashgate on Saturday eager for the news his letters brought. She told him how beautiful the flowers were on the splendid orchids, particularly the *wallichiana*, which had just bloomed in what little George called the 'orkediffidushouse'. She wrote that 'time does not hang heavy for I have so much to do the days are never long enough'. Nevertheless, she wanted him home, or at least news of when he might be expected to turn his face northwards again. The children, she said, would 'devour you with kisses'.

From Venice, the Duke's party moved off to Bologna, Ancona, Loreto and on to Rome, arriving there towards the end of November. The Duke was a world apart from the modern grand tourist rushing all over Rome to see the sights – those trippers that Byron reviled as 'a parcel of staring Boobies' and who were tolerated by the Italians only for the money they spent. The Duke's stepmother, Elizabeth, had lived in Rome following his father's death and shared her stepson's profound interest in and patronage of Italian art, sculpture and antiquity. Stendhal noted that Bess and the Duke were about the only exceptions to the Romans' hatred of the English tourist. Paxton told Sarah that Rome was a wild and dangerous city in which the 'fashionables' slept all day and partied all night; the valet Meynell was frequently drunk to the annoyance of the Duke and Paxton detested the Romans – 'a cut throat people . . . two persons stabbed since we came'.

Throwing caution to the winds, Paxton was living up to the reputation of English tourists and was out spending money – around £100

---

[*]   Which Paxton thought 'an outlandish name'.

or a third his yearly salary. The Duke had already spent £2,000 on works of art and sculpture for Chatsworth, including new works commissioned from Canova. Paxton was thirsty for all he could learn, writing to Sarah 'you will be astonished by my knowledge of sculpture and pictures and other things belonging to fine arts. I know a good picture or a fine piece of sculpture at first sight and in nine cases out of ten can tell the master who executed them. I have likewise acquired considerable knowledge and taste in various matters . . . I believe I know as much of Rome and its contents as any person in it. I have bought the history of the Ancient Romans and read it on the spot.' Their plans were to leave for Naples, visit Leghorn, Florence and Genoa and return via Paris the following February. The Duke, however, delayed their departure from Rome on account of Paxton's rheumatic pains and, promptly, fell ill himself. Tender, long letters followed for all the children to read, painting gloriously amusing pictures of his life abroad. In one church, he saw a model of the nativity scene, with the Virgin Mary and 'Joseph, her husband, stands opposite looking as if the child before him is a bastard. At a little distance stand Wise Men from the East . . . Blanche and Toey would laugh at them, while Emily would say "Oh father, what nonsense". Even poor dear little George would, I think, laugh at the fun.' To Emily he wrote that the Pope was dressed like a fine doll, wearing a fool's cap, and that he would not kneel in the street to him when he passed, for fear of scuffing the knees of his trousers.

Back home, in the bleaker, colder world of Derbyshire, Sarah was disappointed and stoical, writing that 'jobs crowd thick upon me at times, but my health is so good, I am able to get through them'. Laura was growing to look like William ('and God grant that she may have a disposition like his, which was truly heavenly'), whereas George was becoming spoiled and difficult. At the Stove, the boilers were now being installed; John Gibson, who considered himself master in Paxton's absence, was becoming a precious puppy. *Amherstia*, she noted, was growing vigorously in her husband's absence.

With her five children around her, Sarah's spirits had rallied by the start of January 1839 as she began to hope that he would turn back to England – 'I'll venture to say you should like to see Palermo. But don't go any further,' she wrote. Paxton was torn between her need for him at home and his indispensability to his employer. He did not commit himself to staying abroad but he could not see how the Duke would manage without him to help with his purchases, settle his accounts and calm disputes among the servants. Casting his eye towards home, he held out hope of his return, warning her that he was about to board ship where he could receive and send no letters. He ended his latest and then, at least as far as Sarah was concerned, he disappeared.

The group did not embark immediately as planned but remained three more weeks in Naples, visiting Pompeii, Herculaneum and Vesuvius, where the rocks flew around and where the glow from the volcano at night was sublime. Paxton's Italian was becoming almost fluent, and the Duke was taking as much trouble to introduce him to all the wonders as when he first arrived in Geneva – no waterfall was too small to visit and 'nothing can exceed the Duke's kindness and attention to me'. The Duke took it into his head that there was nothing worth returning to England for until the work was finished at Chatsworth, to which Paxton quipped that he may as well stay on the continent a long time, for there was plenty more opportunity for enrichment of the grounds. In the middle of February, they embarked on a ten-day voyage which took them to Palermo – where Paxton rhapsodised about the Botanic Garden – to Messina, Catania and Syracuse and on to Malta. The Duke gave him no chance to leave and Sarah's worst fears that he would continue beyond Europe with the Duke were about to be confirmed.

'I could not get away from the Duke on any pretence whatever,' he wrote.

> In vain did I represent the urgent business at home, and how well he might spare me. His Grace replied . . . 'all that you have said is true . . . but I care not how much work is retarded . . . it is my particular wish that you would go . . . I have longed all my life to see Greece . . . but if you strongly object to going, I will not go at all but all my after life it will be a source of regret and I shall reproach you' . . . Of course I was obliged to comply. You may perhaps think I did not want much persuading, but I assure you to the contrary. I could go all over the world without a murmur, indeed I should be delighted to do so if you and my dear children and my various occupations did not require my attendance at home. Pray write <u>the moment</u> you receive this and tell me all you can of what is going on with the works.

Sarah did not receive these, or any other letters, until the first week of March, by which time the party had reached Athens and visited the

Acropolis, the Parthenon and the King and Queen of Greece. For Paxton, the astonishing whiteness of the buildings and the antiquity of his surroundings was almost a dream. He and the Duke bought themselves red capes and cloaks in the bazaar and went out in a boat together, laughing on the clear blue water. Though it would be another two months before he turned for home, Paxton's thoughts flew more regularly to Chatsworth, grieved at how worried Sarah must be at his prolonged absence and torn between equal desires to press on to Constantinople and to return to his family.

Sarah's anxious suspense was relieved when his letter from Naples finally arrived. She still hoped he would return from there, despite 'all the people here [who] say you will accompany his Grace if he goes further than Malta', and she had dispatched the dependable Andrew Stewart, head of the kitchen garden, to meet him in Paris. Stewart went in untypically bad spirits, never having been abroad before and certain that Paxton would not be in Paris to meet him. Indeed, the Duke's party was off again, across the Dardanelles, 'the place where Leander swam across the Helispont [*sic*] and more recently Lord Byron . . . I think I could do it myself without much difficulty', and on to Constantinople and the astonishing sights that crowded in on them there – the fine doors, the Grand Seraglio, the masks and the minarets. There were no other English travellers in Istanbul. The Duke and Paxton visited the magical Hagia Sophia and the Sultan's garden, bought Turkish slippers and carpets in the bazaars, and feasted on 84-course dinners thrown in their honour, seated on cushions on the floor ('I ate of 47, the Duke could not manage so many'). The Duke, perhaps in recognition of Sarah's fortitude, bought her a Persian silk gown. Paxton wore a Greek cap and a long Italian cloak. Thoroughly entering into the romantic spirit of the adventure, freed from the constraints of English rural mores, he had let his hair grow long.

Meanwhile, Sarah was in despair, writing, 'I was excessively unhappy when I read your letter, my hopes of seeing you . . . in a moment crushed.' She wrote that the intermediate ribs of the Stove were raised, the earthwork finished, the wide drive into the pleasure grounds from the kitchen garden was complete and now descended into the tunnel under the cascade, and that the arches on one side of the building were done. The first tree, an *Araucaria braziliensis* (unsurprisingly, a variety of monkey puzzle) had been moved into the unglazed structure. In the gardens, not a single plant was lost all winter, and the yellow rose had bloomed throughout the snows.

Returning from Constantinople, the Duke and Paxton sat in obligatory quarantine in Malta, where Sarah's letters and those from Stewart, who was still waiting in Paris, were handed to him with tongs. Then, Paxton finally cut his hair short again and set sail in the middle of April, leaving the Duke, Meynell, Condell and the others to return to England at a more leisurely pace. As he left their company on the steamship *Acheron*, he wept. He travelled back past Algiers, up the coast of Africa to Gibraltar, on to Lisbon and from there swiftly to Paris, where he met the ever-patient Stewart before setting sail for Falmouth. He arrived in London at the start of May, longing 'to rush and kiss you and my dear, dear, children', delayed only by the Duke's business and the necessity of clearing all their boxes through customs. He assured his wife that he did nothing but dream of her and the children every night, and that he longed to be introduced to the little stranger, his new daughter, Laura. Sarah was overcome with joy and could scarcely hold her pen as she replied to him, teasing: 'it is reported in the country that you have been <u>dubbed</u> Sir Joseph. I doubt I shall make a bad lady but you can leave me at home you know.'

And so he returned home. The children laughed and cried and laughed again they were so excited to see him. On his instructions, the trunks he had sent from Rome had not been opened, and now presents for Sarah and the children poured out — necklaces and toys, prints from Venice, and guide books to tell the story of the journey he had made.

Amidst the whirl of his return, Paxton quietly visited the sculpture gallery. After months in the Duke's cultured and improving company, he now stood and looked at the pictures and sketches with quite new eyes, writing to the Duke that he 'saw a thousand beauties in them which I had not appreciated before'. He was full of gratitude. 'The kindness which I have so beautifully received at your hands on all occasions and particularly for the delightful tour . . . has so much improved my mind. I will exert myself in every way to deserve the continuance of your Grace's good opinion and every day of my life I will pray for your health and safety.'

⌐⌐

The village at Edensor had progressed but slowly while he was away and he was disappointed, though he admired Wyatville's now completed lodges very much. He wrote to the Duke that he would put more men to work there and gradually started to reorder the estate work into its natural channels again. Then came a crushing blow. Letters had been received at Hudson's Bay House from Fort Vancouver dated 7 November 1838 – they had taken six months to arrive by boat and were forwarded immediately to Paxton, arriving within days of his own return to Chatsworth. They reported that, two weeks before, as they were descending the Columbia River, one of the boats carrying Wallace and Banks and nine other passengers, including children, had struck a rock in the rapids below Dalles des Morts. All the passengers had drowned. Wallace and Banks were within four days of the headquarters at Fort Vancouver where they would have begun to harvest plants and seeds. Paxton's inquiries as to their route had been exhaustive, but he was no doubt plagued by the fact that, had he taken Lindley's advice and sent the men via the sea route, this tragedy would have been avoided.

It fell to him, however, to break the news to Wallace and Banks' parents and to draft and have printed a circular to all the subscribers. The Duke had made a 'sacred' promise to Wallace that, should he not return, his parents would be looked after. Paxton had to find them a house and settle them into it. News of the failure of the expedition was also circulated among the gardeners and published in the *Magazine of Botany*. Despite the glorious success of Gibson's expedition, Paxton swore that he would never again send men abroad in search of new and rare plants. His distress was compounded by the death that same week of Andrew Stewart's 7-year-old boy, whose pinafore had caught in some machinery attached to the sawmill. Paxton was riven with sadness.

If he felt a pang for the minarets and bazaars of the east, he threw himself into work in the gardens and on the construction of two more new features in them. The Duke had been inspired by the sight of a huge broken aqueduct in the gardens of Wilhelmshoehe, Cassel, and had asked Paxton to build a replica at Chatsworth. Construction of the 'ruined' or 'cyclopean' aqueduct was probably begun almost immediately he returned home, marking the start of a much greater system of rockworks and streams that would develop on the hillside above the formal cascade. The theatrical ruin was made of loose blocks of gritstone cut from the cliffs above, over which water tumbled in a fall of 150 feet.

That summer, Paxton also fashioned a new heated wall, or

'conservative wall', 300 feet long and 18 feet high, rising up the steep slope from the house to the stables. Although he claimed some years later that conservative walls were 'a new type of garden erection', the idea had, in fact, sprung from the 'hot walls' of early English gardens. These had generally been used for the growth of fruit trees, which were espaliered on to the south face of the wall while rotting dung was piled up at the back to prevent the temperature dropping too low in winter. The wall to be converted at Chatsworth had been over-grown with dark and damp trees for years and it was here that the yellow china rose mentioned by Sarah in her letters had braved its winter. When it was cleared, Paxton realised that it would be a perfect position for half-hardy plants. Developing the ancient gardening idea, he added a flue and fires to the rear of the wall to keep the tempera-ture above zero. In front, wide wooden panels projected, from which curtains could be hung in winter to prevent draughts. The wall was then ornamented with architectural features that Paxton called 'occa-sional small stone projections or piers', so that the structure appeared to ascend the slope in a series of broad steps, each section higher than the last. A glorious new magnolia was almost immediately planted there.

Unsurprisingly, the amounts spent on the garden in the last half of the 1830s had escalated again. Between 1836 and 1840, glasshouses alone accounted for £5,704, and this did not include any of the expenses of the Great Stove. Prior to 1838 the total cost of the gardens in Paxton's accounts averaged £5,000 a year, but from the 1840s it regularly topped £10,000. Labour costs alone more than doubled.

There was another, far smaller, event in the gardens that summer which rattled Paxton. In mid-July, one of the gardeners, George Norkett, who had been at Chatsworth thirteen years, in the course of which he had accompanied thousands of visitors around the gardens, was involved in a potentially amusing incident which had turned sour. A visiting group was standing by the cascade house when the water was turned on rather too precipitously, drenching one of the gentlemen. He failed to be amused, considered it a malicious humiliation and ran at Norkett with a stick. Norkett defended himself by pulling a knife from his coat. For a brief moment, anarchy ruled on the manicured lawn. There were complaints and cross-examinations and, when George apologised, it appears that Paxton drew a line under the unfor-tunate incident with little more ado.

Paxton's intellectual and social trajectory since arriving at

Chatsworth fourteen years earlier mirrored, to a great extent, the social and political changes that were sweeping through the country. His relationship with the Duke had been transformed into that of sometime confidant and adviser such that, on their return from the grand tour, it was Paxton rather than the auditor Currey who renegotiated the premium on the Duke's life insurance policy. Throughout the 1830s, Britain had basked in a surge of optimism, putting its faith in the material progress rapid industrialisation would bring. As one decade now slipped into the next, the country was becoming the workshop of the world. If time had not before been a pressing consideration, the new *sense* of time evolving out of the progress and discoveries of geological science began to elide with a practical acceleration in the pace of life made possible by the steam locomotives whose speeds were now approaching 50 m.p.h. By 1840, the journey from Chatsworth to London could be made in a crowded train in eight or nine hours, cutting by four or five hours the same trip in a coach and six. The steam-power revolution had stimulated the iron, steel, coal and engineering industries, it had improved the transportation of manufactured goods and, among other things, led to the introduction of the quick, cheap and reliable penny post. Speed was the word on everyone's lips. Everything was becoming faster.

CHAPTER TEN

By the start of 1840, over three years after its first conception, the Great Stove was ready to be glazed. Glass was still taxed and therefore expensive, but Paxton was not content to make use of the small crown glass that was generally available. He therefore visited Chance Brothers, glass manufacturers in Birmingham, who had recently introduced a sheet-glass-making process – the cylinder process – from the continent. The use of sheet-glass for horticultural purposes was wholly experimental, but this was a substantial order and the Great Stove, if successful, would provide the best possible advertisement for Chance Brothers' new process. With some effort, they were able to manufacture the sheets to Paxton's specifications – at precisely 48 inches long, these were the largest panes they had ever made. They fitted the length of Paxton's sash bars exactly, and entirely obviated the overlaps he so loathed. Encouraged that the fame of the stove would bring benefits to their company, Chance Brothers supplied the glass at cost.

The Stove was webbed in scaffolding, but the curved form of its roof still presented its own glazing problems. These were overcome by the use of a wooden wagon whose wheels ran along the grooves in the 24,500 sash bars. In each wagon, two men and a boy were able to propel themselves backwards, spider-like, over the fragile surface of the structure, fixing the narrow 6-inch panes as they went. It was dangerous work and occasionally there were falls, but gradually the roof was completed. A similar system would be used eleven years later with the Crystal Palace in Hyde Park.

The Duke had finally arrived back in England late the previous summer and from January he was back at Chatsworth. He and Paxton again took up their long walks together through the woods in wind and rain. John Robertson, Loudon's draughtsman, whose cottage designs had been purchased before Paxton left for the continent, now joined him at Chatsworth as his architectural assistant, ostensibly to oversee the rebuilding at Edensor and to make designs in response to the regular need for new housing in the ducal villages. Decimus Burton also arrived to discuss his plans for a new park entrance and to witness the Stove near completion.* To date, Paxton had fulfilled the duties of architect as well as gardener, which was not entirely unusual – Loudon, after all, was the supreme example of an untrained designer relying on apprenticed draughtsmen. But although Paxton had clearly mastered the crucial elements of architecture, the sheer scale of the work for the Stove and the money that would be sunk into its construction had dictated that he seek Burton's advice, if only to confirm his own calculations. Now, the need to have this technical training on hand permanently, in the form of Robertson, had evidently become essential.

By March that year, the Stove was finally freed from scaffold. Paxton wrote to the Society of Arts – possibly his first connection with them – describing his perfected sash-bar cutting machine and subsequently received their silver medal for design and innovation. Assisted by John Lindley, he was also working on a *Pocket Botanical Dictionary*, which would include the names and history of all plants known in Britain. In his introduction, Paxton was at pains to point out that the work was compiled wholly with practicability in mind. The multi-volume works available could hardly be carried further than the front door and, with a keen sense of the market, Paxton's dictionary provided an instant resource, a popular synopsis which could be taken to public gardens, horticultural shows or nurseries. It described the best method – and likely expense – of cultivating each individual plant, along with a full glossary explaining all the more abstruse terms. The dictionary was still in print at his death.

---

* Once finished, and as its glorious reputation rippled into drawing-room conversations around Britain, Burton began to claim that he was the primary architect of the Stove. He even wrote to the Duke to ask him to confirm the fact. The Duke's reply does not survive, but only the following year he appeared to clarify matters when he wrote in his *Handbook* that the edifice was an extraordinary monument to Mr Paxton's talent and skill in which he was 'cordially met and assisted by Mr Decimus Burton in its execution'. Burton, wisely, did not pursue his claim.

In Paris for April, the Duke heard of the grave illness of his darling niece, Blanche. He returned, but it was too late. He had lost not only one of his dearest companions, but the wife of his heir, in whose family he had vested all his dreams for the future of Chatsworth. When her husband, Lord William Burlington, declined the Duke's offer to move with his children to Chatsworth, the Duke, about to turn 50, was devastated and felt more than ever isolated and alone. Immersing himself in the plants he loved, he set off on a round of visits to horticultural shows and nurseries. He went with John Gibson to Rollinson's nursery and offered a blank cheque for the enchanting epiphytic orchid *Phalaenopsis amabelis*, the first thing to give him any pleasure since Blanche's death. On his return to Chatsworth, he found himself surprisingly soothed to be there, walking again with Paxton, who had just become father to a fifth daughter, Rosa.

Paxton and Lindley then began to plan what was to be the greatest revolution in horticultural publishing – a weekly gardening newspaper to be called *The Gardener's Chronicle*. Along with all his other monographs and activities, Lindley had edited *Edwards' Botanical Register* for over ten years. He was well known to the Duke, who, however, was not particularly pleased with the idea of this new venture, writing to Paxton that he had 'seen nothing in your letter to diminish the great objection and dislike I feel to your being connected with a newspaper'. But Paxton was not to be diverted. He felt urgently that a respectable, affordable paper was needed and he abhorred shoddy publications like Glenny's *Gardener's Gazette* which he thought was a disgrace to gardeners and the profession.

Plans for the paper progressed, but with the stove completed, the Tankerville palms could finally be moved from their home at Walton in Buckinghamshire. Lindley was sceptical about their chances of survival – one plant alone weighed an astonishing 12 tons and the cart needed to draw it would require eleven horses. But in the closing days of August, Paxton supervised the gigantic job – the Tankerville glasshouse had to be entirely dismantled and reconstructed in the process. Most of the local neighbourhood at Walton, up in arms that the palms were being moved to Chatsworth, came to watch the huge carts collect their loads. The Duke meanwhile, with too much time on his hands, showed remarkable forbearance in accepting Paxton's request that he remove himself from the whole exercise. But he was desperate for news of the enterprise. Finally, he could bear the suspense no longer, writing to Paxton for reassurance that the palms were likely to survive. They did.

Well into the following year, great numbers of plants streamed into the Stove. A collection from Wimbledon House that had outgrown its own stove was donated. Baron Hugel – whom Gibson had met at the Cape during his travels – stripped his garden and shipped off his greatest beauties. The Stove had become a temple to flowers and as it was filled, so its fame spread – Paxton's name writ large upon it.

Around 30,000 feet of ground space under the enormous elliptical roof were filled with the best garden soils, varied according to the needs of each of the plants, and the roots of the larger ones were contained in compartments within the soil in order to let weaker ones stand a chance against them. The beds were bisected by a long carriage drive running from end to end, with a broad walkway running around the whole building. There were folding glass doors at either end and the entire arrangement was divided according to the geographical regions from which the plants derived. A set of winding steps led up to a light wrought-iron gallery and platform, from which a visitor could stare into the canopy of enormous tropical trees, or down on to their smaller cousins. The eight subterranean boilers maintained the temperature to mimic both a temperate zone at one end and a sub-tropical zone at the other, while ventilators were fitted into the masonry foundations and into the roof. It was, by all accounts, the greatest glass structure in the world. Its height and span were greater than Liverpool Lime Street Station (1836), Euston Terminus (1839) or the first Great Western Terminus in London completed in the same year, and it required neither wooden nor iron trussing. The Palm Stove at Kew was still four years off.

Later, Paxton would construct a large mass of rockwork to conceal the staircase, planted with ferns and cacti. Gleaming rock crystals from the Duke's collection were also brought here for display, exotic birds flew among the branches and silver fish swam in the pools beneath a plant collection that was simply unrivalled. There were massive, exotic foliage plants and ferns brought from the jungles and mountains of distant continents, orange trees collected in Malta, altingias and araucarias, date palms from the Tankerville collection, the feathery cocoa palm and the giant palm *Sabal blackburneana.* There was a silk cotton tree with its creamy flowers. There were hibiscus, bougainvillea, bananas, bignonias, cassias, pepper and cinnamon trees, massive strelitzias – the bird of paradise flower – and hanging baskets of maidenhair fern. In the south-east corner were sugar canes, papyrus, arum lilies and cycas,

in the north-west corner, aloes from the Mediterranean and
Stephanotis floribunda rising to the roof. When Charles Darwin
visited this miniature floral world in 1845, he wrote that he was
'transported with delight . . . the water part is more wonderfully
like tropical nature than I could have conceived possible. Art beats
nature altogether there.'

CHAPTER ELEVEN

While all this planting was ongoing, the particularly restless Duke insisted that Paxton – who was having nightmares that the watering of the stove plants would soften the undersoil and cause the glasshouse to come crashing down – accompany him to his castle at Lismore in County Waterford. He had been absent for eighteen years.

The estates at Lismore represented around a third of the Duke's revenue. He was among the largest landowners in all Ireland and his castle, with its 42,000-acre estate, was certainly the most romantic, set in the ancient seat of learning among the wild scenery of the Blackwater with its mountains, river and meadows. On his return there, the Duke found the castle embellished one hundredfold and was enchanted by what he saw, and by his agent there, Francis Currey. Paxton found a degree of grandeur he had not been prepared to expect and a garden, nursed by the soft climate, in which dahlias, myrtles, hydrangeas and other greenhouse plants grew without protection. He went salmon fishing for the first time, walked, rode, laughed and sported. The Duke, Paxton commented, was happier than he had seen him in months.

Sarah wrote to her 'Dear Dob' every day. Arrangements for the *Gardener's Chronicle* were moving forward – she thought it likely to be a troublesome affair. Five-month-old Rosa was rolling over, the *Amherstia* was throwing up new shoots and, she reported, people were beginning to talk about the growing closeness between her husband and the Duke: 'You are got into the London papers, travelling with the Duke of D, they call you Mr Paxton the celebrated florist and botanist, well you have nice times of it . . . long may they last'. But soon Paxton was getting bored, he hated 'dandling about when there is nothing to see' and he was longing to return to meetings with Lindley and the organisation of the launch of their paper. The first issue of the *Gardener's Chronicle*, jointly edited by Paxton and John Lindley, appeared two months later, in January 1841, priced at sixpence.

Announcing itself as 'a weekly record of everything the bears upon horticulture or garden botany . . . a full and comprehensive <u>record of facts only – a newspaper in the true sense of the word</u>', the paper was printed in a much larger format than Paxton's previous two magazines, as befitted a newspaper. It was packed with the broadest array of reviews, advertisements and articles, with contributions from the most distinguished nurserymen, botanists and plant collectors of the time. Unlike other gardening magazines, it also included the kind of digest of domestic and political news found in other weekly newspapers, though the editors were clear that it would entertain no political party bias. It was an absolute novelty in the horticultural press and immediately popular.

The *Gardener's Chronicle* was ahead of its time. Born when a surfeit of new periodicals and magazines covering all sorts of subjects were being launched – *Punch* that same year, the *Illustrated London News* the next, with *Blackwood's Magazine* hard on its heels – it outlived most of them. Indeed, it became the longest surviving of all horticultural publications and continued until well into the second half of the twentieth century. A direct descendant of the original paper survives to this day.

At home, Paxton was still transforming the Stove while sending large boxes of trees and shrubs to the gardens at Lismore, with detailed instructions on their planting and care, and also travelling widely with the Duke. They visited the nurseries in London, and the garden of Mrs Lawrence at Drayton Green, some 7 miles west of London. Mrs Lawrence had a considerable reputation as an amateur plantswoman, and in her tiny 2-acre garden she cultivated over 200 orchids and over 500 varieties of roses, long before hybrid tea roses and perpetuals were fashionable. Her garden included rockwork, Italian walks, a French parterre, a span-roofed greenhouse, a stove and an orchid house. She exhibited regularly at the Horticultural Society in London and had won 53 medals including the coveted Knightian medal. Extremely competitive, Louisa Lawrence was in many ways the keenest rival to the Duke and Paxton. Clearly, Paxton did not have a great deal of time for her. Both brilliant plant-cultivators, she matched his straightforwardness with a bubbling wordiness which irritated him intensely. When she visited Chatsworth later that year, it was reported to Paxton, away in Paris at the time, that her flattery was overdone and that she had looked in vain for a weed.

On that trip to Paris, Paxton had, for the first time, taken Sarah with him – her first trip abroad. He showed her Versailles, and the Jardin des Plantes. They shopped for exotic birds for the Stove and visited several of the Duke's aristocratic friends, including the Baron Marvaille in Rouen and Baron James, the head of the Rothschild family in Europe, who had financed the first iron railway between Paris and St Germain a few years earlier. Rothschild's grand hotel in the Bois de Boulogne had been reconstructed in the 1830s on an elaborate scale with famously sumptuous gardens filled with rare orchids. He also owned parkland outside Paris where he indulged his passion for rare birds and animals in an extraordinary collection said to outdo the Jardin des Plantes. Sarah was completely entranced.

Paxton wrote detailed letters to the Duke who was now in Italy, knowing that he, too, would be delighted by Sarah's excitement. He poked fun at Baron James' odd English accent, told the Duke of a new way of growing pineapples at Versailles and listed the plants he had bought or collected. It was as if they could not stop talking to one another despite the distance between them, united in their love of gardens and the memory of their own travels together two years earlier. The Duke was missing Paxton dreadfully, demanding that he write regularly and in the smallest detail. He was disappointed that Paxton had not called on his sister Lady Granville in Paris, nor his friend Lady Hunloke, demonstrating in so doing how particularly his gardener was accepted and esteemed by the Duke's own circle, such that they *expected* him to visit.

Back at home again, Paxton's association with Bradbury, the printer of his various magazines, deepened into a lasting friendship. One of the small handful of her husband's business associates that Sarah actually liked, he and Paxton shared a liberal view of politics, an entrepreneurial nature and as vigorous a sense of humour as of business. By the end of 1841 the fortunes of *Punch* were foundering. Bradbury and his business partner, Frederick Evans (known to the *Punch* staff as 'Pater'), lent the magazine £150 and soon found themselves the proprietors. Almost immediately, they introduced a weekly

Wednesday-night dinner for its contributors and staff, including
Charles Dickens, whose books they had printed since the late 1830s,
the editor Mark Lemon – who was to become a particular friend of
Paxton – Douglas Jerrold, the dramatist, caustic wit and champion
of people's rights, William Makepeace Thackeray, John Tenniel, the
illustrator of *Alice in Wonderland*, and Henry Silver. Uniquely, Paxton
was regularly invited into this exclusive group, to the dinners dubbed
by Thackeray as 'the Mahogany Tree', which, in fact, took place
around a table made of ordinary deal.

Paxton was also often with George Ridgway, the Duke's steward
in London. The two men had spent a great deal of time together, along
with the Duke, from their earliest trip to Paris – and Paxton consulted
Ridgway regularly when the Duke was abroad. He asked Ridgway for
advice on schools for his daughters, and would support him through
the vagaries of his later life, remaining firm friends into their sixties.
By now, John Lindley had become a close ally as well as business
partner – with two daughters slightly older than Emily and Victoria,
he, too, was consulted by Paxton about their schooling in London. In
fact, Emily was to be sent not to Lindley's daughter's school in Hendon,
but to Brighton, and when Paxton visited her towards the end of 1842
he borrowed the Duke's smart brougham and a pair of coach horses,
in order to arrive with 'quite a bustle'.

By 1842 the village at Edensor was all but completed; boilers and grates
had been installed and the cottages had been aired with hot coals to
make them ready. It was a Victorian pattern-book come to life, a fantasy
jumble of architectural styles landscaped carefully into its surroundings. It was also an essay in social welfare and all the houses were
supplied with water and sewer drainage. One of the last villages of its
type to be constructed in England, its Victorian solidity and durability
was broadly admired, though it had its critics. Two years earlier, the
great Gothic revivalist, Pugin, had already roundly condemned such
ventures as mere games, deriding them as 'the worst kind of English
architecture'. Today, its artificiality has been weathered and softened
by 160 winters.

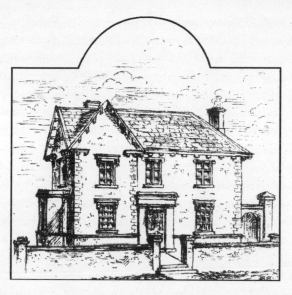

That summer, the sanitarian and public health reformer, Edwin Chadwick, sent Paxton a copy of his new and outspoken report into the relationship between unsanitary conditions, disease and the escalating death rates of the labouring poor in overcrowded cities, the *Report on the Sanitary Condition of the Labouring Population of Great Britain.* Cholera had arrived in England from India via the Sunerland docks in the previous decade, ravaging London with its first epidemic in 1831–2 in which over 6,500 people had died. The link between the poor disposal of untreated sewage and the disease was not to be proved for two decades more, Chadwick himself believing, along with Florence Nightingale, in 'the miasmic theory', in other words that cholera was spread through fetid vapours. Nevertheless, the relationship between filth, drainage and disease, especially in the growing cities, was just beginning to be understood, and Chadwick was one of the earliest campaigners on interventionist methods of social improvement.

Paxton agreed at length with Chadwick's comments on the preservation of health through efficient drainage, but he felt that Chadwick's own recommendations for bettering the dwellings of the poor could be much improved themselves. He argued that the provision of a garden in which labourers could cultivate their own vegetables as well as enjoy decorative flowers, made them happier and prouder of their homes and thereby raised their 'moral character'. Acutely aware of the practical realities of rural life, he was at pains to point out to Chadwick that so long as tenants were given little more than a yearly interest in their farms, there would be no incentive for them to improve drainage at their own expense. He offered to contribute to future reports or supplements to Chadwick's report. It was a subject about which he felt strongly, and one with which he would continue to be involved throughout his life.

Paxton's last child and his sixth daughter, Annie, had been born in March. Within a month she and Rosa had caught measles and the spectre of William's death again hovered over their home. Sarah had Annie baptised swiftly and privately, incurring the disapproval of Mr Money, the latest vicar of Edensor, who wrote at length to Paxton insisting that private baptisms were evil, that the Paxtons were living examples of one rule for the rich, and another for the poor. Paxton was incensed, his reply bitterly indignant. He was not a man to be bothered by rigid trivialities of convention where they were heartless or impractical, and especially at such a time.

In May, with Rosa and Annie fully recovered, Paxton escorted the Queen and Prince Albert around the gardens at Chiswick House. Later the same month his sister, Sarah, at 41 only three years older than him, died in Bicester and he attended her funeral in pouring rain, before visiting his family at Milton Bryant. Looking over his shoulder while there, he might have noted that the glory of the gardens at Woburn had fled with the death of the late Duke. He returned to Chatsworth to supervise plans for a new family house, to be called Barbrook. Plans for this large Italian villa, close to their cottage in the kitchen garden, were being prepared by Robertson. After sixteen years with the Duke, the new house represented a significant visual measure of Paxton's success and it was probably conceived of and paid for by the Duke entirely from his private accounts.

There were new, grand plans, too, for the pleasure grounds, in the formation of an elaborate rockery below the broken aqueduct that would, unusually for Paxton, take several years to complete. Rockeries were becoming fashionable, with new examples at Blenheim Palace and at Syon House, and Paxton had developed his own clear theories about them. He insisted that large rockworks should be isolated from the flower garden and pleasure grounds, a distinct feature whose enormous theatricality should be happened upon unexpectedly. Rockeries, he said in the *Magazine of Botany*, could easily be grand disappointments and errors of taste, 'no subject in the gardening profession [calls] for a more vigorous exercise of skill and talent . . . It is here that those who have studied from nature, frequented her most savage territories and drunk in with avidity their inspiring influence . . . is vividly manifest.'

With all this in mind, he set out to design a massive structure, recalling his journey through the Alps, using gritstone from the abandoned workings at Dob Edge above the estate. Stately and wild rock forms would cover over six acres, with the largest boulders cantilevered at the top of immensely high formations for the most dramatic effect. The grandest of all the single rocks, named after the Duke of Wellington, was 45 feet high, with a waterfall coursing over its face. To blend this massive man-made feature into the natural environment, plants were introduced into crevices and spaces between the rocks, trees were planted and pools created. This was theatre, a rugged drama into which plants should only be carefully woven and always subordinate to the rocks themselves. Paxton recommended in particular rock roses, zinnia, phlox and lobelia, along with half-hardy perennials, the common scarlet geranium and even amaryllis and iris at the lower edges where the rocks met the smoother contour of a water basin.

Initially, at least, progress was rapid. Soon there was a labyrinth of rocky walks, a cobbled flight of steps with balustrades of Irish yew, the Queen's Rock and Prince Albert's. 'The spirit of some Druid seems to animate Mr Paxton in these bulky removals,' the Duke noted with pride in his *Handbook*. The work continued for some five years and later still, in 1851, the *Art Journal* gushed that 'here, Art has been triumphant; the rocks which have been all brought hither are so skilfully combined, so richly clad in mosses, so luxuriantly covered in heather, so judiciously based with ferns and water plants, that you move among, or beside them, in rare delight at the sudden change which transports you from trim parterres to the utmost wildness of natural beauty'.

In 1842, Paxton also began excavations for 'the strid' or 'Bolton stride', an imitation of a feature near the Duke's estate at Bolton Hall in Yorkshire, where a watercourse rushed through a chasm in the rock with stepping stones across it. Once contrived, large native beeches overlooked the pool and the whole area was planted with berberis and cotoneaster, with bilberries and wild currants brought from Fountains Abbey for what has been described as one of the earliest examples of ground-cover planting. The aqueduct was linked to the rockery and the strid by the waterfalls. Many years later, the whole system was eulogised by the *Gardener's Chronicle* as the most extensive and most ambitious rock garden made by the hand of man.

With successful magazines supporting his growing prosperity, his establishment within the Duke's affections and social circle secure, a deepening network of his own close friends and a grand new house in construction, Paxton no longer displayed innocent wonder at his fortune. He was growing into it, and out into the world. In August, he visited Liverpool once more, this time at the invitation of a prominent industrialist and town councillor, Richard Vaughan Yates.

Liverpool was now a thriving city whose new industrialists were profiting from their easy access to transatlantic traffic and the trade that came with it.[*] With a population approaching 100,000, it was becoming possibly the greatest industrial city in England, its growth fed by the opening of the Liverpool to Manchester railway and the manifest power of steam. With his relatively new wealth, Yates had bought 97 acres of land from the Earl of Sefton as a speculative development for around £50,000. It was about a mile and a half from the

---

[*]   The mail, slaves, sugar and tobacco in particular. While the *SS Great Western* had sailed from Bristol in 1837, Liverpool was rapidly catching up with its trading rival in the south, modernising its docks and infrastructure so that once the *SS Great Britain* left her dock in Bristol in 1843, the biggest iron ship in the world, propelled by the new screw propeller, she worked out of Liverpool thereafter. Cunard, however, had already won the mail contract for Liverpool.

city centre, on a slight rise, comprising meadow and farmland formerly part of the ancient Toxteth Deer Park. Yates wanted to set aside around forty acres of land for a park, developing the remainder as exclusive housing in the form of terraces and single villas. His invitation to Paxton to develop the park – which would become known as Prince's Park in honour of the birth of the Prince of Wales in 1841 – was a marketing coup for Yates. For Paxton it represented his first essay in municipal design, setting a pattern that would be developed and extended in all his future public projects.

It is worth remembering that, at that time, London was the only British city with a number of large parks – mostly royal – including Regent's Park, designed between 1811 and 1826 by John Nash, though here public access was restricted. In effect, only the pleasure gardens in London, the most famous of which were at Vauxhall, offered public access to walks and gardens, music, dancing and sideshows. With the growth of cities, public open spaces were diminishing. Concerned at the overcrowding of the new industrial towns, a movement for public parks was established and, in 1833, a Select Committee on Public Walks had been appointed, the first of its kind.

As a result of the committee's recommendation that open spaces should be made available for ordinary people in cities, Primrose Hill in London was secured for the public, Victoria Park in the East End was proposed* and Parliament took the first faltering steps towards securing Battersea as a public park. The Derby arboretum, opened in 1840 and designed by Loudon, who had been advocating open space design since 1822, had been donated to the town by the mayor, on the understanding that it would be freely available to all. Trees were planted on mounds, walks were provided with seats and shelters, statues were set on pedestals and the entrances boasted pretty Elizabethan lodges. Three days of celebrations marked its opening. In the event, however, the maintenance costs prevented the dream of free access – the arboretum was open only to those who could afford it, with only one day set aside for the enjoyment of ordinary people.

Yates' plan in Liverpool was also to provide a park at least part of

---

* Designed by James Pennethorne, student of Nash, it did not open until 1845. Later, John Gibson became superintendent there and altered it extensively to provide a more beautiful park designed along the lines of Paxton's principles, before moving on to become superintendent of Battersea Park.

which would be reserved only for the use of residents. Yet it showed an appreciation of the economic advantages of the marriage of parkland with housing development, providing a manicured open space in a city where only the Botanic Garden and the Cathedral Gardens existed as alternatives.

With this new commission in Liverpool, Paxton practised with wide and narrow walks and the creation of different designed spaces within a coherent whole. As early as 1831, in the second number of the *Horticultural Register*, he had set out nascent ideas for the formation of subscription gardens in the vicinity of large towns, recommending that 12½ acres be split into 50 small gardens of a quarter of an acre each for growing fruit and vegetables, with a 4-acre flower garden at the centre. The addition of a house on each plot and a carriage drive around the perimeter gave him the basic formula for the design of Prince's Park.

Paxton's design for Yates separated the park in into two principal areas. Wide open, undulating grass parkland, planted with informal groups and single trees contrasted with a more intimate, private garden. The small garden surrounded an irregular, sinuous lake with its own island linked by a bridge. There was a boathouse, probably designed by Robertson, formal patterned bedding and narrow paths winding through plantations of shrubs. Ornamental bedding fronted the proposed terraces, linking them to the park itself, and a broad curving perimeter drive, flanked by a separate, narrower footpath, linked the four road entrances. Trees – native hardwoods with their broad silhouettes, tall firs and pines and some exotic varieties – were planted sometimes to frame, sometimes to interrupt the views of the park, especially from the entrances, before they were allowed to open out again in imitation of an ideal estate park.

Once the plans had been drawn up by Robertson, delivered and approved, Paxton deputed Edward Milner, a senior gardener at Chatsworth, to oversee the landscaping of the park in his absence. Work started at the end of 1842 and continued throughout the following year. Large, mature trees were transported to the site, operations avidly reported by the *Liverpool Mercury*: 'we may notice the removal of large full grown trees from one spot to another for the formation of avenues and other desirable objects. One tree, 30 years old, has just been removed. The plan adopted for this important process is that invented by Sir Henry Steuart and improved upon by Paxton.'

'Paxton's Plan of Prince's Park'

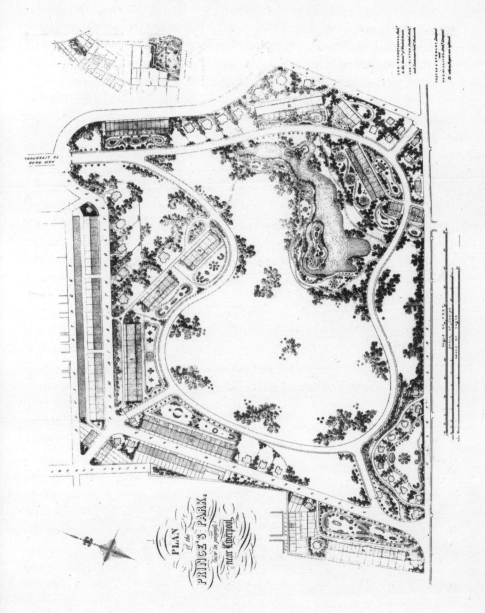

Progress was rapid and the landscaping and planting was all but complete by 1844.

Prince's Park was a forerunner of later Victorian parks, with its principle of exclusive housing built around the edges of the park on individual plots sold for profit. While the land plots sold far slower than Yates had expected, and most of the proposed terraces were never built, it enabled Paxton to try out ideas he had been developing for years. In particular the making of a clear distinction between vehicular and pedestrian traffic, the inclusion of water in the overall plan, the landscaping of open meadow, and the juxtaposition between private and open space, wide views and winding paths. It was the prototype of all his future park design.

CHAPTER TWELVE

The commission for the design and layout of Prince's Park marked the enhancement of Paxton's reputation and the start of a professional career running in parallel with his responsibilities at Chatsworth. By the time it was completed in the summer of the following year, 1843, Paxton was approaching his fortieth birthday and there were seven children at home with Sarah or away at school locally. Sarah and Paxton continued to write fond and affectionate letters to one another almost every day that they were apart, and little George, now almost seven, was becoming increasingly masterful and unmanageable as he took advantage of his father's growing absences from home.

A small town on the other side of the Mersey now approached him to create a new park for them, too. The population of rural Birkenhead had grown rapidly since the advent of steam ferries in the 1820s linked it to the great city of Liverpool, from a few hundred souls in the early years of the century to over 8,000 by the early 1840s. Liverpool's over-crowding, poor sanitation and high death rate served as a warning to them. A decade before, a parliamentary act created a town commission to manage and develop the infrastructure of the budding town – communications, drainage and sewerage, and a large public park were prioritised.

The commission was chaired by William Jackson, a railway contractor and prominent industrialist, and included MacGregor Laird, the shipbuilder, and Thomas Brassey, who would become one of the greatest of all England's railway contractors. Pending a private parliamentary bill allowing them to finance the development of a park from town funds, these men had already personally purchased the proposed 185 acres. Once the bill was passed, they sold it back to the town, creating the very first public park in the world, to be managed by the municipal authorities on behalf of every member of the community. Sixty acres of land around the margins of the park would be set aside for housing, sold at a profit to offset some of the costs.

At the start of August, Paxton walked and measured the huge 125 acres of land set aside for the park with his architectural assistant Robertson and one of the senior Chatsworth gardeners, Thomas Bailey. The land was made up of fields, marsh and bog, requiring sophisticated drainage to make it useful. It was entirely flat and the earth was predominantly sterile clay. Relishing the challenge, and the £800 fee offered, he wrote to Sarah, 'I think I must have lost a lb. of perspiration for I walked at least thirty miles about to make myself master of the locality and it is not a very good position for a park . . . The land is generally poor . . . but of course it will be more to my credit and honour to make something handsome and good out of bad materials.'

Robertson swiftly drew up plans to Paxton's designs. By the beginning of September, the committee resolved that he proceed with the setting out of the park and, as he had done in Liverpool, he appointed a superintendent to manage and direct the whole project, Edward Kemp, a protégé from Chatsworth who assisted Paxton for years with the running of his magazines.

We naturally expect grand civic projects to take months, if not years, to come to fruition. The confidence and drive of these early Victorians are salutary – the future was a blank page on which they could plan the transformation of space, utilities, transport and industry. The design and building of the town's sewer system, road system, docks and railways were proceeding in parallel as tenders went out for levelling the park, building the roads and for pulling up hedges. By the autumn, Paxton was asked to provide sketches for the seven lodges needed for the entrances – Robertson's plans for these were heavily influenced by his work at Edensor, including Norman, Tudor, Castellated, Gothic and Italian styles – and for the railings to surround the land. Kemp was given a permanent office, a monthly salary of £13 10s and, after some to-ing and fro-ing between the committee and Paxton, a budget for materials including a spirit level and measuring tape. Soon there were hundreds of labourers excavating the lakes, setting drains and landscaping the park into mounds and sweeping contours.

Paxton's plan for the park developed many of the ideas he had tested in Liverpool, in particular the separation of different kinds of traffic and the opposition of open and intimate spaces. Groups of trees on raised mounds with luxuriant underplanting and pedestrian walks cutting across the expanse of the park were set against sinuous lakes with bridges and boathouses, a small rockery and narrower, winding paths. Once again, formal bedding around the edges of the land was designed to link it to the proposed houses on the perimeter.

From November that year to the following spring, Kemp was authorised to spend thousands of pounds on plants, including mature trees, tree-moving equipment and shrubs. None of Paxton's planting plans has survived, but Kemp left a clear indication of the kinds of trees used in a book he published some years later. Underlining the importance of evergreens throughout the winter months, he recommended the use of the evergreen oak, the Scots fir and Austrian pine, cedar of Lebanon and the Deodar cedar as well as the *Pinus excelsa* and the Douglas fir. These were mixed with the broader shapes of hardwoods and native trees, with exotic specimens added for interest and individuality to provide a tapestry of finely crafted form, colour and texture.

‿

With their children growing up around them and with their income supplemented by his private commissions, life was comfortable for Paxton and for Sarah. Though with all this new, public work, Sarah began to worry that he was being torn in too many directions, taking on too much responsibility to be able to maintain his precious health. The Duke appears to have sanctioned Paxton's increasing absences from his responsibilities in Derbyshire since it suited him perfectly well for the reputation of Chatsworth to grow in tandem to that of his gardener. Right in the middle of the Birkenhead plans, the Duke took him to Bolton Hall, his estate in Yorkshire, where he was shown all over the estate in detail, joined the shooting party and outshot everyone.*

* On the way to the Hall, the Duke and Paxton stopped for lunch at an inn. Paxton became so sick of waiting for the food to arrive that he stormed into the kitchens, cut up some mutton and cooked some eggs and had the maid take it in. The Duke was so delighted that he tipped her, until he found to his astonishment that his gardener could even turn his hand to cooking.

The Duke did not go abroad at all during 1843 – and his visit to Bolton Abbey was the first for five years. He fell to planning again – Paxton was to succeed William Carr as agent for the estate there, and he was to make alterations to the grounds and extensions to the house itself, including a new wing to the north and new bathrooms. They stayed for a month, interspersing their days' shooting on the moors with visits to Ripon Cathedral and Studley Royal. After seeing the ruins of Fountains Abbey he wrote to Sarah in the same excited tone that had enriched his letters from the Grand Tour – he said that he was almost turned mad by the beauty of the place. Benjamin Currey came up from London to approve the expenditure on the estate, after which Paxton wrote to his wife 'I shall have full orders to proceed without the slightest alteration [to his plans] . . . it will be a big job . . . do me great credit.' Once again he appointed a deputy – this time Robert Lindgate from Chatsworth, who came immediately.

Paxton was riding high on a wave of self-confidence, working and – at Bolton Abbey – playing hard. His letters to Sarah are exuberant, at the same time tinged with a kind of nervous excitement. It was not only the scope of his projects but the considerable quantity of business now on his hands. It seemed he could do no wrong. He was beating them all at shooting and having a ball with the Duke, travelling around the countryside and concocting plans for the aggrandisement of the house. John Gregory Crace – decorator to the rich and famous who had already worked extensively at Chatsworth and Devonshire House for the Duke – was there already and Paxton had to be consulted on every question. The Duke even ordered that he was to send his accounts direct to Currey rather than through the Chatsworth agent, Smithers, or the London steward, Ridgway – in effect creating for him a mini empire – and he spoke of increasing his wages yet again. Even the staff were beginning to treat Paxton differently – he wrote to Sarah that 'everybody [is] paying court and cringing to me which . . . rather annoys me'. Everything was going right, he could relax a little in the holiday atmosphere of Bolton Abbey, speculate a bit more on the railways with his extra cash; and he could rely on Sarah to keep everything ticking over at Chatsworth while he was away. His only regret was that the Duke was to stay at Chatsworth well into October, putting paid to a fortnight's jaunt with her.

The Birkenhead project was proceeding at full throttle, though the increasingly unstable political and economic climate meant that over half the housing plots were left unsold. Then, in November, the Duke heard from Buckingham Palace that the diminutive Queen (she was 4 feet 11 inches high) and her equally small husband Prince Albert had decided to come and stay at Chatsworth at the end of the month. The Duke thought it was a bore and a great deal of bother better over with quickly and Paxton was ordered to discuss arrangements with Ridgway in London, both men utterly nervous at the lack of notice and the secrecy to which they were enjoined. Ridgway wrote to the Duke: 'Pray don't visit Chatsworth at present is the wish of Mr Paxton as well as myself; your Grace's presence would retard what may be necessary to be done.'

Paxton went into overdrive, scribbling hasty letters to Sarah from London in a florid hand listing the jobs to be put in hand: 'pray tell Andrew all the garden walks must be in the most perfect order', roads must be cut, and Andrew could employ ten extra men. 'The lime trees at Edensor must be pruned immediately and every part of Edensor made perfect' in case Victoria and Albert wanted to visit the church there – for this they could take on 20 men. 'The road from the arboretum walk is to be covered with white and yellow gravel . . . there must not be a drop of water on the arboretum walks . . . I have ten thousand things to tell you as well as the ten thousand kisses . . .' No water on the paths in November was quite a request, but Sarah galvanised the men. One thousand three hundred and eighty oil lamps were ordered, along with at least 12,000 more to illuminate the Great Stove.

Paxton rushed back from London to supervise. This was to be the greatest event in the living memory of the Peak District. Rooms at the inns for miles around were booked. Paxton even briefed the local newspapers who applied for details of the operations being planned. One at least took the opportunity of 'acknowledging [this] courtesy which when every moment of that gentleman's time was so fully occupied, we felt to be particularly obliging – and yet everything was conducted with such order and quietness that a stranger passing near . . . would scarcely have imagined that anything extraordinary was about to occur'.

In London the Duke prepared the guest list and sent out invitations. He liaised with the Palace over arrival times at Chesterfield station, and over the schedule of breakfasts, lunches, balls and dinners. He communicated with the Yeomanry about providing an escort to Chatsworth, and with the army about the provision of powder and cannon for a 21 gun salute from the hunting tower. One hundred and ninety-four gallons of ale were ordered, 436 gallons of beer, cases of port, moselle, hock, champagne, sauternes and brandy; 6 oxen and 20 sheep were slaughtered. New beds were bought for the guests and their servants (including the Palmerstons, Lord Melbourne and the Duke of Wellington – 45 bedrooms were needed in all, some impro-vised), gilding was touched up and a grand ball and supper for 140 organised for their second night. The silver was polished and the Russian gold plate brought from the safe. Coote, the Duke's musician, composed new music for the dances, red druggets[*] were bought and the band practised 'God Save the Queen'. The Duke's London deco-rator, John Gregory Crace, arrived to supervise the finishing touches to the state-rooms and Paxton prepared to decorate the staircases with green and white flowering winter shrubs.

Crowds of people met the royal party at Chesterfield on Saturday, 1 December, and lined the 12-mile route to Chatsworth. The park was teeming, the waterworks and fountains playing and the royal standard floated out over the entrance. After lunch the Queen visited the tree she had planted as a girl, Albert added another, and they toured the grounds with Paxton, who showed them the conservative wall, the arboretum and the flower gardens. At six o'clock, in the winter dark, the royal party were driven in carriages, to the strains of the National

[*]   Carpet coverings. These, according to the Duke in his *Handbook*, p. 24, were later turned to good effect as portières and curtains – a very rare example of the Duke's household economy, for the rest of the rooms were swathed in silks, damasks and velvet.

THE GREAT CHATSWORTH CONSERVATORY.

Anthem, past the unfinished rockery, and along the carriage path until they reached and entered (still in their carriages) the Great Stove, illuminated like a fairy castle. Here, Paxton introduced the Queen to vegetable wonders, garnered from the four corners of the globe. They returned for dinner and a ball, past the orangery illuminated with a series of Chinese globe lanterns, while thousands of the public, having applied for the appropriate entry tickets, swarmed into the Stove to see its glories for themselves.

At nine o'clock exactly, Paxton's dramatic pièce de résistance was watched from the south-front windows of the great house. The cascade was lit with coloured Bengal lights, changing from white to blue and then red. Three thousand Russian lanterns blinked from the trees and the waterworks were lit by lamps. The gardens were ablaze, the fountains sparkled and, at 10 o'clock, Paxton gave the signal for a single rocket to be launched. Cannons shot from the cascade and the hunting tower, coloured lights burst from the robber's stone, and all the while magnificent fireworks exploded over the park.[*]

Descriptions of the night exhausted the superlatives of all the papers sent to cover the events. The *Illustrated London News* reported that the Duke of Wellington had remarked 'I have travelled Europe

---

[*] Fireworks had been a part of national celebrations for centuries but increased in popularity in the 1840s because of commercial production methods reducing their costs. In 1844 Bruhl published *The Art of Making Fireworks* and several boys' journals carried recipes for simple fireworks. Bengal lights were used for large displays and burned in open pans placed by trees or water.

through and through and witnessed scenes of surpassing grandeur on many occasions but never before did I see so magnificent a coup d'oeil as that now extended before me.' When the curtains were closed after 45 minutes, an army of garden staff poured out on to the lawns and paths with baskets, rakes and brushes, and when the royal party walked out the next morning there was no trace of the previous night's extravaganza – not a burnt touchpaper in sight, not a piece of gravel out of place or leaf on the lawn. Wellington praised Paxton's skill and organisation so highly that, it is said, he announced that he would have liked him as one of his generals.

On Sunday the royal party walked over the park to the Paxtons' house at Barbrook where he presented the Queen with the first nine volumes of the *Magazine of Botany*, and secured her permission to dedicate the tenth volume to her. They inspected the glasshouses in the kitchen garden and the orchids in particular, and when the Queen departed the next day she left an exhausted Chatsworth behind her. Lady Palmerston, writing her thanks and congratulations to the Duke, singled out Paxton: 'how pleased [he] must be at his success. I hope it won't turn his head – but I believe nothing can.'

CHAPTER THIRTEEN

The strain beginning to appear in the social and economic climate of Britain during the mid-1840s began to be reflected in Paxton's own life and, occasionally, in his relationship with Sarah. The late 1830s had been a boom time in Britain. Now that sense of awe and wonder at the progress made possible by industrialisation was giving way to angst as the price being paid proclaimed itself in the sickeningly over-crowded cities – over half the population of Britain now lived in dirty towns – and the often brutal regime of the factory system. During the 1840s, in the race for profit and amidst an export slump, tens of thousands of workers began to be laid off at the start of a trade depres-sion sometimes blamed on overpromotion of and investment in the railways.

For the new middle classes – and Paxton and Sarah were resolutely in the upper stratum of this class now – life was becoming, at worst, a scrabble to hold their own in the churning waters between the contin-uing profligacy of the aristocracy and the misery of the poor. At Chatsworth, and in his devotion to the Duke, Paxton was to an extent protected and cushioned. Nevertheless, if 'idle' had become a dirty word for the Victorians, his own schedule exemplified the 'sick hurry' of modern life described by Matthew Arnold. He and Sarah were increasingly apart. One trip in September 1845 typified his workload:

> I arrived safe in London and lay down for two hours; then got
> up and began business. Our meeting at the Isle of Wight lasted

for two hours. I had from one to two to go and see Cannon; at two we commenced upon the Southampton project which lasted till five. Without getting a morsel of food, I started off again for Derby and from 8 in the morning until we arrived . . . I had not touched food or drank even a glass of water . . . Got to Derby about half past 11 where I found the Sheffield deputation waiting for me. We sat discussing matters over until three in the morning. I had to be at breakfast at seven o'clock to be ready to start with the Midland Directors to Gloucester and Bristol. After a hard day at Birmingham on Cheltenham & Glos., we got to dinner at Bristol at about eight o'clock. We had a very large party and did not break up until two o'clock in the morning. The next morning was engaged in seeing the Corporation of Bristol and other things . . . [Then] it was agreed I should start by the half past five o'clock train to London next morning [but he was diverted for 24 hours to Bristol]. I got up next morning at a quarter before five and went along to London to see Mr Currey. After a good deal of bother I found out that he was at . . . Kent, nine miles from London. I therefore took a cab and called up Bradbury who went with me, and on my return I called at Cannon's and got Bradbury to write you a few lines while I did business with Cannon. I then started . . . to Birmingham; got there at half past twelve and got a deputation of railway people out of bed at one o'clock; sat till three; went to bed and started off at six o'clock this morning to Derby and came on to York . . . I am sure you will say 'prodigious'. The truth is I never had a moment even to write my name, and out of the five nights I have been from you, I have not altogether had one good night in bed . . . Home tomorrow . . . come and meet me, that's a dear . . . I bless and long for you at all times.

Paxton was now increasingly involved in railway business. In 1844, Gladstone's Railway Act had tried to make sense out of the chaos of lines which proliferated in an atmosphere of unbridled competition. It failed, in effect only managing to introduce compulsory third-class travel on each line in each direction every day, and to limit the ticket cost of these journeys to one penny a mile. But now, the easy wealth to be gained by speculators eager to invest in new lines at the end of the 1830s was, by the mid-1840s, more tenuous. In 1845 alone,

Parliament authorised the building of over 2,000 miles of new track, at an estimated cost of over £50 million. Despite the new class of investing public rushing for shares as soon as new companies were announced, there was justifiable concern in the city that so much capital, labour and material could not be found easily by every prospective line. Consequently, share prices began to fluctuate madly and fortunes were being lost as well as won. Speculation had become more dangerous.

Rail was unquestionably the strongest symbol of the 1840s. It represented the wealth and expansion of the nation and Paxton and Sarah had been investing heavily. Paxton's desk was always overflowing with prospectuses for new companies and promotions of new lines, and he was in the enviable position of being able to take advantage of the advice of many of the most famous in the business, whom he counted among his acquaintances and friends. But it was nerve-racking. In a rare note of serious discord with Sarah, he blew up over money and left home without saying goodbye. She was so miserable that even the sight of the new lambs playing could not lift her spirits.

Paxton met with Isambard Kingdom Brunel, the great designer and engineer of the Great Western Railway's broad-gauge line and of the technological triumph the *SS Great Britain*, the biggest iron ship in the world. In 1845 alone, Brunel was involved as a director or promoter of the Sheffield, Bakewell and West Midlands Railway, the North Derbyshire Union Railway, the Churnet Valley Railway and the Manchester and Southampton Railway, to name but a tiny proportion of his interests. Each of these lines required not only investors but acts of Parliament to proceed. The acts were often preceded by tortuous days of 'committee' in which lines were justified or derided, discussions in which Paxton was often called to give evidence by Brunel, William Jackson, Robert Stephenson or the 'Railway King', George Hudson. He was often overcome with the anxiety of business and the 'confounded hassle' that was starting to dominate his life.

Sarah worried about the extraordinary pressure of business under which he began to labour. They both felt, on occasion, overwhelmed. Paxton was investing fortunes, on one day £500 for an adventure that he thought might make £10,000. On another, he had made up his mind 'either to lose £300 in this matter or gain £4000 – the die is cast'. Sarah sat at her desk one evening while he was in London and looked over their shares. She was astonished to calculate that they had sold over £18,000 worth of shares in the past few months alone. In the space of two years, they subscribed to over £136,000 worth of shares, risking a substantial amount of capital, though they were more often than not successful. Against the backdrop of the sometimes erratic behaviour of their investments and the whirlwind of activity surrounding the railways, Paxton managed the completion of his Liverpool and Birkenhead projects, planned a further monstrously grand project at Chatsworth and was called upon as never before to support the Duke. There seemed to be no stopping him.

⌒

At the start of 1844, the Duke heard that his great friend, Tsar Nicholas of Russia, was to visit England and, he greatly hoped, Chatsworth. The Duke had been impressed by the fountain at Peterhof in Russia which played to 120 feet. Only the previous year he had admired another at Wilhelmshohe in Cassel which achieved 190 feet. Now, in honour of Nicholas, he and Paxton conceived the 'Emperor Fountain', a single jet of water that would burst out of the formal canal in front of the house to a height of over 260 feet – the highest gravity-fed fountain in the world. It would replace the canal's original fountain of 1690 by Grillet, designed as a 30-foot jet and later elevated to 50 feet.

The site for a massive reservoir lake to feed the fountain was chosen 350 feet up on the top of the hills to the east of the house. Men were set to work against the clock to excavate a 9-acre area to a depth of between 7 and 13 feet, often working through the nights with braziers and flares in order to remove over 100,000 cubic yards of soil by spade, barrow and cart. To fill the lake, a stream was diverted by a 2½ mile conduit cut into the moor and, over the next six months, over 200 tons of iron pipes were laid.

Paxton experimented with hydraulics and pneumatics and, to reduce the effect of hammer shock, designed a double-acting valve at some distance from the fountain which took at least five minutes to open or shut. With the work unfinished, word was sent in June of the Tsar's sudden arrival in London. The Duke wrote 'the autocrat likes to arrive like a bomb', which prompted Paxton to scrawl in the margin 'and so does your Grace'. The labourers began temporary measures to finish the works at least to enable the fountain to play should Nicholas visit. It was soon clear, however, that Nicholas would not make it to Chatsworth, and the Duke summoned a disappointed Paxton

to London to meet him there. The Tsar never saw the fountain named
in his honour, though he gave Paxton permission to dedicate the
eleventh volume of the *Magazine of Botany*, which carried a description of it, to him.

The fountain was finally completed later that summer and, with
only 2 feet of water in the reservoir, and without the audience of the
man for whom it had been designed, it raged up into the heavens for
the first time, pluming like a firework. The Duke wrote in his diary
'it is a glorious success. The most imaginative object and a new glory
of Chatsworth. O Paxton!' Visitors flocked to see this engineering
wonder of the day. It was to be Paxton's last great work at Chatsworth
and, like many of his other projects there, it set a new fashion.

Loudon might also have rushed to Chatsworth to report news of
the fountain for his own magazine but, just over a week after the Queen
had glided through Paxton's great glass bubble the previous December,
he had died, leaving his younger rival undisputedly the leading
botanist-gardener in the country. Loudon left only debts for his wife,
Jane, despite being the most indefatigable and extensive horticultural
author of his day. In the *Magazine of Botany*, Paxton remembered him
as a man who 'laboured nearly day and night for the advancement of
science, and wasted his constitution in pursuit of his favourite studies'.
Along with Lindley, he helped to raise funds for Loudon's destitute
family, writing widely to his horticultural contacts across the world
and inviting them to contribute to a special fund.

⤳

Debt on a grand scale ran rife in nineteenth-century aristocracy.
Already the Duke of Buckingham was teetering on the brink of the
bankruptcy that would envelop him in 1848 with debts of £1.5 million,
and the Duke of Bedford was sitting on debts of half a million pounds.
The new wing at Chatsworth had cost over £269,000, the Stove over
£36,000, improvements in the villages, including Edensor, over
£97,000. Paxton was taken aback when he was told that the Duke
had inherited not only an immense fortune but crippling debts from
his parents and that the estates were heavily mortgaged. Over half of
the Duke's income of between £80,000 and £100,000 a year was spent
on compound interest payable on a debt of just under £1 million.

Currey pressured the Duke to make economies, in particular on
any new building, and suggested that small, outlying parts of his

estates could be sold. Paxton, fully aware of the Duke's real financial position for the first time, felt that Currey had failed the Duke in allowing the state of affairs to lie unattended and escalating for 20 years. He thought that a large sale of ducal land should be put into effect as swiftly as possible in order to liquidate the debt entirely. He advised against the sale of the Yorkshire estates, suggesting instead the immediate sale of Lismore in Ireland. He applied himself to the problem in detail and his report to the Duke was lengthy. It urged him to consider 'common sense' in freeing himself entirely from financial obligation and cautioned swift action in the face of the possible repeal of the Corn Laws* which would likely reduce the value of the estates. He felt the most dreadful, pressing responsibility for his part in the profligate expenditure, writing 'I have been the cause of your Grace spending a deal of money; had I been at all aware of your real position I certainly should never have done so – I most truly regret my responsibility . . . the great pleasure I have had in adding to your enjoyment of this princely seat can be my only excuse.'

The Duke's eyes were opened to the horror of his mortgages. He listened to Paxton and he took issue with Currey over the tardiness of his advice. Currey, an honourable man, defended himself – he was of a generation that believed, perhaps rightly, that large debts curbed large spending, and he had tried in this way alone to rein in his spendthrift employer. Currey was adamantly against the sale of Lismore, which he believed would double in value given time. George Cavendish, the Duke's nephew and friend, was also consulted. He spoke at length with Currey, who already suspected that Paxton was influencing the Duke's decisions behind the scenes. Far from feeling rancorous towards him, as he might well have done, he actually confided to Cavendish that he thought Paxton quite 'a sensible fellow'.

Immediately, the Duke left for Lismore, taking Paxton and George Cavendish with him. Paxton did not even have a chance to see Sarah, with whom he had been fighting over money again, and over their son George, who was misbehaving at school in London. As her husband calculated how best to free the Duke of his encumbrances, Sarah wrote to him in Ireland defending her own position: 'I know I have a great love of money, as regards scraping it together, but that has been a

---

* The tariff on imported corn which maintained the high price of corn in England was being vigorously opposed by free-traders, and those who saw that a reduction in the price of grain would enormously benefit the poor. He was right; the Corn Law Act was repealed in 1846.

great blessing to you, you should not find fault with me for that, how many men have to complain of the reverse . . . If I have but your smile I am richly paid.'

The Duke, Paxton and Cavendish stayed at Lismore throughout August. Cavendish agreed with Currey that neither the castle nor its lands should be sold. Despite the sombreness of the trip, the Duke could not refrain from throwing at least one grand ball. As Paxton was laying his own supper below stairs, the Duke came down to ask why he was not dressed to join them and urged him to do so quickly. When the Duke came to look for him again, Paxton was ready. Taking him by the arm, the Duke led him into the centre of the company and introduced him to the leading gentry. If his guests felt that the gardener's conspicuousness was slightly eccentric, they did not show it.

The Duke, Cavendish and Paxton soon returned to Bolton Abbey, where Currey joined them from London, his arms full of papers and account books. Paxton sweated over the outcome of their discussions, confiding to Sarah 'O it is a dreadful load to have on one's shoulders . . . pray for me . . . to get through this giant undertaking.' The four men thrashed through the accounts, the debts and all possible plans for their resolution. Sarah knew quite how deeply her husband felt for the Duke and at Chatsworth she had been fighting for him all day in her mind, quite distracted from anything else. And then there was a breakthrough. The next day, Paxton wrote 'The victory is gained.' All the debt was to be paid off.

> Strange to say, Mr Currey had not a word to say against my plan except the sale of Ireland . . . I felt it prudent to give way on that point rather than engender a bad feeling and a want of cordiality . . . had I persisted in this he would have thrown every obstacle in my way. The Duke told Mr Currey in my presence that there was nothing in his affairs which he might not commu-nicate with me . . . your own darling love is made assistant auditor. Mr Currey behaves beautifully . . . This is the grandest triumph your fond love has ever achieved . . . The Duke appears . . . quite delighted . . . I am truly wild at having carried my great project so successfully.

Land at Lismore would not be sold. Instead, Currey's initial recom-mendation of the sale of the Duke's land at Londesborough and at Baldersby, both in Yorkshire, held sway.

The meeting marked a watershed for Paxton and his involvement in the Duke's affairs. Having consulted him so deeply, the Duke felt that times had changed irrevocably and that Paxton should now be a partner with Currey in his affairs, consulted on all matters large and small. Clear-sighted Sarah saw immediately what this would mean for him. She recognised that he was now in bondage to the Duke in an unprecedented way, writing, 'his affairs are cruelly managed but yet it is very cruel to make you the slave which I am but too certain must be the case now'.

Paxton's innate charm and goodwill, his quick intelligence and tireless ability to enrich the Duke's world had, however, made him indispensable to the aristocrat not only as an employee, but as a friend. There is no more striking proof of this than in the Duke's *Handbook to Chatsworth*, written throughout 1844 and published privately the following year, in which he praised the man almost above the palatial house and exquisite gardens. Paxton, he said, excited 'the goodwill and praise of the highest and lowest, unspoiled and unaltered, he has risen to something like command over all persons who approach him, without one instance of a complaint, or a word said or insinuated against anybody, to me, or to any other person. Beloved and blessed by the poor, considered and respected by all, to me a friend, if ever man had one.'

Wherever he travelled now Paxton found himself 'a lion'. Dinner invitations would be delivered to his hotel, his time was prevailed upon and he rarely had a moment to write quietly to Sarah. By the end of the year, he had sold the Duke's estate at Baldersby to George Hudson and was negotiating with him for the sale of the 12,000-acre Londesborough estate, the ownership of which would allow Hudson to block rival railway lines. While not resenting his change of fortune, Sarah felt that everyone wanted a piece of her husband for their own gain. She was suspicious of the Birkenhead crowd, whom she considered 'purse proud', and she was particularly scathing of them when they did not invite her to a ball that autumn which Paxton attended. Sarah hated 'society' and being on display and she probably felt herself to be a cut above the crowd. A feisty and independent woman, she managed everything at Chatsworth in Paxton's absences, maintaining order, paying and directing the men, but she intensely disliked being ignored. The Paxtons had, in many ways, an unusually equal marriage within the constraints of Victorian convention and, unlike many of her sisters, she refused to stay quiet when she felt crossed.

During 1845, the Duke experienced a crisis in his health and was indisposed for much of the time. Paxton tore by train between Devonshire House and Chiswick House in London, Bolton Abbey, Kemp Town – the Duke's house in Brighton – and Chatsworth on the Duke's whim, while rushing between railway meetings and committees (and stock markets) all over the country. Railways, railway men and railway shares drenched the public consciousness. Charles Dickens said of Paxton that he 'has the command of every railway influence in England and abroad except the Great Western, he is in it heart and purse'.

In May, Tsar Nicholas made him a Knight of St Vladimir and sent him a handsome present of three silver gilt vases and a glorious sable coat. Paxton had been slightly put out when the Tsar had conferred the Order of St Anne on Coote, the Duke's musician, the previous year and was pleased to note that his decoration was 'one degree superior'. Sarah was delighted, but at home she was now regularly distracted by the increasingly unmanageable 9-year-old George. He was unruly, he would swear and he took absolutely no notice of any authority if he could possibly get away with it. It was decided to move him to a school in Sheffield in an attempt to correct his behaviour.

Paxton, meanwhile, was concentrating again on the last phases of Birkenhead Park. The local architect working under him, Hornblower, had already designed a boathouse on the lower lake as well as the park railings and gates. He had recently submitted to the committee a plan for a grand entrance to the park without first seeking approval from Paxton who had left the development of the park in the hands of Kemp. When he saw the designs, Paxton roundly criticised them and communicated his disapproval to the committee. Possibly, he felt that the proposed grandeur of the entrance was at odds with the rural beauty of the park he had created. But more than that, he hated to lose control of the overall design of his plan. In the event, the amendments he made to Hornblower's designs did not include a reduction in its size. The triumphant entrance was constructed, turning its face directly to Liverpool across the water – one of the world's most prosperous cities – and proclaiming loudly its own civic pride in the world's first municipal park.

Commentators raved about the new town of Birkenhead and its magnificent park. The *Edinburgh Journal* noted that 'by far the greater number of our readers will have never heard of this place . . . yet it is one of the greatest wonders of the age'. Paxton, indeed, did himself honour – his reputation for water management and park design soared.

A decade later, when New York City was preparing plans for the development of 700 acres of land, they held a competition for a designer. F. L. Olmstead and the architect Calvert Vaux won. They consulted Kemp and visited Birkenhead, finding there a thick, luxuriant and diversified garden, consummately maintained, which became the direct model for their own plans for Central Park. Here they followed Paxton's lead in incorporating an outer carriage drive, separate pedestrian walks, open and enclosed spaces, water and architectural ornament. Olmstead went on to become perhaps the most famous of all American park designers. He said of Birkenhead 'in democratic America there is nothing to be thought of as comparable with this People's garden. Indeed, gardening had here reached a perfection that I had never before dreamed of.' Birkenhead Park brought the ideal of a huge rural landscape right into the centre of the city as a founding principle of its development. It is now the only grade one-listed landscape in England to have been designed from the outset as a public space.

At the request of the commissioners, Paxton made a new plan for the sale of land for houses by dividing the land into smaller and less expensive parcels. Even this did not meet with total success, but it marked the completion of his responsibilities to the town. On his recommendation, Kemp remained as permanent park superintendent, later working concurrently on his own designs for the layout of Stanley, Newsham and Sefton Parks in Liverpool as well as parks in Southport, Gateshead and on the River Dee. Paxton became a director of the Birkenhead railway and docks and remained friends with William Jackson and Thomas Brassey throughout his life.

Two years later, on Easter Monday 1847, the park celebrated its grand opening, delayed to coincide with the completion of the new Birkenhead docks and warehouses and the extension of the Birkenhead and Chester railway out to them. It was a day of sleet and hail, then rain. Lord Morpeth opened the docks and a 'breakfast' was laid on for 800 people, before the guests processed up through the town to the park where a crowd of 56,000 people had gathered, many given a day's holiday by their employers. The weather cleared, and the sun came out. There were bands, bell ringers, sack and hurdle races, a women's race, a slippery pole, catching the greasy pig, a grinning match and a donkey race.[*] Later, fireworks exploded over the town. It was a fitting opening for Paxton's great park.

[*]   The cricket ground, introduced some years later, is one of the oldest in England, and hosted several of the earliest national matches.

In the summer of 1845, Sarah took the children for the first time to Scarborough on holiday.* She was frustrated and rather bored. Her girls wanted to stay in all day reading books and she longed for her husband to come to relieve the tedium – she could never get used to being unproductive for long. But Paxton, as usual, was busy. The building of their new house, Barbrook, was complete, but it was full of plasterers and painters, with Paxton whipping it along in time for their return. He was also involved in the formation of the Manchester, Buxton, Matlock and Midland Junction Railway (or MBMMJR), designed as a trunk line linking Manchester to the existing Midland line running between Derby and London. The line was proposed to run either through the Derwent valley, which would take it through the Chatsworth estate, or through the Wye valley and the Duke of Rutland's estate. Rutland was vehemently opposed to either alternative. The Duke of Devonshire was overjoyed at the prospect of the railway coming to Chatsworth, and subscribed £50,000 to the company so long as the Derwent line was successful. He stipulated that should the railway come to the park, it should be hidden from view in a tunnel, but since he quite loathed the experience of travelling at speed through railway tunnels, he also insisted that there should be a station at either end of it. In that way, should he want to travel south he could join the line at Rowsley or, if north, at Baslow.

With some of their railway profits, Paxton and Sarah bought Darley House, a Georgian farmhouse with a 1½-acre garden on the Bakewell Road in Darley Dale. It was a sign of their established prosperity and they may have lived there from the time they took possession that autumn until the end of the year, while Barbrook (pictured overleaf) was completed, though it was leased fairly quickly after that to a Mr Adam Washington. Paxton laid out the gardens there and, a couple of years later, built a small conservatory attached to the house.

It was about this time that Paxton became deeply engaged with Bradbury and Evans in plans for a new national, liberal daily newspaper to rival *The Times* and the *Morning Chronicle*, promoting the interests of free-traders, industrialists and manufacturers. It was a dangerous and unusual move for him to make, an indication of his

---

* The sea air had become more popular since the discovery of ozone in the late 1830s, which was believed to be beneficial to health. Seaside resorts began to develop throughout the early 1840s as labourers began to be liberated from their work on Saturdays, too – creating the idea of the 'weekend' and the pursuit of leisure for the working classes that was a particular feature of mid-Victorian Britain.

profitable investments in the railways and that he continued to be willing to grasp all opportunities with both hands. Reading had become the middle-class habit and his own magazines had already joined the enormous literature of information available on a baffling range of subjects. Paxton risked himself as the major investor, subscribing £25,000, more than Bradbury and Evans between them. The Duke supported and Hudson backed them, too – though one feels he might have endorsed any rival to *The Times*, which was already beginning to question his control over so many of the railway lines in England.

Bradbury and Evans were particularly keen on Charles Dickens becoming the editor of the new paper. He visited Paxton at Chatsworth and, according to Dickens' biographer, found a gifted, energetic and ingenious man. Dickens too, of course, was self made. Both he and Paxton, as well as most of the great contemporary engineers, had practised the tenets of Samuel Smiles long before his first self-help manual advocated a set of more-or-less formulated 'rules' in the pursuit of rapid upward mobility.

Paxton spent entire days with Bradbury working out the detail of their newspaper plan. Bradbury seemed in no doubt of their likely success and the time Paxton spent with him was not only because he had an enormous stake in the paper. The two had now been associates for over ten years and they were firm friends. Nevertheless, Paxton was discovering that the newspaper business was not really suited to his temperament – he detested being cooped up inside all day, but he could not go back to Chatsworth at such a critical point. In an attempt to mollify Sarah, his friends at *Punch* sent her a note: 'at the urgent request of the undersigned, Mr Paxton has agreed to remain in London until Tuesday morning'. Among others, it was signed by Douglas Jerrold, William Bradbury, John Leech, Horace Mayhew, Frederick Evans and Mark Lemon. As share prices continued to fall and fortunes were sliding with them, Paxton felt himself being swallowed up by London and by the paper.

CHAPTER FOURTEEN

Although Sarah said that she had become inured to the disappointment of letters that continually postponed her husband's return to Chatsworth, she now seriously feared for the loss of his health. Even Dr Condell, watching Paxton's frenetic activity increase, believed his wellbeing was precarious. He warned of an imminent collapse – a 'brain fever' or something equally bad – if he did not slow down. 'The railways have harassed you for years', wrote Sarah, 'and I certainly think you are acting improperly in giving up so much of your time to them. If you did just half as much as you do, you would be quite as well thought of, or perhaps better; nobody works like you – and what for? Your expenses are very, very great and who pays them? Why yourself. Come home for a little rest and things will go just as well without you – besides, things want looking after here.'

Aside from the railways, the paper was certainly worrying Paxton almost to death. He raced from one meeting to the next, carrying an increasingly large bundle of papers, letters and contracts. Occasionally, he mislaid a cheque or share certificate so that he was forced to retrace his steps, or rummage through the pockets of clothes in his travelling trunk or his white waistcoat to locate it. *The Botanical Dictionary* was reprinted, occasioning many minor distractions, railway shares were falling fast again and George, nine and a half, was an increasing handful – he threw stones and on one occasion hit Emily so hard that she bled copiously from her nose and mouth. The school in Sheffield was not working and Sarah wanted him sent to a public school such as Harrow, where he would be taken in hand. George's behaviour was a conundrum to his father, but Paxton did not have enough time for a lengthy consideration of his son's future. Firefighting on all fronts, neither he nor his wife had noticed the embers smoking in their own drawing room. Paxton took advice from Bradbury, Lindley and Sarah's cousin, George Cottingham, and finally settled on a small 'family' school in London, Lower Grove in Brompton. It cost 100 guineas a year but it was not the forcefully disciplinarian type of public school that Sarah had in mind.

The severe pressure of launching the *Daily News* was in sharpest focus. Charles Dickens, fresh from writing *Dombey and Son*, had agreed, after initial vacillation, to edit it on a salary of £2,000. Scott Russell, the engineering contractor whose fame was growing steadily, was persuaded to become railway editor. Douglas Jerrold, wit and key *Punch* contributor, also joined with John Forster, both to write leaders. Dickens seduced some of the best-known journalists from rival newspapers, as well as hiring some of his own family as staff. In art criticism, literature, politics and news, he had managed to draw around him one of the best journalistic teams in London. Rival papers were concerned and forced to pay higher salaries to stave off defections.

By the end of January, a new deed of partnership had been drawn up, now with nine men forming the company of proprietors. Paxton managed substantially to reduce his own investment to £16,500 by bringing in Cottingham for £3,000, Smithers, Ridgway and Allcard for £1,000 each and two other investors, but he was still investing more capital than anyone else. To encourage the key staff, plans were put in place to pay a fifth of the company profits as dividends to them – Dickens was the main potential beneficiary. He now wrote the prospectus, setting out the paper's guiding liberal philosophy. It would, he said, be swayed by no personal influence or party bias, devoting itself to the advocacy of rational social welfare and issues concerning the rights of man. But right at the outset, one of their brokers went bankrupt and Dickens resigned. A fortnight later, with new capital investment of around £100,000, he reversed his resignation. Advertisement sales had gone well and, for a while, concerns abated. Sarah was rallied by the thought that the paper would make their fortune, buy them a house in London and the time to enjoy it.

The offices of the paper were located in a block of partly tumble-down buildings in Whitefriars principally owned by Bradbury and Evans for their printing works, with an approach from Fleet Street.

Editors were housed on the ground and first floors, with sub-editors crammed around large tables stacked with papers and inkwells on the second. The compositors were high up a wooden staircase on the third floor. The London fog pervaded the lanes and penetrated the doorways, creeping up the staircases and

> lodging in the pipes of the inmates. Add to this the worn steps, the soiled cocoa matting, the walls that seemed ever to require painting and polishing, the windows grimed with smoke, the gas and the glare and the smell of oil and paper. The ceaseless noise of the presses, moved by hand or by steam, produced a busy hum whilst in the foggy atmosphere one could see flitting, like ghosts, the forms of men in paper caps and dirty shirt-sleeves.

Dickens' father John was quite a feature in the turmoil. Short, fat and full of fun, he sat like a beached whale, often with a glass of grog in hand. Sweat trickled down his face since he lacked the means to mop it up – he could not move fast enough to stop the street thieves who regularly relieved him of his silk handkerchiefs as he arrived for work.[*]

The first issue of the *Daily News* appeared on 21 January 1846, following the day of Peel's great speech for the reform of the Corn Laws. It had been quite a scramble and Paxton, Bradbury and the team pulling it together had not slept all night. Dickens had apparently become increasingly drunk as the night wore on. At four o'clock in the morning the printer was pronounced incompetent and Paxton wrote to Sarah that it was only by a 'superhuman effort' and 'suspense worse than her labours' that the paper was produced at all. There was a clamour at the stands for the first number, which was badly printed on second-rate paper. Dickens' piece about his Italian travels was the best thing in it. The editors of other national papers breathed a sigh of relief. Nevertheless, they had beaten *The Times* on to the barrows that morning and sold 10,000 copies on the first day – a figure that fell back to 5,000 over the next few days before regaining its launch sale within the week.

John Gibson was dragooned to help, running between Westminster and the paper's offices with parliamentary reports – often beating the runner from their greatest rival, the Thunderer, which was so furious at the competition that it refused to run *Daily News* advertisements.

[*] John Dickens, manager of the parliamentary reporting staff on the paper, was possibly the original model for Mr Micawber.

But the high spirits of their initial success did not last. Dickens was in the wrong job – he was the best reporter in London but he was not cut out for a newspaper office, unable to manage interference from Bradbury and taking particular offence at what he considered to be a slight against his father working in the back office. Ten days after the first issue was produced, Dickens walked out exhausted, and disappeared abroad.* John Forster, historian, amateur actor, a member of the *Punch* team and, later, Dickens' first biographer, replaced him as editor, persuading Dickens to continue to write the popular series of letters describing his Italian travels as well as occasional letters on important social questions.†

Within a month, the management of the paper was in chaos and its circulation had dwindled to 4,000 copies a day. Paxton was terrified that it would fold, in which case he stood to lose a fortune. Finding it almost too much to bear, his peace of mind and characteristic fortitude momentarily evaporated. Sarah vacillated between optimism, an almost blind reliance on his 'hitherto lucky star' and despondency as she realised that they were balanced on the edge of a precipice. Something was needed, and fast, to pull them back from the brink of financial disaster. Help arrived in the form of Charles Wentworth Dilke, editor of the literary journal the *Athenaeum*, who agreed to take over the management and finances of the paper, immediately reducing the price from 5½*d* to 2½*d*. Forster remained as editor. Sales began to rise, reaching 19,500 in July, and outselling *The Times*. Within months, as a truly radical newspaper, the *Daily News* began to flourish.

～

Throughout the worst of the crisis in March, Paxton had continued to juggle the separate demands of private commissions. The newly established Coventry Cemetery Committee, in need of the drainage and landscaping skills employed at Birkenhead Park, had invited Paxton to submit plans for a new burial ground. It was to be one of the first municipal burial grounds in the country, on the edge of the growing city's boundaries, relieving the shockingly overcrowded parish cemeteries and accommodating the increasing death rate resulting

*   Dickens described his foray into daily journalism as 'a brief mistake' but his desire to establish a newspaper was channelled into the creation of *Household Words*, launched in March 1850.

†   The series was later printed as the book *Pictures from Italy* by Bradbury and Evans.

from cholera and the squalid conditions of the industrial labourers. Only the finest landscape designer in the country would do. Paxton was asked to transform a disused and waterlogged stone quarry into a place of beauty.

Ten years earlier, in his article on arboreta in the *Gardener's Magazine*, Paxton had suggested that collections of trees could, in metropolitan areas, double as cemeteries and now he had a chance to put these ideas into practice. His was a vision of a graceful gentleman's park in which the dead would be cradled within the harmony of harnessed, ordered nature. It would have an embanked terrace, walls with parapets, fine cypress, cedar and yew trees and groups of many different flowering shrubs. In Paxton's cemetery, death would lose its sting. The plans were accepted and work began immediately.

In May, Paxton took George to Hammersmith to dine with horticultural friends. His son behaved impeccably until after dinner when he started to contradict his father outright and ignore everyone else. Paxton was mortified by his outrageous behaviour. As they walked back to London, he discovered that George had got hold of a glass of strong brandy and that he was drunk. He flogged him soundly right there on the side of the road, but he had little time to think more about the incident – an insurrection of quite a different sort was occurring at Chatsworth.

Hannah Gregory, who had died just before the Queen visited Chatsworth three years earlier, had been replaced as housekeeper by Elizabeth Bicknell, previously a barmaid at Buxton. Sarah had written to her husband that the 'upstart' Bicknell was reported to be eating off silver and entertaining her friends at the Duke's expense during his absences from the house. This was an affront of no mean proportions, tongues wagged and the workers in the villages around the estate twittered and trembled at the explosion they expected. The Duke duly flew into a rage and Paxton into such a passion that he felt his hair standing on end and had to restrain himself from flying to Derbyshire to throw Bicknell, physically, from the house. Ridgway and Currey were galvanised, meetings and recriminations followed, and the housekeeper was smartly dispatched to be replaced by the far more suitable Mrs Hastie, a woman in the mould of Mrs Gregory.

Across the Irish Sea, human tragedy on a scale never before witnessed was lurking. The previous autumn, the *Gardener's Chronicle* had announced that the potato blight had reached Ireland from northern Europe. There was no known cure. The poor in Ireland were beginning to starve. Pressure to repeal the Corn Laws finally met success in June* and, with the domestic price of corn no longer artificially maintained, bread became less expensive. The market regained a little of its confidence and shares began to rise falteringly. Benjamin Currey delivered the Duke's statement of accounts for the year, showing that the successful sales of land in Yorkshire had reduced the Duke's debt so far that interest on his outstanding mortgages was reduced to less than a third of his income. For the first time, his accounts showed a surplus. The Duke was in the black.

While tearing backwards and forwards between the *Daily News* offices in London, the scene of Bicknell's treachery in Derbyshire and the cemetery commissioners in Coventry, a significant new opportunity presented itself. A Quaker stockbroker and friend of his, John Allcard, had bought a small estate on the edge of Bakewell from the Duke of Rutland the previous year and asked Paxton to design and build him a house with landscaped grounds. He duly prepared designs for a neat, ornamental Tudor-Gothic-style house. Since Allcard shared Paxton's passion for rare plants, an integral part of the plan was a large, eight-bay conservatory with a ridge and furrow roof, attached to the house and overlooking grounds designed by Paxton that stretched out 100 feet above the River Wye.

The famous builder, George Myers (dubbed 'Pugin's builder' since Pugin would work with no one else), won the contract for building the house. John Marples, who had built the model of the Great Stove in 1835, was to be the foreman builder, and Robertson provided the completed architectural drawings. Burton Closes, as the house was named, was Paxton's first large-scale domestic commission. Inside, the walls, ceilings, woodwork and much of the furniture were lavishly designed and supplied by the team of Augustus Pugin and John Gregory Crace, whose ongoing work on the new Houses of Parliament at Westminster was so striking.

Modest in size, Burton Closes was yet a showpiece of a house, taking over two years to complete. Over a century later, it thrilled Pevsner who was to call it 'a virtual epitome of early Victorian taste'. With Marples in charge of the building and the pressure of business distracting him Paxton appeared, though, to have little opportunity to enjoy this exciting commission, never referring to it in his letters.

---

*   Though, of course, since the landlords continued to export grain *from* Ireland, the Irish were no better off.

It was the last project that Robertson worked on for him; as soon as the plans were completed and accepted, he left. Possibly, he was dismissed. Two years earlier, Sarah had written to her husband that Robertson had disgraced himself by not showing up at Birkenhead as arranged, and suggesting that he be 'discarded'. That May, she voiced her irritation again, telling Paxton that she had paid other men in his office for the work that the 'idle' Robertson had not completed. Whatever the reason, Robertson departed, and Paxton searched for a new architectural assistant, settling on the very young George Stokes, formerly apprenticed to the architect George Gilbert Scott, an exponent of the Gothic style. The shy and stuttering Stokes joined Paxton's practice later that year.

By the autumn Paxton was able to escape. He prepared for a swift tour of parts of northern Europe by train, accompanied by old George Stephenson, Sarah's cousin (and now one of the Duke's agents) John Cottingham and a Derbyshire friend, Richard Barrow. Lord Palmerston provided eight letters of introduction to principal ministers abroad and they travelled fast through Ostend, Ghent, Antwerp and Brussels and on to Liège and Cologne. They took a boat up the Rhine. In Frankfurt, Paxton was welcomed by an invitation from Baron Rothschild to visit his estate at Baden Baden. As they travelled, Paxton bought lace for Sarah and several curious plants for Chatsworth. The party's reputations preceded them, and he and Stephenson were fêted 'by all sorts of attention'.

Eager to see his friend, the Duke had delayed his own travels to wait in Munich, where Paxton arrived in late September. They continued as one party. In Linz, Stephenson and Paxton were presented to the King of Bavaria who 'concluded his audience by saying he was very happy to know such distinguished men'. With time to relax, Paxton was charmed by the advantages of his own advancing reputation. He travelled as a self-made man and all doors were open to him, yet he was most proud of his ability to manage with the Bavarian king who, like the Duke, was partly deaf. Stephenson, on the other hand, had been able to make no headway at all with him. Becoming rather careless about seeing sights, Paxton now filled his days in Vienna and Berlin with purchases, garden visits and grand dinners in his honour – here he was introduced to the Austrian Chancellor, Prince Metternich, and to Prince Lichtenstein. Used to the experiences of travel, to the different architectural, horticultural and artistic styles on display, even to meetings with aristocracy and royalty, he wondered more at the fact that married couples traditionally slept in separate beds, and young women served in taverns. In Cassel, since the Grand Duke refused his request for the fountains there to be played out of season – envious perhaps of the Emperor Fountain at Chatsworth – Paxton bribed the workmen to play them for him in secret and allow him to measure the jets. He was pleased to find that they could not all play at once or for more than 40 minutes at a time, despite their very great expense.

In Hanover, Paxton received news from home that Sarah's father had died of cholera. By the time he reached Cologne he learnt that, in nursing him, Sarah and her mother had both contracted the disease and Dr Condell despaired of their lives. He was 'in a state of madness' and decided to leave for England without the rest of his party.

Sarah was sick for five weeks, but she held on tenaciously and by the time Paxton arrived in London at the start of November, Bradbury was able to tell him that she was recovering, though her mother was not. The speed of the trip and the dampness of the beds in Germany had taken their own toll – Paxton had developed inflammatory rheumatism in his hip and groin, reaching Chatsworth only to take to his own bed. He and Sarah passed a sickly Christmas together and, in January, Sarah's mother died.*

What they both needed was time to recover their health and discover a new sense of equilibrium but Paxton was not given the opportunity fully to recuperate. Before he went abroad, he had thought that the line of the new tracks to be built by the Manchester, Buxton, Matlock and Midland Junction Railway from the Ambergate junction had been agreed. Now, however, the Duke of Rutland was resolutely for blocking any new line and asking for huge compensation for the parts of the track passing through his land at Haddon Hall. With the two alternative routes, villages in all directions, desperate for the prosperity the railways would bring, each lobbied for the line that would pass closest to them. The directors, and Paxton in particular, went between the groups, hoping to convince them that a line through Chatsworth would be the better alternative. Ironically, as time passed,

---

* In the period 1848–9 the second great national outbreak of cholera in Britain, spread rapidly through contaminated water supplies, killed over 60,000 people, twice as many as the first outbreak in the early 1830s. The disease killed two-thirds of those who contracted it, and over 14,000 deaths were in London alone. When it appeared to have passed, the Queen announced a day of national mourning at the end of 1849.

Rutland realised the profitable potential of large land-compensation payments, and changed his mind, petitioning now in favour of the route that passed through his land. Plans went through four separate committee stages before the Chatsworth route was finally defeated the following summer. The Duke of Rutland had won.

Work at Coventry Cemetery had moved fast. By November 1847, within two years of the first plans being delivered, it was ready for opening. The poor quarry land had been transformed into an idealised landscape, bounded by irregular belts of trees and vegetation to enclose the views, and planted with winding walks lined with different varieties of weeping trees, with the grave-plots aligned behind each of the paths. Mature silver birches contrasted with an avenue of weeping limes espaliered into horizontal lines before being allowed to spring upwards. There were monkey puzzles, Scots pines and specimen oaks and a broad formal terrace raised above the burial ground for walks. The cemetery superintendent was housed in an Italianate entrance lodge similar in design to Barbrook and the Italian cottage in Edensor. A Norman church and a classical non-conformist chapel both provided retreat for the grieving while ornamenting the landscape. It was one of the first garden cemeteries of the nineteenth century and, four years later, the government's Board of Health announced that 'in beauty and convenience, this cemetery is superior to any other that has been formed'.

As ever, everything was happening at once. Back at Chatsworth, the final and greatest of the rocks in the rockery was being formed. Two massive pieces of gritstone, invisibly cemented together would soon make up the Wellington rock, named after the venerable duke. In London, the *Daily News* company was broken up and re-established, with a further £15,000 of new capital. Paxton's liability was reduced to £1,500 and, although he had still seen no return on his initial investment and was unlikely to do so for many years, he still dreamed of its financial success matching its increasing popularity.

⌒

Over the previous two years, more than one and a half million people had died of hunger or fever in Ireland where the famine had now reached its peak. One million more emigrated, predominantly to America, Liverpool and Glasgow, reducing the total population of the country by a quarter. At Lismore, the agent Francis Currey lost his three-year-old to the fever and his wife to the mental hospital as a result. The Duke cut his rents by up to 50 per cent, occasionally waiving them altogether, and provided wood for shelters to tenants who were forced to leave their land. Nevertheless, the population of Lismore was halved during these years.

Britain was tense. The railway bubble burst in earnest in 1848. By the end of the year, there were over 5,000 miles of track in Britain and Paxton had been made director of two more companies – the Furness and the Midland railways. George Hudson operated over 1,500 miles of British track, but as the economy continued to contract, *The Times'* crusade against him was gaining steam. Chartism, with its People's Charter calling for universal manhood suffrage, the ballot and other democratic principles – one of the many symptoms of a working-class sense of injustice – had somewhat lost its force since their original petition was rejected by the Commons a decade before. Now the movement found its focus and energy again in the militant persona of Feargus O'Connor, and a new petition was prepared.

In March, Benjamin Currey died of a sudden seizure at the House of Lords where he had for many years been one of the clerks of the Parliament. The Duke was grief-stricken, and panicked. He called for Paxton, and looked for him hourly until he arrived with George Cavendish two days later. The Duke may have thought that Paxton would take on Currey's responsibilities too, but nothing was further from Paxton's mind. Instead, he recommended that Benjamin's son William should continue to run the Duke's financial affairs displaying, in the Duke's opinion, noble and disinterested conduct in his suggestion. Paxton probably already realised that the fine attention to the detail of figures required of an auditor was not his forté and, besides, he simply did not have the time.

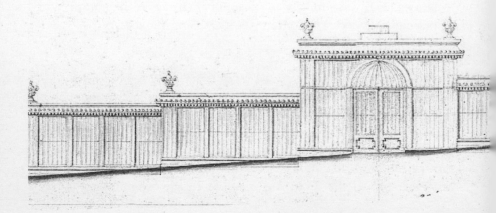

Revolution was sweeping through European cities. In March, Louis-Philippe and his queen fled France and Napoleon became President of the Second Republic. In Britain, it seemed, the industrial engine of in-humanity might also drive the masses to revolt. There had been outbreaks of Chartist violence all over Britain throughout the early forties. Now they prepared to march in force on Parliament to deliver their petition on 10 April. Massive mob violence was feared. Parliament drafted the support of military units and thousands of new special volun-tary officers,* the Bank of England and other key institutions were sand-bagged, Parliament prepared for a siege and the country held its breath.

Paxton, sanguine, wrote to Sarah from London, where he had been called to quieten the Duke, that he expected no more than a few broken windows. In the event, 10 April marked the death of Chartism. It rained all day and the crowd was far smaller than expected, and rather well-behaved. The marchers, who compromised with the authorities and delivered their petition to Westminster by cab rather than in person, were easily dispersed. At the *Punch* table one evening years later, Paxton recalled that he had passed Kennington Common (a famous gathering-place for demonstrations)† in the early hours of that day and, noticing how small the crowd was, went direct to his brokers and bought stock, making an immediate profit of £500. 'That's the way to profit by a panic,' he is reported to have told them. Clearly, he could keep a remarkably cool head.

---

*   Isambard Kingdom Brunel was one of the many who volunteered to be a special
     constable, though he thought it all rather ridiculous.
†   The first known photograph of a crowd scene was taken at this meeting at
     Kennington Common. The *Illustrated London News* published a large engraving
     based on it.

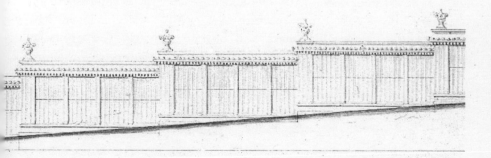

That summer, Gibson left Chatsworth to become superintendent of Victoria Park in the East End of London. The bustle and clamour of the world of business seemed to quieten somewhat and Paxton was able to spend more time at home. He replaced Gibson with a Mr Isles, with whom he spent much of the rest of the summer modifying the conservative wall. It was widened and extended, divided into ten bays with an ornamental centre that projected slightly from the line of the structure. The temporary, thick blue-striped curtains and their rods and hooks were taken away and the whole was glazed with vertical panels that could be removed in summer and with a slightly inclining ridge and furrow roof. Planted with luxuriant *Camellia reticulata* and *Camellia japonica*, trained on to trellising at the back, the conservative wall had become, in effect, a permanent, architectural, covered walkway, its glass catching the light as it 'stepped' up the hill.

Still hoping for a Chatsworth railway line, Paxton and Stephenson had prepared plans for a new deviation to the Wye route already agreed by Parliament in 1846. Success came at the start of August, with parliamentary sanction for a line that would not pass through the park, but would come close to it. On the 10th, Paxton arrived back from London in triumph. For the last part of the journey, from Baslow, his carriage was pulled on ropes by local people, ecstatic at his success. The Duke met him in the gardens to congratulate him, ordering all the estate and garden labourers to return early that evening to celebrate. He provided ale for all, and fireworks. Paxton made a speech and the estate workers and villagers danced to bands throughout the balmy night.

As he watched the dancing, Paxton might have reflected that over the previous 22 years, the garden and grounds at Chatsworth had been transformed and were now flourishing under his guiding hand. No longer the inexperienced youth that scaled the kitchen garden wall, he now stood side by side with the Duke his friend, loved and respected. As the summer rolled into autumn, back at the estate he loved, Mr Paxton, the celebrated florist and botanist, clearly the greatest gardener of his time, was again in his element.

PART 2

AIR

CHAPTER FIFTEEN

Britain now presented a different landscape from that of Paxton's youth. Streets were paved, vast Gothic town halls dominated market towns and cities, the latest machinery roared and, above all, there was the iron horse with its belching funnel, its tracks, bridges, tunnels and viaducts. Britain's goods were finding new markets in the growing empire, in America and in Europe and, for those who had survived the strain and grind of the 'hungry forties', the tide appeared at last to be turning. There was a renewal of confidence in the economy and in the country's place as the leading industrialised nation.

By the end of 1848, the *Magazine of Botany* was faced with diminishing profits and competition from a new generation of horticultural and botanical magazines. Paxton wound it up with the publication of the sixteenth volume the following year. Now he could return to his plants and 1849 was a year in which he spent more time at Chatsworth than he had for almost a decade. Douglas Jerrold, his friend from *Punch*, sent his 16-year-old son, Tom, to work in the thriving gardens, which, he found, were providing the most exquisite baskets of flowering plants for the Duke at Chiswick, Devonshire House and Brighton. Fruit also poured from the forcing houses and greenhouses throughout the year to supply His Grace's tables. At the start of March, William Currey accompanied the Duke to Chatsworth to formalise what was already in effect. Everything there was to be united under Paxton, promoted as sole agent for the estate. He was to work closely with Currey, and examine all the London expenses, too. Effectively, Paxton's elevation made Ridgway's position as the Duke's steward in London superfluous, but as one man fell to another's rise, there was a surprising lack of bitterness or envy. These two men were friends and Paxton's affability and lack of condescension or superiority ensured that they continued to be friends to the ends of their lives. Once again, quite remarkably, not a word was said against him.

Paxton now controlled all the accounts at Chatsworth, for land, farms, house and garden, for the schools and villages, disbursements and pensions, for game, fisheries, annuities and for all taxes due from property, land and mines. The money he controlled rose from around £9,000 a year to upwards of £26,000, and his pay leapt from £276 to £500 a year, with an allowance for two assistants. These were Samuel Hereman who had been employed in Paxton's office from the earliest days, and a more junior clerk to assist him.* The Duke's accounts were rosy. In April the following year, William Currey sent the completed books to Paxton before presenting them to the Duke, remarking that they were better than had been presented to the Duke in any previous year of his life.

With such enormous responsibility, Paxton nevertheless remained at the beck and call of the Duke even over trivialities. On one occasion, he was called on to drop everything in order to arrange the supply of billiard balls to the house in Brighton, where the new table and cues had been delivered without them. On another, the Duke's portrait was to be painted by Landseer, paid for by subscription from the Duke's own tenants at Chatsworth, and Paxton was required to chase the reluctant artist around the country with his letters, trying to pin down dates for sittings to complete the picture. Landseer was not a portrait painter and the fact that the Duke's dogs were to be included did little to mollify him. It took years to complete the work.

By late March, the race to produce the first flower of the *Amherstia nobilis*, so long the desire of the Duke and Paxton, was lost to them. Mrs Lawrence at Ealing Park proudly announced her success with a

*   Samuel Hereman revised and corrected the *Botanical Dictionary* in 1868 after Paxton's death – in his preface he stated that he had been 'secretary for nearly forty years to the late Sir Joseph Paxton'. Much of Paxton's (business) correspondence is in Hereman's hand – including the contract between Paxton, Wallace and Banks signed prior to their departure for America. Hereman was, it seems, responsible for assisting with much of Paxton's journalism, also. While only his *handwriting* appears in the Paxton correspondence he was, throughout Paxton's life in Derbyshire, his invisible but indispensable secretary.

plant she had forced up quickly. She invited the Duke to come and inspect it, sending the first spike to the Queen and the second to be engraved. A further spike arrived at Chatsworth where the crimson and gold labellum exceeded their greatest expectations and sent both the Duke and Paxton into raptures at its beauty. Sportingly, the Duke wrote to Mrs Lawrence of his own 'severe disappointment . . . that my tree has not flowered, [but] I cannot but rejoice that you have proved that it is to be accomplished'. Paxton was game enough to include an illustration of the flower in the *Magazine of Botany* and ceded the race to his horticultural rival with a grace deeply tinged with disappointment. His inability to induce the *Amherstia* to flower was, in effect, his only horticultural failure.

But, as usual, he had other distractions. On 4 June the line from Ambergate to Rowsley – three miles from Chatsworth – was completed. This was as far as the railway would approach the park, but the Duke and Paxton were happy, and they both made speeches at the grand opening and prepared for the onslaught of day trippers that the new line would bring to the gardens. The day was not entirely free from worry for Paxton – his coachman overturned their carriage at Rowsley and was promptly sacked. Later in the day he had to dismiss one of the gardeners, too, for disobeying the orders of his foreman. Two weeks later, the first large party of around 600 visitors arrived in the morning by special train from Derby, and was shown around the house and gardens in small groups of 20 to 30. They were soon followed by a party of at least 2,000 teetotallers from Sheffield, who were allowed to wander around alone, the paths guarded by the gardening staff.

Large groups of 'pleasure seekers' continued to arrive, from Birmingham, Chesterfield, Leicester and Leeds, throughout the summer and into the start of September. Many of the visiting temperance men and women had booked and paid for their day out through the budding firm of Thomas Cook and Son, pioneers of excursion trains in the Midlands during the 1840s. When Thomas Cook first left school aged ten years old, he, too, had worked in a garden. In the summer of 1841 he had arranged his first group tour, taking the members of a temperance society from Leicester to Loughborough using Midland trains. By booking in advance, they could pay for their tickets in more affordable weekly instalments, the company undertaking to accompany the group, to provide meals and transfers to and from the stations. Thomas Cook's business developed, investigating and booking hotels, and extending their 'package tours' further afield to Scotland. During the summer of 1849 Cook tours added to the large numbers of visitors to Chatsworth and contributed to making it the most visited country house in England.

In the same week that Rowsley station opened, the Duke received a key to the Royal Botanic Gardens at Kew from William Hooker, in recognition of his devotion to botany. A month later, Hooker wrote to Paxton to tell him that he had succeeded in propagating seeds of the *Victoria regia*, the giant Amazonian water lily. This news initiated a new contest for Paxton, a horticultural battle for which he was richly suited.

Like much of England, he had fallen under the spell of the vast, yet elusive, water lily. It had been discovered in Peru in the early years of the century by Haenke and descriptions of its extraordinary loveliness had caused ripples of excitement throughout the horticultural world. A quarter of a century later, Monsieur d'Orbigny sent some dried flowers and leaves to the Natural History Museum in Paris where they lay unnoticed. The lily appeared to have been lost, and the most established plant collectors in South America were challenged to trace it again. On New Year's Day, 1837, the famous collector, Sir Robert Schomburgk, paddling up the River Berbice in Demerera, Guyana, saw what Dickens later described as 'an extraordinary object . . . a titanic water plant'. Its round leaves were up to 6 feet in diameter and its luxuriant flowers were made up of an immense number of petals. The surface of the water was covered with blossoms and he paddled between the leaves in a daze of excitement. News of the rediscovery reached England, where it was celebrated; Lindley was among the first to publish a monograph on the plant that year with drawings by Schomburgk himself.

Schomburgk dug up many plants, but failed entirely to deliver one to England alive. Then, at the end of 1840 he sent seeds – one packet for the Queen and one to the Duke at Chatsworth, with whom he had become a regular correspondent. Schomburgk knew the reputation of Chatsworth and, while he was honour-bound to send the first packet to the sovereign, he was convinced that Chatsworth provided the environment and expertise to induce the lily to flower in England for the first time. For six years Paxton had attempted to germinate the seeds at Chatsworth and then, in 1846, Kew Gardens, under William Hooker, attempted to do the same. The race was on.

Now, three years later, Hooker was distributing its seedlings. Paxton wrote immediately that he would start to build a large tank for the plant, which would take about three weeks to heat and finish. He was taking his family on holiday to Scotland for a fortnight and he would collect a plant from Kew on his return. Emily, Blanche, Victoria, George, Rosa and Annie – now ranging from 21 years old to little Annie, 7 – went with him to tour Inverness, Glasgow, Dumbarton, Loch Lomond and Greenoch, while Sarah stayed at home with Laura who was not well. Paxton and his six children travelled by train and carriage on one of the few holidays that he ever took with them, often remembered in later years with fondness. Sarah and the children did now more regularly take a house by the sea in Scarborough or Hastings, where Paxton would join them if he could, but the concept of a family holiday was still far from defined as a Victorian norm.

He returned to Chatsworth focused on the test ahead of him, writing to Hooker at the end of July that he would arrive at Kew at six o'clock in the morning of 3 August – his 46th birthday – to collect the plant and return with it on the express train leaving Euston at nine o'clock. The little lily had four leaves, merely 6 inches in diameter, and its new tank was ready. Paxton had set about recreating as closely as possible the conditions of its native habitat, embedding heating pipes in the soil and adding liquid sewage and small wheels to keep the water in motion, constantly monitoring the light, heat and ventilation in the glasshouse.*

The lily began to grow. In August, Dr Wallich – now retired from the Botanic Gardens in Calcutta – visited and was entirely astonished by what he saw in the Great Stove. In September, the Duke left for Lismore with instructions for Paxton to follow in due course. At the start of October, Paxton wrote to inform him that one of the lily leaves had reached 4 feet across. He needed to build another tank for it, half as big again. The plants at Kew, on the other hand, had not grown at all. But the timing could not have been worse, the nights had drawn in and it was wet and cloudy. If electricity were not so expensive, he told the Duke, he would use the bright 'daylight' it created for two or three hours each morning and evening to make up for the short winter days. Without it, he expected the plant's extraordinary growth to wane.

He was wrong. The lily continued to thrive and on 2 November

---

* Kew gave away from 30 to 40 plants – some to nurseries who began to market them to their best customers. Some reports suggest that the Duke of Norfolk at Syon House received a plant, installing it at his great glasshouse and throwing himself into the race to produce the first flower.

Paxton wrote with trembling excitement to the Duke that a bud had appeared the day before – enormous, like a great poppy head or a large peach placed in a cup. 'From what I can see it will be eight or ten days before it comes with flower and therefore I am in a great stew about going to Lismore at the time I appointed, but I shall do whatever your Grace may wish. I have paid so much personal attention to it and it has been entirely under my own direction since I brought it from Kew, that I should not like to be out of the way when it flowers.' Confident now, he recommended that the first flower be sent to the Queen, along with a large leaf. The entire garden staff was seduced by the grandeur of the lily's appearance, even the labourers took a great interest in it. The leaf was by now 4 feet 8½ inches across, turning up at the edges like the sides of an inverted bottle top. More buds were expected.

On the eighth, in the silence of the evening, the bud swelled, rose six inches out of the water and began to expand. The opening flower was of the purest white, almost a foot across, and it smelled of ripe fruit, something like a pineapple. Over the following evenings as it opened further, its outside petals fell back on to the surface of the water and a pink glow spread out on to the petals from the centre. For three evenings it continued to entrance Paxton and his men before, fully tinged pink, it wilted and fell away. Other buds had emerged, and Paxton left for Windsor with Andrew Stewart to deliver a blossom to the Queen. Mark Lemon, the editor of *Punch*, was there when the bud was cut. He reported that it faded disastrously and almost immediately. Paxton revived it by pouring warm water into the stalk and putting fine sand near its root to imitate the activity of nibbling fish.

As the fame of the flowering lily spread, 'all the world comes to look' wrote Paxton to Sarah, who was in Brighton. William Hooker came, drawn by Paxton's promise that it was worth a journey of a thousand miles. John Lindley came and William Currey, Edmonds from the Chiswick garden, and the Earl of Carlisle. When the Duke returned from Ireland, he was drawn to an illuminated greenhouse lit to welcome him home and lure him out to see the flowers. There were now thirteen leaves on the plant and a succession of new buds met every new visitor. The Duke's friend and neighbour, Lady Newburgh, famously sat on a plank over the water to examine it while artists from the *Illustrated London News* were busy making its likeness. The leaves were so thick and broad, supported so firmly on their undersides by a network of bracing ribs, that Paxton, Lady Newburgh and the Duke

conceived the idea of putting little Annie on to one of the leaves to
test out the theory that it could support a child. Paxton stood her on
a tin tray to spread the load, and later reported to Hooker that he
believed the leaf would have held up to 100 pounds. It was a PR coup.
The *Illustrated London News* printed a long report, with an engraving
of Annie standing on the leaf in the middle of the tank. Jerrold at
Punch, was moved to verse:

> On unbent leaf, in fairy guise
> Reflected in the water
> Beloved, admired by hearts and eyes,
> Stands Annie, Paxton's daughter.

Louisa Lawrence declined the Duke's invitation to see in person
the highlight of the horticultural world that had entirely eclipsed her
own success with *Amherstia*, pleading a sore throat. However, she sent
her warmest congratulations to 'the best practical botanist in the world
. . . on the unexampled triumph of skill exemplified in growing and
flowering of Victoria regia'. Another of the Duke's friends suggested
a trial of Mrs Lawrence herself upon the leaf, followed by other notable
gardeners – perhaps hoping that one or other of them would sink. Sir
William Hooker set straight away to work on his own book *Victoria
Regia* to be published in 1851.

Paxton's lily continued to grow, and to put forth buds and flowers.

He had done everything that his experience had taught him to induce her to flower, he had nurtured her and willed her to reveal herself in her ultimate beauty. Now her most ardent admirer created for her a unique glasshouse. It was to be in the kitchen gardens, right next to his own home, Barbrook.

The pitch of the roof of the conservative wall was very gentle, and the small conservatory Paxton had built attached to his house in Darley Dale also had an almost flat roof. But this new lily house would be the first of all Paxton's glass buildings to have a completely flat ridge and furrow roof. It was the ultimate development of his structural experimentation with glass.

Taking the form of a large glass box, the new house was just over 60 feet long, by 47 feet broad, almost completely filled by a large circular tank. Only four, very thin, wrought iron beams supported the roof, with eight slender, hollow cast-iron columns to brace the structure, doubling as drains for water from the roof. Ventilation was provided by openings in the stone basement and movable roof lights. Air and water temperature were maintained at between 80 and 90°F by heating pipes which ran around the outside of the house as well as through the water in the tank itself. Four small wheels kept the water moving. There were eight smaller tanks to hold smaller aquatic plants.

The unique new house was completed in four months, and the lily moved into it in April 1850, where it continued to produce 112 flowers, 140 leaves and many seeds within the year. In his lecture to the Society of Arts later the same year, Paxton emphasised that the inspiration for his structural system had come from the lily leaf itself, and its extraordinary load-bearing capacity, which he called a 'natural feat of engineering'. This unique structure had also been noted by Richard Spruce, a collector in the Amazon, who reported that he had found 'a leaf . . . suggesting some strange fabric of cast iron just taken from the furnace, its ruddy colour and the enormous ribs with which it is strengthened, increasing the similarity'. Paxton now pointed out the cantilevers radiating from the centre of the leaf, with large bottom flanges and very thick middle ribs with cross girders between each pair to stop the leaf from buckling. In his new lily house, the great horizontal surface of the ridge and furrow roof acted like the cross girders on the leaf.

The completion of the lily house marked the last stage of Paxton's glasshouse improvements at Chatsworth and the repeal of the glass tax five years earlier made it economical. It cost only around £800.

Now the gardens were replete with forcing houses, several orchid houses, an *Amherstia* house, many different greenhouses for fruit, as well as separate houses for the cultivation of mushrooms, cucumbers and vines. The arboretum and pinetum were fully planted with a new pattern of walks laid out. In the Great Stove, plants were maturing to their fullest potential, and in the rockery the leviathan works were finished. The daily diary left by one of the Chatsworth gardeners, Robert Aughtie, between 1848 and 1850, provides a snapshot of a garden running like clockwork. Here the men were swapped between departments to broaden their knowledge and many of them participated in a 'freemasonry of gardening', regularly visiting other gardens and gardeners to share plants and experiences.

Chatsworth displayed the art of the gardener at a perfect pitch. There were examples of technological advance in the form of the greenhouses, of horticultural style typified in the many new garden features and of plantsmanship. The gardens were a fine example of the mixing of the new 'gardenesque' style of gardening with the 'natural' and 'picturesque' parklands of Capability Brown and Repton. Here, nature was subjected to cultivation, a love of plants demonstrated in mass plantings, specimen trees and shrubs displayed to their greatest advantage and matched by ostentatious botanical collections. Chatsworth was not only the most excellent garden in England to visit, it had become effectively the finest school of gardening in Europe.

CHAPTER SIXTEEN

Whatile Paxton was tending his lily, constructing the perfect environment in which to house it, and launching yet another new magazine with John Lindley, *Paxton's Flower Garden*, a small group of wildly enthusiastic men was conceiving an event which – through its extraordinary success – would become the symbol of the age, and provide a showcase for Britain's engineering progress. The Great Exhibition of the Works of Industry of all Nations was planned to take place in London from May to October 1851.

The first exhibition in London was held in 1756 by the Society of Arts, designed to promote the improvements of textiles and porcelain, but Europe's first attempts at large scale exhibitions were in France during the 1789 French Revolution when the Palais de St-Cloud was purchased for the purpose. The success of the second French exhibition led Napoleon Bonaparte to erect a simple wooden construction on the Champs de Mars specifically for such occasions, exhibitions followed regularly and, in 1849, an exhibition larger than ever before was proposed. In parallel, the Society of Arts in London had continued to form several small collections for public exhibition and these were attracting increasing numbers. In 1847, over 20,000 visited their show.

Henry Cole was to be a guiding light in the conception of a great, international exhibition in London. He had been an assistant in the Public Record Office and campaigned, successfully, for its reorganisation. He had also been instrumental in creating the Penny Post and, under his pseudonym Felix Summerley, had published Britain's very first Christmas card. In the summer of 1849, Cole visited the Paris exhibition with two other members of the society, Matthew Digby Wyatt and Francis Fuller, with the view to reporting on its success. On their return journey, Fuller met William Cubitt, President of the Institution of Civil Engineers, and they discussed Fuller's conviction that Britain should arrange an international exhibition in London to which the whole world of manufacture should be invited.

The idea was planted. Cubitt spoke to Prince Albert and by the end of June they all met, joined by John Scott Russell, the secretary to the Society of Arts, an industrial designer and engineer who had also been one of the first journalists employed on the *Daily News* by Dickens.* These men were to form the executive committee for the Great Exhibition of 1851 – the first exhibition to be called 'great'. They drew up the broad principles of their scheme and worked assiduously over the summer to drum up capital support as well as manufacturing commitment, travelling all over Britain to sell their idea and encourage participation.

The goals of the proposed exhibition were unprecedented. It was soon apparent that its sheer scale and its much-vaunted intention of promoting free trade and peace among all the nations of the world required the power of a royal commission to drive it. Accordingly, the Queen announced the formation of one in January 1850. The president was her own Consort, and the vice-president and chairman was the Duke of Devonshire's nephew, the Whig Earl Granville, whose attention to detail, extraordinary diplomacy and intelligent motivation manoeuvred the commissioners through the mountain of planning that lay ahead. Other members of the commission included several aristocrats, the Prime Minister Lord John Russell, the Leader of the Opposition Sir Robert Peel, the President of the Board of Trade Henry Labouchère, William Cubitt, Charles Barry (the architect still struggling to complete the new Houses of Parliament), the engineer Robert Stephenson, the chairman of the East India Company, the president of the Royal Geographical Society and the president of the Royal Society. The two permanent secretaries appointed to the commissioners were John Scott Russell and Stafford Northcote. They met for the first time on 11 January 1850.

* Scott Russell would later partner Isambard Kingdom Brunel in the building of the *SS Great Eastern*, the largest iron ship in the world, launched in 1858.

The date of 1 May 1851 was set for the opening, less than sixteen months away. The royal commissioners would have to encourage the participation of exhibitors from Britain and from every other known country, co-ordinating hundreds of committees and subcommittees. They would have to work from first principles on every detail of the massive event – from the logistical arrangements for the arrival of goods, to the safe management of crowds, the provision of power for machines and refreshments for visitors and the formation of rules about the labelling of goods. They had to consider the effect of the arrival in London of over one million visitors from abroad, let alone the thousands of British visitors they hoped would attend, the pricing of tickets and where walking sticks and umbrellas would be deposited. Above all, they had agreed that the exhibition would be funded not by the government but by the people of the nation, through public subscription managed by local committees. This was crucial: the principle ensured that, if the people were paying for their exhibition, then it belonged to them. From the start there was a growing sense of national ownership in the event. National pride was at stake. Newspapers reported the commission's activities at length. Initially, *The Times* was particularly sceptical of the possibility of achieving the desired outcome of international peace. They thought that the idea was in danger of being engulfed by its own magnitude and that the causes of war were far too deep-seated to be overcome by a contest of manufacturing and design prowess. The *Evening Standard* had no doubt whatsoever that the thing would eventually fail.

Evidently, the need for a building to house this vast undertaking was paramount and an elite Building Committee was formed including Isambard Kingdom Brunel, Robert Stephenson, Charles Barry, the Professor of Architecture at University College, T. L. Donaldson, the Duke of Buccleuch and the Earl of Ellesmere. It was chaired by William Cubitt. By 15 March they were ready to invite suggestions for the design of a building which must conform to several key specifications. It must be temporary, simple and economic to construct given the very short time available, and it should be as cheap as possible. It should, they insisted, contain some striking feature to exemplify the present state of science and construction in Britain.

A week later, there was a great dinner at the Mansion House, drawing together mayors, provosts, aristocrats, politicians, foreign ministers, ambassadors and the Court and intended to spur them all into action on behalf of the exhibition. At the top of the room hung

a great painting showing ships from around the globe discharging
their cargoes at the Port of London. At the opposite end of the hall
hung another, depicting Britannia's angels proclaiming an invitation
to the four corners of the world. Prince Albert spoke with evangelical zeal of the differences between nations vanishing in the face of
new invention, of the potential for the unity of mankind. He gave voice
to a particularly Victorian self-consciousness, to their almost visceral
appreciation that they were living in an age of transition. He believed
that 'the Exhibition of 1851 is to give us a true test and a living picture
of the point of development at which the whole of mankind has arrived
. . . and a new starting point from which all nations will be able to
direct their future exertions . . .' In one respect, at the very least, he
was right. The Great Exhibition was to be talismanic, its iconic status,
for a brief moment, uniting the family of mankind.

Within three weeks, the Building Committee had received 245
plans, including over 38 designs submitted from abroad: from Australia,
Holland, Belgium, Hanover, Brunswick, Hamburg and Switzerland
and, predominantly, from France. Eighteen designs were commended,
including only three from England, riling the British press, who now
feared that Britannia would be beaten by her foreign rivals before the
exhibition had even started. Two were singled out for their daring
and ingenious construction. Both of iron and glass, one by Hector
Horeau, the architect of fantastic glass buildings in Paris, and one by
Richard Turner, the Dublin architect/engineer responsible for the
glasshouse in Regent's Park and for the Palm House at Kew. Turner
and his son had gone to the trouble of supplying the Building
Committee with a block-model of his design at a very early stage. But
the committee considered none of the submissions suitable and they
went ahead and proposed their own design. Turner, in particular, was
simply furious and besieged the royal commissioners with correspondence for months asking for compensation. But at an estimated cost
of £300,000 to build, his design was, like Horeau's, simply far too
expensive.

The site for the building was not yet confirmed. While a position
on the southern edge of Hyde Park abutting Kensington Road by
Prince's Gate had been mooted from an early stage, debate raged in
the press and in Parliament. Wormwood Scrubs, Battersea Park, the
Isle of Dogs, Victoria Park and Regent's Park, in particular, were
thrown up for consideration. The residents around Hyde Park and the
regular riders in Rotten Row lobbied against the use of Hyde Park

and *The Times* joined them in raging against the closure of a public amenity for over a year. Then appeared the most arch of all Tory killjoys, Colonel Charles de Laet Waldo Sibthorp, MP for Lincoln. Sibthorp had previously attacked Catholic emancipation and the principles of free trade, social reform and the railways and had voted for the reduction of Prince Albert's parliamentary grant in 1840. In the battle in the House of Commons over where the building would be sited, Sibthorp now rushed to the defence of a group of ten elm trees, which would have to be felled to make way for it. He denounced the Exhibition as 'one of the greatest humbugs, frauds and absurdities ever known'.

Amidst the high profile debate over the site, and growing fears of pestilence and potential revolutionary incitement that would arrive from abroad, the Building Committee's own plan, drawn up by Matthew Digby Wyatt, Owen Jones and Charles Heard Wild, became unofficially public after a meeting on 16 May. The committee proposed a long, low brick structure with an iron dome designed by Brunel, 200 feet in diameter, which was twice the size of the dome of St Paul's. Their plan would require between thirteen and twenty million bricks. There was outcry in the press who thought the design ugly and hardly provisional. With such a permanent structure, Hyde Park would, indeed, be desecrated.

Paxton, busy with the completion of his new lily house and fully engaged at Chatsworth in his first year as agent, appeared isolated from the arguments batting back and forth across London and the pages of the national press. Until, at a meeting at Westminster with the chairman of the Midland Railway, John Ellis MP, at the start of June, his attention was caught. Comparing the acoustic and ventilation problems already becoming apparent in the new building at Westminster with the potentially disastrous exhibition building, he mused on the potential of a construction similar to the lily house, multiplied indefinitely, to provide a perfect structure. A great believer in the abilities of Paxton to get a job done, Ellis whisked him off to the offices of the Board of Trade to see Lord Granville. Granville was out, but Henry Cole was in, and as he listened to Paxton's ideas he became convinced that they should be aired more widely. Although it was considered far too late to entertain any new design proposals, Cole encouraged Paxton to work up his ideas as quickly as possible. In the meantime he went back to the royal commissioners and persuaded them to add an unusual clause to the prospectus for tender that was to be sent imminently to contractors to establish the cost of constructing the brick monstrosity. The clause stipulated that if any contractor wished to tender for an amended design, he could do so. It ensured that the door remained open, albeit slightly, for alternatives to come forward.

It was Friday. Paxton went straight out to 'step over' the proposed site in Hyde Park before boarding a train back to Chatsworth. On Monday, he went north-west to witness the floating of the third tube of Stephenson's Britannia railway bridge over the Menai Straits.[*] On Tuesday, he was in Derby to chair a disciplinary meeting of the Midland Railway on a trivial matter over a pointsman's irregularity. Throughout the meeting he doodled on blotting paper. The result was the first sketch of the building for the Great Exhibition.

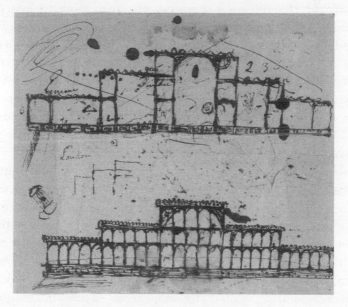

During the whole of the following week, Paxton single-mindedly prepared detailed plans for the proposed building at his office at Chatsworth, assisted by W.H. Barlow, the chief engineer of the Midland Railway. Time was against him, but he wrote to the secretary for the Society of Arts suggesting that he give a lecture on his plans – he knew that he had to marshal his advocates and manipulate public opinion if he was to stand any chance. On 20 June, with the plans

[*] The first had been floated into position in June 1849 before an audience of many of Britain's finest engineers.

rolled under his arm, he set off again for London, fortuitously meeting Robert Stephenson – returning from the Menai Bridge – on the train and travelling with him to Euston. The encounter was providential. Stephenson was a friend and a member of the Building Committee, and he was so impressed that he did not notice that his pipe had extinguished for the whole time he pored over the plans. He advised Paxton to do something else he was good at: charm. Using every advantage offered by the Duke's great standing, Paxton called on one of the staunchest enemies of the exhibition, Lord Brougham, who suggested that he go to see Wellington in secret. In all probability, Paxton did not go to see the Great Duke, who would have remembered him from his visit to Chatsworth.* But he did visit the vice-president of the royal commission, Lord Granville, who 'was so pleased with the plan that he would not let me take it away'. He also went to see Charles Wentworth Dilke, an original member of the executive committee at the Society of Arts, erstwhile manager of the *Daily News* and a fervent disciple of the Great Exhibition. In general, the Building Committee had been obstructive, Barry in particular who was wedded to their own plan. But one member at least, Stephenson, 'helped me like a brother' Paxton told Sarah, and said there was no plan to be compared to his. Granville also arranged for Paxton to meet Prince Albert and, two days later, he took the plans to Buckingham Palace.

As soon as his designs had been completed, Paxton had sent copies to Charles Fox, a Derby man who, with his partner Henderson, fabricated iron products of all descriptions at their works in Smethwick, Birmingham. Fox, Henderson and Co. were also engineers – they had built the roofs for the Pembroke Docks in the mid-1840s, and had just completed the roof of the station at Tithbarn Street, Liverpool. Nothing in Paxton's own career had prepared him for a project of such magnitude, requiring such extensive use of cast and wrought iron. Fox, Henderson were a natural choice as contractors, to mature and realise his scheme. Paxton also sent copies of the plans to Chance Brothers, the glass manufacturers in Brimingham with whom he had worked on the Great Stove at Chatsworth, priming both companies to be ready to produce tenders for his design at a moment's notice.

On 22 June the Building Committee published their brick design in

---

*   He did, however, visit him on 23 July at the Lords, and wrote to Sarah that 'the old Duke said he knew it would all come right as soon as [he] heard [Paxton] had it in hand'.

the *Illustrated London News*, right at the height of polarised opinion and
a storm of debate over the exhibition itself. It was a public relations
blunder. The 200,000 readers of the paper were horrified. Three days
later, the royal commissioners held a special meeting to consider
tenders received for their own design as well as Paxton's plans. Since
only three firms had tendered out of the nineteen asked, Henry Cole
was now sent out to Liverpool, Birmingham and Manchester to
encourage more, lower tenders. Cole also visited Fox, Henderson both
to solicit a tender for the brick building, and to assist them with their
own calculations for Paxton's glass palace. Cole had already been won
over, writing to the Prince's secretary that he 'had great hopes the
cost of Mr P.'s plan would be lower than the Committee's'. He advised
Fox, Henderson, as, separately, did Brunel, to be rigorous and sober
in their tenders.

Paxton was all the while on tenterhooks, writing to Sarah 'this
grand plan will kill me'. He visited Fox, Henderson several times at
their London offices in New Street, Spring Gardens, to go over the
designs; Robert Lucas Chance was telegraphed to come to London for
a meeting. Messrs Fox and Henderson also visited Chatsworth to see
for themselves the lily house, and to pore over the details of their
quotation. Over the following days they worked through the nights
on a mountain of mathematical equations, quantity analyses and structural calculations.

A week after the brick design was made public, Paxton signed an
agreement with Fox, Henderson and with Chance Brothers, which
bound them together in partnership for the construction of his glass
design. It promised that, in the event of their success, Fox, Henderson
would pay £2,500 to Paxton and Chance Brothers would supply 16-
ounce glass at the rate of three pence per foot. On the same day, the
Commons debated the Hyde Park site and, on his way home, Peel, the
Leader of the Opposition and a firm supporter of Paxton's plan, fell
disastrously from his horse and died three days later.

Peel's sudden death shocked Westminster and, perhaps, it brought
them to their senses. Opposition to the Hyde Park site fell away and
when the debate resumed on 4 July an overwhelming majority defeated
Colonel Sibthorp's motion, though not before he had decried the exhibition again, railing that some of the Hyde Park elms had already
been illegally felled.

Paxton was waiting to play his ace. In a provocative effort to give
publicity to his plans, a full description of the building, with engraved

illustrations, had been prepared for publication in the *Illustrated London News*. On the advice of Charles Fox, however, he delayed publication until a patent for his ridge and furrow roof had been lodged successfully and then, two days after the vote, he was ready, and his designs were published.

This was a building designed for spectacle, 1,848 feet long,[*] 456 feet wide at its broadest point, and 108 feet high at the transept. The ground floor and galleries would provide over 10 miles of exhibition frontage. Paxton argued that it could be dismantled and removed as easily and quickly as it could be constructed and suggested that it could later be transformed into a winter garden or massive horticultural structure, either in Hyde Park or elsewhere. He pointed out that the building itself would form the most singular and peculiar feature of the exhibition itself – a vast structure covering almost 21 acres, supported only by thin cast-iron columns.

The building Paxton had designed was extremely simple. Requiring no mortar, stone or brick, it could be assembled at speed, with its parts prefabricated off-site and brought to the park only for assembly. Ventilation was provided at basement and gallery level, and parts of the flat roof, constructed as ridge and furrow, as well as the southern elevations, would be covered with white calico. This would not only provide shade but, when water was poured over it, would also cool the building in a primitive form of air-conditioning. The *Illustrated London News* clearly favoured this design over that of the Building Committee. It suggested that 'the structure as a whole, would form a peculiar novelty in mechanical science' and reported 'when we consider the manner of supporting a vast glass roof, covering twenty-one acres on the most secure and scientific principles, and filling in a structure of such magnitude wholly with glass, Mr Paxton ventures to think that such a plan would meet with the almost universal approval of the British Public, whilst it would be unrivalled in the world'.

The public were convinced. This building, an entirely novel and graceful conception compared to the lumpy brick design of the committee, caught its imagination and the cry went up for its adoption. Douglas Jerrold, at *Punch*, christened it the 'Crystal Palace', emphasising its fairy-like transparency. Only *The Times*, still resolutely hostile towards the whole enterprise, called it a monstrous greenhouse

---

[*] There was a small confusion about the measurement in the press and it was often referred to, even by the Royal Commissioners in their reports, as 1,851 feet long, a happy coincidence with the date of the exhibition.

and swore that it would leak, that the internal heat would be intense and that the exhibits would not be safe. Builders and architects were united, it said, against the employment of 'mere' glass and iron on such a mighty scale.

The Building Committee met five days later on Saturday, 11 July, to report on the tenders they had received. Paxton was optimistic, assured that only the two designs were under consideration. The committee agreed that his plans provided a greater facility to add galleries should exhibition space become oversubscribed and, indeed, it was clear that Fox, Henderson's tender was far lower than that for their own design at £88,000, against £141,000. At the last minute, however, the committee added a further design, now omitting Brunel's vast dome, and calculated to cost 10 per cent less than Paxton's palace.

Paxton's nervous tension was palpable. The next day he wrote two separate letters to his wife. In one he has 'made up my mind to a disappointment . . . a great effort will be made but don't be bothered if we lose', in the other he writes that 'nothing is settled but I believe we will win'. He berated himself for spending so much time on the project. Meanwhile, the Duke was so 'anxious for me to have it he is almost wild about it'. All they could do was wait.

Despite William Cubitt's desire to see the Building Committee's own design succeed, the tide had turned. Samuel Morton Peto, railway contractor and engineer, and member of the Finance Committee, was fiercely in favour of Paxton's design and strongly advised the Prince to support it. In addition, Fox, Henderson had stipulated that they only required payment of 40 per cent of the cost during the construction of Paxton's design, with the remainder to be paid later with interest. This would give the commissioners more time to continue to raise capital through subscription and the opportunity of applying ticket sales to their funds.

The Building Committee was irresolute and Paxton's heart was in his mouth as he waited. As they reconsidered his designs, Barry believed that the roof should be vaulted rather than monotonously flat and threatened to withdraw if the amendment was not made. Cubitt, on the other hand, threatened to resign if a vaulted design was accepted, simply refusing to believe that it could be completed in time. Stephenson supported the plan as it stood and Brunel, convinced of its beauty, would not stand in its way. Indeed, he advised Paxton that in order to conform to specifications, the interior columns should be recalculated to be 24 feet apart instead of 20. He also demonstrated

his generosity by arriving at Devonshire House early one morning
with a note of the height of the remaining Hyde Park elms, which
were in the middle of the proposed site, but which could not be felled.
Paxton later reported that Brunel told him that morning that he meant
to try to win with his own plan, but thought it right to give Paxton's
beautiful design every possible advantage.

Despite their investment in their own design, there were now grave
doubts that the brick building could be constructed in time. The
Committee met yet again on 15 July, and took evidence from Paxton
and Fox, Henderson before asking them to leave the room. When they
were called back in, they were privately assured of their success, at a
reduced estimate for construction of £75,000. Finally, after six weeks
on the rack, Paxton allowed himself to believe that he had won. At
7.28 p.m. he cabled the station master at Derby station: 'my plan has
been approved by the Royal Commission – send this to Chatsworth'.
How Sarah's hands must have trembled as she read it. The cable was
followed swiftly by an exultant letter: 'it has been a hard fight but it
is glorious to win. The Duke is enchanted.' The Duke wrote in his
diary that 'Paxton was . . . triumphant being chosen for the great
building'. The next day, Sarah wrote of their great excitement at his
glorious success. The village bells had been rung all day, and visitors
had poured through her doors to congratulate her. It was all almost
inconceivable.

Nothing of the Committee's decision had been made officially public.
The following week several of the commissioners visited the lily house
at Chatsworth to see at first hand the prototype of Paxton's design
and the proof of its success. Every pane of glass was cleaned and
polished for the occasion. There was further discussion about relieving
the long flat line of the roof by the addition of a flat-roofed transept
bisecting the length of the building. Since the elms were now protected
by government order, this would have to be positioned off-centre if it
was to contain them effectively. Much later, it was suggested that this
transept was designed by the committee themselves but Paxton was
to be absolutely clear that this was not so. In a speech to the Mechanics
Institute in Derby in October, he confirmed that Fox, Henderson had
originally suggested it as a device to relieve the monotony of the long,
flat building. They had convinced him of the superiority of their idea
when it was calculated that its addition would add stability to the
building, even if it did give some exhibitors an unfair advantage. Barry
then suggested that the whole length of the roof should be arched –

but Paxton had demurred, believing that it would not be possible to erect such a design in the time given. However, this gave him food for thought. If the transept alone were to have a curved roof, he reasoned, it could be designed high enough to arch above the trees, and could therefore be repositioned right at the centre of the building.

A week and a half after the Building Committee's private decision, the Duke and Paxton returned as heroes to Chatsworth, to a crowd of 700 who cheered the Duke as if he were in Ireland. Paxton, said the Duke, remained 'quite [the] unaltered gardener'. With Sarah, he sat down to read the mountains of mail: letters of hearty congratulations from Smithers, from his railway and horticultural contacts and from his family. In particular, his eldest brother William wrote that 'father and mother . . . would leap for joy could they but have a peep from the grave'. Paxton had come a long way from Milton Bryant.

Two days later, on 26 July, the Building Committee formally recognised Paxton's design, including the new bisecting transept with its arched roof. The final tender, including this amendment, was for £85,500. Fox, Henderson retained ownership of the materials used, but £150,000 would be paid to them in total if it should be decided to maintain the building permanently. Within a week, Fox, Henderson had taken possession of the site. Three hundred workmen began to erect fences and wooden hoarding, laying drains in the ground and preparing the foundations. In the first week of September the first iron columns were delivered to the site from the Midlands.

They had 22 weeks to complete a building on a scale and principle entirely untested and make it ready for internal decoration and the influx of exhibits. Charles Wild, Owen Jones and Matthew Digby Wyatt were on hand as supervisors of the works on behalf of the royal commissioners.

Paxton, meanwhile, had been called to Lismore and to the Duke, leaving London only with an assurance that no alteration would be made without his approval. Since the start of the year and in parallel with their work on the new Houses of Parliament, John Gregory Crace had been refurbishing and redecorating the central rooms and new great hall to plans supplied by Pugin. Paxton had made a flying visit to Lismore at the end of March to check on their progress, since when Crace had hounded him regularly with queries about wallpaper or lighting – relatively trivial matters about which, apparently, only Paxton could decide on behalf of the Duke. On a larger scale, Paxton was fashioning plans to rebuild the derelict towers and other uninhabitable parts of the castle in what the Duke would call his 'second great work of 1850'. Paxton's three eldest daughters, Emily, Blanche and Victoria, as well as his son, George, accompanied him to Lismore, staying with Francis Currey and his wife, who had returned from the mental hospital, recovered but still rather odd. There was a whirl of balls and visits and the Duke was entirely thrilled with Paxton's girls, writing to Sarah that they were 'in appearance, and manners and intelligence . . . everything that could be wished. It must make you and Paxton very happy to see them turn out so well.'

By the start of October, as the great skeleton of the building rose inexorably out of the mud of Hyde Park, Paxton was back in London, being bothered with applications of all sorts – invitations to dinner, requests to paint his portrait, and demands to make public speeches. He found it all a great bore and declined them all. As the structure went up, more and more people flocked to see it. In addition, at the end of November, Baron Mayer de Rothschild, whose brother Lionel acted as one of the trustees to the royal commission funds, invited Paxton to a meeting to discuss a commission for the design of the first Rothschild mansion in England. The Rothschild family was already established as one of the most powerful families in Europe, building properties in France, Italy and Germany on a vast scale to house their great collections of art and antiques. Despite the fact that Paxton had only designed small ducal houses and the moderately sized Burton Closes, Rothschild wanted the most famous architect in Britain to build him a vast, expensive stone mansion to outrival all others. Paxton wrote to Sarah, after several meetings, that he was sure the Baron was going to engage him for the work. He was quite clear that the commission would be worth a very great deal to him, and he was apparently unfazed at this comparative leap into the unknown. By December, he was already seeking estimates for stone from Derbyshire quarries to use in construction.

With all the fuss and adulation, Paxton could not possibly have been quite the unaltered gardener, but he maintained an unbounded warmth and sense of debt towards his Duke. Many times over the next year, in particular, he would have opportunity to express his gratitude to him publicly. Now, though, he wrote privately that 'it was to your fostering hand that I am indebted for all that I possess in the world and in everything I do, I only consider I am shadowing . . . your great kindness and liberality'.

CHAPTER SEVENTEEN

No one thought that before the nineteenth century was half out, England would see the largest building ever made by human hands, without mortar, brick or stone, without a piece of timber thicker than one's arm, but indestructible . . . covering more than twenty acres but begun and completed in one autumn . . .

Some said that genius had dashed off the design. Now it was down to Fox, Henderson to realise the dream through minute and careful calculation of all aspects of a type of construction for which there was no real precedent. Newspapers reported its progress keenly. In early November, the artists from the *Illustrated London News* were allowed on to the building site to witness the raising of the vast transept ribs, which had to be completed on the ground and then hoisted aloft, and about which most anxiety was felt. The paper published a special supplement, packed with engravings of the work in progress, and showing quite how fast it was growing. It was partly the speed of construction and partly the fact that the method was so easy to grasp, that the now popularly called Crystal Palace had entered the public imagination as no other secular building had ever done.

Even the drawn-out construction of the new Houses of Parliament had not received so many column inches. In fact, *Punch* jested that that tardy new edifice – Barry's building took twelve years to complete and was finally opened in 1852 – should now be rejected in favour of a Paxtonian glass Parliament. He had only to clap on his 'considering

cap', said *Punch*, 'that pretty tasteful thing bent from the leaf of the Victoria regia – and the matter is done'. The novelty and magnitude of the building, the extraordinary skill, energy and celerity of its erection were a media dream, and they deified it. Even *The Times* had swung in its favour.

The workforce grew to over 2,000 men and as much iron and glass went up each day as for a moderate railway station. As Brunel had suggested, all dimensions were now worked on multiples of 24, allowing these multi-functioning parts to be prefabricated en masse. Most of it was brought direct from the Fox, Henderson foundry in Birmingham by the North Western Railway, and fixed into its assigned place within eighteen hours of beginning its journey. Reports centred on the building's daily mutations into something yet more wonderful, and on its dimensions, almost every detail of which was significant. Over its three tiers, the building would contain 33,000 iron columns, 2,224 girders and 600,000 cubic feet of timber. At 49 x 12 inches, the panes were the largest sheet-glass ever made; over 900,000 square feet of it were produced, to be held in place by over 205 miles of sash bars. There would be nearly one million square feet of floor-space.

The Prince Consort visited. Expressing astonishment at the magnitude of the undertaking, he watched the girders being tested under 22 tons of pressure before being swung into position. He inspected the portable forges and the four steam engines which drove various machines for punching and drilling the iron work. As he left, a bell was rung and the 2,000 workmen slipped down columns, skipped across joists and balanced along girders to form a semicircle around his carriage and cheer. His gratitude was marked by the gift of 250 gallons of beer for them.

In the middle of November, Paxton finally addressed the Society of Arts at a regular Wednesday night meeting at St John Street, Adelphi. He took with him not only plans and drawings of the palace, but a massive leaf of the *Victoria regia* from Chatsworth to demonstrate the engineering inspiration for the flat ridge and furrow roof. It was the first time he had read a paper in public, and although he would become adept at public speaking over the next year in particular, unlike his engineering contemporaries this was probably his only lecture to a learned society. On this evening, he began by detailing the history of his experiments with glasshouses at Chatsworth, at pains to point out that while his design for the Crystal Palace may have been fortunate, it was not fortuitous but was the direct result of years of trial. Clearly, he stood before the audience not as a trained architect nor as an engineer but, with his giant lily leaf, as a genius gardener.

The building he described was cunning. As with the lily house, 8-inch diameter columns provided the structural support as well as the means of collecting water from the roof which ran away into the Kensington sewers. He considered that the flooring could not be made of stone or concrete due to its moisture content, and so it would be constructed from 9-inch boards set at 1-inch intervals to allow water, dust and debris to fall away between the slats – multi-brush machines were developed for the purpose. Much of the hoarding used to surround the site was later reused as floor material, and the royal commissioners would make provision for boys to scramble under it to prevent the accumulation of sawdust, papers and other inflammable materials.

The Crystal Palace was six times the size of St Paul's Cathedral, which had taken 35 years to erect. Paxton's hope was that, at the close of the exhibition, he would be allowed to convert the building into a permanent winter garden with carriage drives and riding facilities. Notwithstanding that possibility, his clear belief was that with the relative cheapness of glass and cast iron, the influence of the Palace would be far-reaching and this type of design limitless in its potential uses, domestic, industrial, medical or horticultural.

However, even before it was up, the seeds of the Crystal Palace's future deconstruction had been sowed. Earlier uproar over Hyde Park being scarred by the permanence of the committee's ugly design had led the commissioners to promise to reinstate the land come what may. By mid-November 1850 they had signed a deed of covenant with the Queen promising to restore the site to the Crown by 1 June 1852.

Violent storms buffeted the building and even Paxton tensed and was frightened for it. The fact that it sustained no damage was proof to many that its stability was vindicated. By the end of November, with the site looking like a gypsy encampment as the men lit fires to keep warm, glazing was in full swing despite a temporary setback when the glaziers struck for more pay. People watched in wonder as high, high up in the air the glaziers swarmed over the pellucid roof and sailed along the rafters in 76 hooded wagons, fixing pane after pane as they pushed themselves along with their feet. The sash bars had been pre-painted on site with the assistance of a special machine that was filled with liquid colour into which they were dipped before being passed through a series of brushes set at angles. At the ends of the building the steam engines puffed their white clouds of steam.

The royal commissioners continued to plan every detail of the forthcoming exhibition. Granville gave orders that food must be cooked off site, though potatoes could be steamed. The Chelsea Water Company laid new pipes to the site and Messrs Schweppes were awarded the contract for providing liquid refreshment from stalls placed around the elms at the centre of the transept. The commissioners even considered the problem of how the thousands of visitors

would relieve themselves. There were at that time no public conveniences and it was evident that tea shops and ladies' clothing shops would not be able to cope. Finally, a decision was made for George Jennings to design urinals for the men and 'monkey closets' for the ladies, which could be used for the price of a penny. Over 827,000 people availed themselves.

Fears about the exhibition and its building prevailed among scaremongers and detractors, neatly summed up by the Consort in a letter to his relation Frederick William IV of Prussia:

> Mathematicians have calculated that the Crystal Palace will blow down in the first strong gales; engineers that the galleries would crash in and destroy the visitors; political economists have prophesied a scarcity of food in London owing to the vast concourse of people; doctors that owing to so many races coming into contact with each other the Black Death of the Middle Ages would make an appearance as it did after the Crusades; moralists that England would be infected by all the scourges of the civilised and uncivilised world; theologians that the second Tower of Babel would draw upon it the vengeance of the offended God.

Despite media adulation for the building rising from the mud, behind the scenes there remained concerns about its stability. Cubitt, in particular, felt that a strong wind might yet blow it over, but Brunel flew to Paxton's defence, poring over the calculations and assuring Cubitt that they 'only prove to demonstrate that all our houses and large buildings are liable to be blown down by a strong gale'. Winds returned and started to lift some of the panes of glass, but the Palace once again withstood the gale, proving that the lateral pressure of wind on a perpendicular wall was mitigated by the great extent of the surface. At a stormy meeting of the Institution of Civil Engineers in January 1851, as the last column was raised, Digby Wyatt, Fox, Brunel and Stephenson all roundly defended its structural integrity to an audience including many of the most eminent men of science.

The commissioners discussed endlessly the price of various public tickets. Paxton, feeling unassailable, dashed off a stinging, open letter to the Prime Minister, Lord John Russell, which was printed in *The Times* on 22 January, agitating for free entrance to the exhibition for working men and women, the 'sinews of the land', as he called them. The experience of the Great Exhibition, he said, should be 'free as the

light which pervades it'. As the designer of the People's Palace, he no
doubt felt strongly that the labouring poor should be championed, but
his method severely annoyed the Prince, whose secretary wrote immediately to reprimand him for choosing such a public channel rather
than corresponding more diplomatically with the commissioners.
Paxton was slapped down firmly and had no choice but to reply with
sincere regret and apologies.

Paxton was a blunt man, who understood the power of the press,
but he was rarely tactless or undiplomatic. On this occasion, though,
even Granville acknowledged the grave blunder, writing that Paxton's
'head has been turned by the events of the last six months, and it is
not surprising that they should have had that effect upon a self-
educated man'. The endless demands and ongoing responsibilities to
the Duke, to the Baron, to Fox, Henderson and to the commissioners
had crowded so fast upon Paxton that he barely had time to consider
any course of action properly. There was still a constant stream of
demands for his attention – requests for invitations, for fruit or flowers,
for advice on shares or aspects of gardening – while many of his
wider family of nieces and nephews would write to him seeking work,
references, or financial assistance. He would often wait until the
evening for a quiet moment in which to write home to Sarah, only
to find it stolen from him. If he could decline the aggravating and
endless invitations from his devotees, he was unable to say no to any
powerful idea that was put to him, or any request, no matter how
trivial, made by the Duke.

By February, only one month late, the building was complete
enough for the internal decoration to begin. Designed by Owen Jones,
the scheme was based on red, yellow and pale blue paint, flags and
banners. Outside, only the gas and water pipes and the calico roof
cover had still to be completed. Two months later, the royal commissioners insisted on structural tests for the galleries before the bulk
of exhibits were admitted. Two hundred and fifty-two cannon balls
were rolled backwards and forwards along them with no discernible
effect and sappers marched in step across them; the galleries vibrated
no more than a drawing room during a ball. The real problem,
however, remained with the weather, which had been wet almost
throughout construction. March rains were delaying the incoming
exhibits and although it was not discussed publicly, there were leaks
in over a thousand places. All could be stopped by putty, but not
until it stopped raining. In the meantime, Fox, Henderson and Co.

was forced to undertake work elsewhere to improve their cash flow.

The Duke continued to visit the site daily with his aristocratic friends, proud as a man with a new baby. In March, he dined with the Queen, who talked of nothing but Paxton – which completely delighted him. Then he gave Paxton an effusive present of £1,000. Writing his thanks, Paxton noted that, come May, he would have worked for the Duke for 25 years.

Paxton had become a household name: 'ask Paxton' was the advice for anyone in any kind of difficulty and 'Paxton vobiscum' joked the fashionables. Dickens contributed to this general adulation in an article in *Household Words* in which he praised the Crystal Palace and described Paxton as one of the busiest men in England, a workaholic 'whose very leisure would kill a man of fashion with its hard work'. He was portrayed as both a visionary and a man with his feet on the ground, a man who could stride through the bureaucracy of committees with a bluff realism while his eye and heart remained nailed to an ideal; a man for whom no obstacle appeared insurmountable.

Sparrows had nested in the branches of the elm trees and no one knew quite how to get rid of them. Guns were, obviously, out of the question. The Duke of Wellington is said to have advised sparrow hawks, and a letter was published in *The Times* suggesting that metal bird-feeders should be charged with an electric current strong enough to kill the birds on contact. With only six weeks to go until opening, the pace of labour increased as the weather deteriorated. Hundreds and hundreds of wagon loads of exhibits were arriving every day as the storms continued to batter the building. There were 15,000 exhibits to be housed, over half of them British and the remainder shipped from 40 nations. There were china and coal, steam engines, patent envelope-making machines; there were knives with seventy blades; hats and ribbons, animal and agricultural produce, locks and jewels and armoury. There were unpickable pockets, stuffed frogs from Würtemberg, a silent alarm clock that turned you out of bed; there was the first gas stove and Pugin's medieval court and there was the greatest diamond in the world, the Koh-i-noor, lent by the Queen. In the centre of the transept, sat Osler's vast crystal fountain.

Outside, piles of rotting orange peel, rags, horse dung and rubbish lay in the mud and carriage ruts around the site. Cubitt doom-mongered that it still could not possibly be finished in time. Granville retained his sense of humour and, by a superhuman final effort from contractors and exhibitors, by the end of 30 April everything that could be done had been done – and activity stopped. Here was the world under a glass case. A world, it was dreamed, that would be freed from the tyrannies of war through liberalism and free trade. As Sarah and the children moved into 34 Portland Place, rented for the summer season, the Crystal Palace stood silent and glittering in the moonlight in Hyde Park, a vast transparent edifice, ready for the millions flocking towards the turnstiles.

⁓

Despite the fiasco with the *Daily News*, Dickens was broadly a great supporter of Paxton and he had developed a warm friendship with the Duke, who was engaged by the attention paid to him and diverted by Dickens' amateur theatricals. The novelist, along with Sir Edward Bulwer Lytton – considered one of the leading dramatists in Britain – had created the Guild of Literature and Art to assist 'distressed men of letters' and had endowed it with several thousands pounds of his own money. Bulwer Lytton wrote a new play, *Not So Bad As We Seem*, to be performed by the Amateur Company, which included Wilkie Collins and several of the *Punch* staff. The play was dedicated to the Duke, and he offered Devonshire House as a venue and his address book as a guest list. The Duke asked Paxton to design and build the stage and the royal box in the drawing room of Devonshire House and generally to manage all technical requirements including working out which windows should be left open and which closed to afford the best possible ventilation. The Queen agreed to attend the first night on 30 April – the very night before the biggest day of Paxton's professional life, the opening of the exhibition.

Dickens' father and tiny daughter died in April, causing the play to be postponed until 16 May. This at least gave Paxton some breathing space. It was not just the stage-building that distracted him. Everyone who was anyone wanted a ticket to the opening night, one of the social events of the year. Anyone and everyone who had even the most tenuous link with Paxton applied to him for help in getting one and the Duke called on him to collect the cheques for £5 a ticket and dispatch them as required. It would not have been in Paxton's nature to fail to attend to every detail that could possibly be conceived to ensure the evening's success.

Two weeks before the exhibition's grand opening ceremony, Edwin Chadwick at the Board of Health, with whom Paxton had earlier corresponded over the cottages at Edensor, joined his demands to the many being made of Paxton. He gave notice of the Board's compulsory purchase of two cemeteries in London and their intention to add a third under the new Metropolitan Interment Act, which proposed the closure of poor graveyards and the creation of new modern burial grounds from public funds.* Only Paxton's advice on their drainage and layout would do, surely he had at least one free day to survey the properties? While he was assisting Chadwick, arranging his court dress and shining his sword, the metropolis was readying itself. Boarding houses and hotels for miles around had been fully booked for months, visitors were pouring in from the continent and, in the West End, on the eve of the opening the pubs and coffee houses stayed open all night.

On 1 May, bunting hung from every building and from every street light. There were boys in the trees and on the roofs and a gridlock of carriages and handsome cabs throughout the city. After another brief controversy, the commissioners had decided that the exhibition would be opened by the Queen in a ceremony open to all season-ticket holders. This meant that she would walk among her subjects for the first time, no insignificant break of protocol with the memory of European revolutions still so fresh in everybody's minds. As her state carriage, with Albert and her children accompanying her, left Buckingham Palace, the drizzle abated and the sun began to burn away the clouds and pour on to the crowds in true story-book style. A fine haze rose from the wet grass, making the Crystal Palace shimmer and gleam as the flags of all the nations streamed from its roof. The Queen passed through swarms of people in their Sunday-best. Three hundred thousand people gathered in Hyde Park alone.

Since early morning the Palace had been filling slowly with the 30,000 season-ticket holders who watched with craned necks as each luminary arrived. The Duke of Wellington on his 82nd birthday, the Prime Minister, the great and the good. When the royal carriage had delivered the royal family and they had taken off their shawls and overcoats, Paxton, in full court dress, sword at his side, walked between Fox and Henderson, leading the procession to the centre of the

---

* None of these cemetery schemes eventuated because of the Treasury's indisposition to fund them.

building. They were followed by the royal commissioners, ministers and the Court. It was the proudest public day of his life. All anxiety had abated.

Victoria's diary entry for that evening charts quite how much she, too, was moved. She recalled a day a thousand times superior to her coronation, with swelling cheers, palms, spectacle, bustle and great excitement. For her, the enormity of the building was magical, glorious and touching; everyone, she said, had seemed truly happy, and no one more so than Paxton 'who may be justly proud; he rose from being a common gardener's boy'. When the Queen had left, the Duke descended from his gallery position to parade Paxton around wearing 'his dress and his cocked hat as if he had been so clad through life. We were incessantly stopped and surrounded with overflowing greetings.' People shouted out 'Look, there's Mr Paxton!' followed, more quietly, by 'and there's the Duke of Devonshire'. The Duke was tickled.

The next day the papers fought over superlatives in their descriptions of a building that dominated the exhibition and its contents completely. Thackeray immortalised it in his May Day Ode. One article called it 'a poet's dream'. A contemporary pastiche novel by *Punch*'s Horace Mayhew, whose plot centred on a provincial family's trip to the metropolis for the opening, spoke of its 'exquisite lightness and tone of colour . . . a visual feast and a rare delight of air, colour and space'. *Punch* itself called it 'a wonder of beauty that seemed to realise the fiction of fairy-land: a structure raised rather by the genie of Sindbad, than materialised through human genius . . .' Some, however, were disappointed. The very transparency of the Palace confused perspective, they said, there were no shadows, no obvious delineation between the interior and exterior, it was impossible to contain in a glance.

Architects and architectural journals such as *The Builder* and *The Ecclesiologist*, praised the Palace but refused to recognise it as architecture, so far had it redefined their structural vocabulary. Carlyle called it a big glass soap bubble and Ruskin a giant monster, though a very admirable conception from an active and intelligent brain. Both were voices in an argument that would rage well into the following century. The building not only fulfilled its purpose, it moved people and left a deep impression on contemporary minds, less a greenhouse than a blue mirage of a building. Official and unofficial guides to it and to the exhibition flooded on to the market, becoming an industry in itself. The Palace's influence was soon seen in, among other things, the vast glass and iron span roof of the Paddington Railway Terminus building, a showpiece built between 1852 and 1854 and designed by the equally indefatigable Brunel.

~

Dickens was, perhaps, a little envious of the complete attention paid to Paxton by the Duke. He wrote on the opening day to the Duke: 'when Paxton is got safe out of his court dress and his sword no longer sticks crosswise in your mind, you may perhaps have a moment's leisure to read the short article I have written about the Guild for next week's Household Words'. In addition to the play, a series of grand balls were thrown at Devonshire House to mark the Duke's 61st birthday and the start of the London Season. Paxton again supervised most of the details, including the flowers.

During the glorious first months of the exhibition, everyone had a cause for grand celebration. A banquet was held at the Hôtel de Ville in Paris to honour those involved in the Great Exhibition, including Paxton. It went disastrously wrong when the majority of the luggage was lost at French customs and the visitors found them- selves forced to borrow evening dress from wherever and whoever they could prevail upon. Great celebratory dinners followed, hosted by the city of Derby. First for Charles Fox — where there was also a misfortune with the luggage which caught fire on the train from London singeing Paxton's coat and hat — and a second in honour of Paxton. Representatives from all the London newspapers attended and the bells of All Saints Church pealed as the guests of honour arrived.

The Derby dinner gave the Duke a public forum to display the lavish pride he felt for his Chatsworth agent, protégé and friend. He spoke of Paxton's mind as well regulated, clear and active, his will as powerful and persevering, and he praised his integrity, his simplicity and his talent. For his part, Paxton never missed an opportunity to show his own devotion and gratitude to the Duke. He sincerely felt that he owed to him everything that he had become. The exhibition, he said, had appeared to him as 'a beam of light of vast magnitude', yet he admitted that from the day he had first sent in his designs his anxieties had been almost overpowering. He was pleased to say that while his 'public duties have been many and onerous . . . yet in the performance of them it is my happiness to know that I have never lost a friend'. This ability to win and maintain great friendships was remarked on throughout his life, and particularly after his death. It was a side of his character that he took completely for granted and one that contributed to his crippling workload.

Other men might finally have returned to the bosom of their families for well-earned rest, but Paxton had more to do. Plans for Mayer de Rothschild's grand romantic mansion in the vale of Aylesbury were being finalised. It was to be called Mentmore and built in an Elizabethan style in a park of over 700 acres. The design was influenced by the Duke's Elizabethan hall, Hardwick, and, more particularly, sixteenth-century Wollaton Hall in Nottinghamshire. He designed a turreted roofline and a rectangular tower at each corner with a massive great hall at the centre, galleried and entirely covered in glass.

Expense was never going to be an issue. Many of the floors and ceilings had already been bought from French palaces requiring, in some instances, the rooms to be designed and built around them. George Stokes worked on detailed plans for Paxton's design and by the autumn George Myers, the builder of Paxton's far smaller Burton Closes, had signed a contract for construction with the Baron, binding himself to a completion date less than eighteen months away.

Also at this time, the zealous Edwin Chadwick was bothering Paxton again. Even the Prince Consort had become interested in the pressing problem presented by the disposal of increasing amounts of sewage from towns. There were many schemes proposing its agricultural use, or its purification for reuse as drinking water, and in early 1850 Prince Albert had invented his own sewage filter which he sent to the Royal Agricultural Society for their comments and to others, including Paxton, for theirs. Chadwick was now preparing various reports on the different solutions being considered across Britain, and he pressed Paxton for his comments based on his experience with using liquid manure on crops and plants at Chatsworth, in particular in the widely reported cultivation of the *Victoria regia*.

The exhibition continued into the autumn of 1851. It seemed that the world 'turned on a shilling', the price of the lowest entry ticket. In the early part of the year, Thomas Cook had opened excursion clubs and ordinary people across the country had been saving for months for the price of an entry ticket and train fare. Train companies had entered into a price war, which, by the summer, meant that excursion fares to London were now at rock-bottom prices. The exhibition would remain open for 140 days, resolutely closed on Sundays, attracting some six million visitors, including a woman of 84 said to have walked all the way from Cornwall.

The railway revolution, and the doubling of the population since the start of the century, had created a new phenomenon – the public, and with it the start of a revolution in leisure. *The Times* reported that the people themselves had now become the exhibition, noting that nothing like it had ever been witnessed before. The six main railway termini were regularly choked with arrivals from the country. Omnibuses were filled inside and out as fast as they were emptied, and cabs were frequently not to be had on the best-attended stands. All streets leading to Hyde Park were jammed by a seemingly inexhaustible stream of public conveyances, and the pavements swarmed with dense columns of pedestrians, a moving panorama of life directed towards the Crystal Palace. The papers wondered where all the people came from.

By October, £356,000 had been taken in entry fees, nearly two million buns and over one million bottles of non-alcoholic drinks had been sold. There was almost no lawbreaking: 12 pickpockets, 11 petty thefts and 3 women assaulted. It was the first, and last, exhibition to make a profit. After much debate, the royal commissioners used the surplus (as it was called), plus a matching parliamentary grant, to purchase a vast acreage of horticultural and market-garden land at South Kensington to be devoted to educational purposes. This is the land now occupied by the Royal Albert Hall, Imperial College, the Victoria and Albert Museum as well as the Science and Natural History Museums, the Royal College of Music, the Royal College of Art and more. Paxton's great temporary building had not just ensured the success of the greatest exhibition the world had ever seen, it had guaranteed a lasting legacy to the people of Britain and the permanent landscape of London.

CHAPTER EIGHTEEN

So sure was Paxton that this combination of glass and iron pointed the way to the future, that he could not rest. As the foundations for the great Rothschild mansion were dug, he was consulted widely on other possible applications for factories, circuses and theatres, none of which eventuated in finished plans. He also proposed a glass roof over the Royal Exchange in London, which again did not happen. When America announced its intention to hold its own world's fair in New York in 1853, he felt compelled to submit his own design. In the event, a design by George Carsten and Charles Gildermeister was chosen for a strange building, a glass octagon clearly inspired by the new techniques displayed in the Crystal Palace, though only one-eighth of its size.

In the summer, Paxton proposed yet another scheme for a 'Crystal Sanatorium' adjoining the City of London Hospital for Diseases of the Chest near Victoria Park. The elaborate building, in which patients could exercise in all weathers, was reminiscent of the Great Stove with its masonry pediment and arched span roof, but here there would be an ornamental tower at each corner. For this building, he described a system of ventilation approximating modern air-conditioning in which there would be a 'free circulation of air without direct currents . . . no cold outer air should enter the building until it has been warmed, purified and rendered fit for easy respiration'.

Espousing one of the preoccupations of the day, highlighted by the Select Committee for Public Walks in the early 1830s, Paxton was

passionate about creating spaces for ordinary city dwellers, quite apart
from invalids, to exercise in all weathers. The Crystal Palace, like the
Jardins d'Hiver in Paris, clearly demonstrated to him that large covered
areas within parks could provide this, especially if they were modular
buildings from which sections of the glass could be removed in summer.
The Crystal Sanatorium project again came to nothing, and as the
summer progressed and thoughts turned to the future of the exhibition building, a war of words erupted in London.

In his own mind, those Sarah described as the Goths and Vandals,
would never dare order the destruction of the great building in Hyde
Park. Paxton had always envisaged it as being transformed to provide
London with a venue for walking and riding in all weathers, surrounded
by luxuriant and exotic plants, the finest sculpture and educational
exhibits. Parliament, however, had promised that any building erected
in the park would be temporary. Only two months after the Great
Exhibition opened, Paxton began to petition Parliament for its retention. His supporters formed a committee for the preservation of the
building, and he wrote and published a pamphlet setting out his ideas
in detail. As is the nature of all pamphlet-driven debate, many others
followed in support, including those by 'A Medical Man' and 'Denarius',
whose essay was called 'Shall We Keep the Crystal Palace, and Have
Riding and Walking in all Weathers among Flowers, Fountains and
Sculpture?' Denarius turned out to be the staunch Henry Cole. A few
answered with their own pamphlets denouncing the monster in the
park.

Paxton, typically public in his vehemence, turned to the media. He
wrote to *The Times*, detailing the likely cost of fitting-out and maintaining the building and describing alternative uses. It could, for
example, form an establishment for horticultural experiments, or for
housing the overflow of artefacts from the Natural History Department
of the British Museum. Above all, it could provide a place of public
resort that would, uniquely, open the field of intellectual as well as
healthy enjoyments. Public opinion, in favour of his plans, fuelled and
echoed by the press, was strong and from July questions about the
building's future were asked regularly in the Commons. The Prime
Minister Lord John Russell argued to keep it, Lord Brougham who
had initially been against the idea of a building in the park, now also
supported Paxton's petition, and Lord Granville admitted that he
would feel a great pang at seeing it come down. In the opposite camp,
Lord Campbell presented his own petition, signed by the residents of

Knightsbridge, denouncing its stability as a permanent structure; Colonel Sibthorp took up the cudgel again and, in the wings, the Prince himself was against the building's retention.

As the pressure mounted to reach a decision, *The Times* cried: 'Mr Paxton's answer is <u>try it</u> . . . there were people who said the building, as it now is, would never stand . . . all these and many other apprehensions have been dispelled by the fact . . . let Mr Paxton's plan be understood before it is rejected.' Henry Cole wrote to the Prince's secretary, Colonel Phipps, that the commissioners were resolved to give up the building but that he feared a public outcry. In August, Parliament voted a stay of execution – the building could stand until May 1852 to give them time to consider all options.

On Tuesday, 7 October, over 109,000 people, including the Duke of Wellington, visited the exhibition. So much money was taken at the door that two cabs had to be hired to take it to the bank at Threadneedle Street. And on the last public day, Saturday, 11 October, 53,000 came and no one wanted to leave, singing and cheering until the very last. The next day the building stood empty, echoing with the memory of the six million who had walked its floors and galleries, the greatest mass movement of people in Britain's history. A quiet and private closing ceremony was held four days later for the commissioners and Prince Albert – it was pouring with rain outside and it dripped through the putty on to the men below; the building had never been made absolutely water-tight. The following week Paxton, who had already received £2,500 from Fox, Henderson under the terms of their tripartite contract, was awarded the highest honorarium of £5,000 by the commission. Later that month, at Windsor Castle, he was knighted by the Queen, along with his friend Charles Fox. The Prime Minister had written that, owing to his ingenious design, his name would be for ever connected with 'one of the most marvellous enterprises of an age so remarkable for invention and discovery'. Paxton was moved to silence. He later said that he was unable to find the words to express his feelings.

'The past year has been to me one of great anxiety and great uncertainty of action . . . I let many things into arrears in the early part of the year that an accumulation of engagements pressed so heavily upon me this autumn that I never could for two days together be certain as to my movements,' wrote Paxton that November. As he passed his 48th birthday, he had began to succumb painfully to rheumatism so that he postponed joining the Duke in Ireland that autumn. The Duke nevertheless wrote regularly from his little kingdom at Lismore, surrounded by his doctor, his band and his pianist, his servants and his aristocratic guests, by balls and fireworks and fun. The kind and affable Duke wrote delightedly about all this but, utterly reliant on Paxton, also of bills and the details of the alterations, about smoking fires and the cost of hiring ferries, all of which he wanted Paxton to investigate. The year of his crowning success had been the most physically, intellectually and emotionally taxing of his life and there was little respite in sight.

On the last day of the year, Baron Mayer de Rothschild's daughter, Hannah, laid the foundation stone of Mentmore. As one grand edifice began to rise above the Aylesbury plain, the prospects of another in Hyde Park appeared more fragile.

⌒

Between trips to Lismore and to Paris at the start of 1852, the new Sir Joseph and Lady Paxton were organising their first family wedding – that of Blanche, their second daughter, aged 20. Digby Wyatt had been married at the start of January, and Paxton had gone to endless trouble to send him flowers and exotic fruit from Chatsworth, including a bridal bouquet already made up, with detailed instructions on their care in order to be perfect for the day. Yet, perhaps because there were two older, unmarried sisters and because their own home was again uninhabitable due to alterations, letters between Sarah and Paxton show that they did not much enjoy making the arrangements for Blanche, 'for this horrid wedding and all its troubles'. Indeed, since everybody seemed to be bothering Paxton for his opinion on it, he quite wished that it was over. Blanche was married on 22 January at Edensor Church, with an evening ball held at Chatsworth at the particular request of the Duke.

The Times now stepped up its campaign to retain the Crystal Palace as a winter garden. In December the government had appointed a commission to review the situation, including Lord Seymour, who was the Chief Commissioner for Woods and Forests, the recently knighted Sir William Cubitt and Paxton's old friend John Lindley. At the end of January, Paxton was called to give evidence. He was reluctant to do so. He knew that two-thirds of the commission, Seymour and Cubitt, were against the building remaining in Hyde Park and that they had already suggested the as yet unformed Battersea Park as an alternative.* He must, however, have hoped that the word of John Lindley might save his glittering creation.

The committee reported in mid-February. Examining the costs of keeping and maintaining the Palace as a public building, either in Hyde Park or elsewhere, they made no resolute recommendation, but they did suggest that, of all the options, perhaps Paxton's plan to convert it into a garden was the most worthy of consideration. But they also damagingly repeated Paxton's own statement that it may still not be 'the best adapted to its purpose, and that for the sum of £150,000 he could put up a much finer, more magnificent and more appropriate structure'.

Paxton, despite applying for the opportunity to review and alter his evidence, was not given the chance, and in fury he wrote to *The Times* that he had been made to murder his own child. The general committee formed to lobby for the retention of the building went into overdrive. Only popular opinion, it felt, could now move Parliament. Private handbills were printed and circulated widely. Huge crowds – larger than on some of the shilling days – were allowed to promenade in the building to sign petitions and inspect a model of Paxton's proposed amendments. Public meetings were arranged around London and at the end of April 4,000 people gathered at the largest of these at Exeter Hall. In total, 192 separate petitions were got up and delivered to the Commons on the eve of the deciding parliamentary vote.

Sibthorp was joined by Benjamin Disraeli, Henry Labouchère and even the great Liberal champion and friend of Paxton, William Gladstone, in a deciding vote against retention of the building. Paxton's allies, including George Cavendish, William Jackson, Viscount Palmerston, Sir Robert Peel† and Samuel Morton Peto, could not save it. The Crystal Palace in Hyde Park was doomed and Fox, Henderson were ordered to remove the building from the park by the first of November.

Sarah feared that he was again exerting himself beyond human strength. Then the Duke became severely ill and Paxton was called to sit with him at Chiswick House, while Stokes managed the details of construction at Mentmore. He was on the point of exhaustion, but still he managed to work behind the scenes on contingency plans for

---

*   Battersea Park opened in 1853 but remained unremarkable until John Gibson moved
      there in 1858 as superintendent, forming the then-famous subtropical gardens there.
†   Nobly voting, as his father would have done, in favour of the building.

EMOTION OF OUR FRIEND SIBTHORP ON READING IN A PUBLIC PRINT THE
PROPOSAL THAT THE CRYSTAL PALACE SHOULD REMAIN IN HYDE PARK.

the future of his building so that on 13 May Prince Albert's secretary
wrote dramatically to the Consort that, swiftly and secretly, the Crystal
Palace had been bought for £70,000. The money had already been
paid by a group of nine men forming the Crystal Palace Company,
backed financially by the London, Brighton and South Coast Railway
on the understanding that the building would be re-erected on land
close to their line. Paxton was to be Director of the Winter Garden,
Park and Conservatory.

The directors of the Crystal Palace Company included Samuel
Laing – the chairman of the railway company – John Scott Russell
and Francis Fuller. George Grove, previously the secretary at the
Society of Arts and later famous for his complete *Dictionary of Music*,
was appointed secretary.* Seeking capital of half a million pounds, the
new company published its prospectus four days later, announcing that

---

* Grove made the earliest annotations of Beethoven's symphonies and became the
first director of the Royal College of Music. It was odd that Henry Cole was not
employed by the company – despite his obvious claim to being the moving force
behind the Great Exhibition. His diary shows that Paxton supported him as
manager. But Fuller supported Scott Russell and distrusted Cole, who was overlooked.

the building would be re-erected by Fox, Henderson on ground at Sydenham in Kent, within easy reach of London. A spur laid from the railway line from London Bridge would ensure that the journey from the city took only 20 minutes. It promised that the Palace would become a miniature of the world, its gardens filled with fountains to rival Versailles, that it would provide refined recreation 'calculated to elevate the intellect, instruct the mind and improve the heart'. A large estate was purchased from Leo Schuster, one of the directors of the railway company, along with his house Penge Place, which became the company offices. More land was bought, including a house called Rockhills, and 30 acres surrounding it. Retaining 200 acres for the park, any land found surplus to their needs was then sold to developers for a profit.

By the beginning of June, splendid new plans were produced to show that the new Crystal Palace would increase vastly in size and, for permanence, the wooden transept ribs would be substituted with iron. After the success of the Great Exhibition, financial optimism was at its zenith. The £5 shares in the company were quickly oversubscribed. The working capital was ready to go to work.

Paxton returned to Sarah at last and they were able to move back home to Barbrook, from which they had been displaced for over a year.

Paid for primarily by the Duke from his private accounts as a gift to Paxton, very grand alterations had been made. The house was now an even more substantial villa, with a square tower, large living rooms, new offices and domestic rooms, all newly decorated and surrounded by landscaped gardens. Despite the fact that he was now also employed by the Crystal Palace Company, and continued to run his own private architectural practice, the Duke increased his salary again, to £650 a year. In August, Paxton's architectural assistant, George Stokes, asked for the hand of their eldest daughter, Emily – and was accepted. For a short while, at least, Paxton was able to rest at last. Affluent, and happy with his family, he celebrated his 49th birthday. Two days later, the first column of the new palace was raised.

CHAPTER NINETEEN

In the early 1850s, Norwood, the village at the top of the new Crystal Palace estate, was still sparsely populated and rural, dominated by its large areas of woodland and rising delightfully clear of the smoke of London a handful of miles away. It was the most significant site on the outskirts of London. Ruskin owned a house on Denmark Hill, and the Regency 'Royal Beulah Spa' nearby was a popular health and pleasure resort. The *Illustrated London News* called it 'a place of perfect solitude. Not a sound, not an object in view, betrays the close vicinity of the great city. The blackbirds and thrushes sing away in harmonious rivalry and the rabbits dashing through the brushwood and wobbling along the fields complete the idea of a rural remote district only disturbed by the occasional thunder of a train dashing along the valley below.' Here Paxton was to write a new chapter in public amusement – creating a spacious exhibition hall and elaborate park available to all for the cost of a train ticket.

Contracts were swiftly negotiated for earthworks and detailed drawings completed. The building was substantially altered and was far more complex than its parent. To correct what some had seen as the monotony of its original flat-roof design, the roof of the new building would be vaulted along its entire length, with the central arched transept increased by over two storeys to a height of 175 feet. Two smaller arched transepts on each side of the centre, and long wings at right angles to each end of the building were added. The overall area was increased by almost half, and would require over

1,650,000 square feet of glass, stronger 21-ounce glass replacing the 16-ounce glass used at Hyde Park. Because the slope of the park fell 26 feet over the width of the building, brick piers supported the columns to one side, forming a half-basement which housed rows of paired furnaces and boilers and a network of over 50 miles of pipes for the hot water heating system, a communications road and store-rooms. Subsequently termed 'the Paxton tunnel', the area adjacent to it would also house exhibitions of moving machinery.

Navvies had cut the canals in the early nineteenth century and then railways, bridges and tunnels for engineers like Stephenson, Brunel and Locke, attracted by high wages and with a legendary capacity for food and drink. They now flooded on to the site from all over England. Eventually there would be 6,000 working there. Some built huts for themselves on the site, others travelled from lodging houses in surrounding villages and as far out as Beckenham and Forest Hill.[*]

Progress was rapid. The first column, brought from Hyde Park, was raised in glorious weather at the start of August at a public cere-mony for 500 invited guests, directors, investors and the British press. The royal standard flew, and a 21-gun salute rang out, followed by toasts and speeches and a programme of music by Mendelssohn, Rossini and Donizetti. The eminent journal *The Builder* proclaimed that it would be the most extraordinary structure in the world, and a thirst for similar projects broke out. There was talk of erecting public glass buildings in Bath and Plymouth, glass roofs were increasingly used for railway sheds and termini, and there were plans afoot all over the country for winter gardens and floral halls.

Surrounded as Paxton was by contracts, bills and quantities for construction, excavation, embankment, ironwork, drainage, masonry and a hundred other urgencies, the Duke was not to be ignored. In June, he relapsed and remained housebound in Brighton. Again, Paxton flew to him, soothed him as he would a father and did not leave until he was satisfied of the older man's comfort. For the Duke this was no trifling care. He relied increasingly on the lasting kindness of his gardener. 'O Paxton, my kind deliverer, how good and kind today,' he wrote in his diary.

For Paxton, the great reputation he had achieved prior to 1851 –

[*] Eventually, what we would now call a housing estate was built to accommodate
them – the first of its kind in the world. It was surrounded by a high wall, and
contained three pubs. It had a reputation for violence and disorder and no one in
their right mind would go near it after dark.

the design of parks, of houses, of glasshouses and of gardens – ensured that his own private practice continued alongside his work for the Crystal Palace Company. The spa town of Buxton in Derbyshire became a particular distraction. The Duke continued to invest in the town and Paxton could not but be involved. He was enlisted to lay out a new system of roads and a park and housing development on a similar plan, though smaller scale, to Prince's Park in Liverpool. Only the park was completed, while the young architect, Henry Currey, no doubt influenced by Paxton, added ridge and furrow glass roofs to his designs for the baths.

Paxton was also taken up with Lismore. A fire had recently devastated the range west of the gatehouse, though it had spared Crace's recently completed redecoration of the principal rooms. Paxton thought it was no bad thing to have had some of the gloomier rooms cleared. Indeed, the fire was the spur for even greater plans. In January 1851, when the first of the old towers had fallen, Paxton had laughingly told the Duke that he would build them up again and now a grand scheme of rebuilding was planned for the medieval castle. The ancient round tower and ruined flag tower were to be extended, with six further towers raised up and new wings designed. Quarried stone for windows and dressing was carted in bulk from Derbyshire to the castle by chartered private ferry and canal. John Brown from the Chatsworth estate supervised the works to Paxton's designs, with detailed plans prepared once again by his assistant, George Stokes. Some of the earliest gas lighting in Ireland was supplied to the castle and the town on Paxton's orders.

Leaving Stokes to the plans, Paxton left for Paris to buy orange trees. Originally owned by the old king at Neuilly and confiscated by the state, they would be a valuable addition to the glorious collections at the finished Palace at Sydenham. All the while, the Duke, still unwell, dragged at Paxton's coat-tails. He fussed so insistently that Paxton only ever managed to achieve half of what he wanted to complete. Irritating it may have been, but this was the one man to whom he owed everything. He could be refused nothing.

⌐

Late that autumn, the directors of the Crystal Palace Company agreed that Paxton could have the use of Rockhills, the property situated at the top of the park site and adjacent to the Palace. He may have initially envisaged this as a suitable house for his offices and in which to stay only when he was obliged to be at the Palace. However, in the turmoil of the following years he spent far more time there than at Barbrook with Sarah, and the lease marked a turning point in their marriage and in his life. Had the Palace stayed in Hyde Park, perhaps his dislocation from Chatsworth would have been less dramatic. In the new venture, he had assumed far more responsibility than his title suggested, and Digby Wyatt and Owen Jones – now popularly dubbed 'Alhambra Jones' for his flair with Moorish decoration – far less than theirs did. While they prepared plans for the lavish courts – among them the Medieval, the Alhambra, the Pompeiian – and scoured Europe for artefacts for display, Paxton assumed responsibility for the construction and the ultimate success of the venture in all its constituent detail. Here there was no royal commission, no committees and subcommittees; just a relatively small band of men, led by a visionary whose shoulders began to bear the entire weight of public and private expectation.

The most graphic illustration of the increasing separation between husband and wife is found in the great volume of letters that now passed between them. Paxton continued to speculate in railways though now the focus had spread to new lines being built abroad and, in particular, in America. With their accumulated wealth, this was large-scale interest – $25,000 alone in the new Cincinnati Railroad. His oldest daughter Emily married Stokes in the spring of 1853 and his son George, misbehaving again, was installed at Woolwich Military Academy where, it was hoped, his adolescent predilections for fast horses, swearing and betting might be tempered. He had already failed at so many schools and with so many tutors that neither Paxton nor Sarah was confident of the restorative powers of the army. Still, they hoped. George was Paxton's blind-spot – the only boy in a family of girls – and he simply did not know what to do with him and had no leisure in which to try to understand the motives for his son's increasingly unruly behaviour.

⌒

The great, brick edifice of Mentmore progressed more reliably. By the time Emily was married to Stokes, the new approach road was in its final stages. One mile long, it was planted with circular clumps of horse chestnut, birch and elm, alternating with Wellingtonia – the most massive of evergreen trees introduced that year, and incredibly expensive. As the road approached the house, it narrowed and curved so that it was only at the last minute that the magnificent house could be seen, rising on its eminence in a drained and manicured parkland.

The 80-room house was built of heavily embellished Ancaster stone, a central square block flanked by a secondary servants' block. The huge grand hall at the very centre of the house rose to a glazed roof which flooded it with light. A richly moulded recessed arcade of alabaster and green marble ran around the first floor level of the hall, backed by side corridors along which the principal apartments were arranged. While Mentmore followed the prevailing fashion for grand new domestic buildings – such as Thomas Cubitt's much illustrated Osborne on the Isle of Wight built for Victoria and Albert by 1848 and the remodelling of Trentham and Highclere by Charles Barry – Mentmore was to be resolutely modern in the technologies Paxton employed. Making architectural use of plate glass for the first time, massive, polished glass doors filled the arches of the hall, running on brass tracks, and vast panes of plate glass were fitted into all the windows. The most advanced underfloor heating was installed, and running hot water provided to all the bathrooms.

The Builder was never quite ready to admit Paxton the untrained architect into its hallowed halls. Gothic was the style of the moment and they derided this Jacobethan mansion. But Mayer de Rothschild, his wife, Julia, and their daughter loved it – as did Paxton – and when it was finally completed in 1855 the journal was forced to modify its criticism in the face of the proven grandeur of its substantial conception. Inside, the Baron made it one of the outstanding treasure houses of the country. The interior light was extraordinary as enormous French antique mirrors reflected the roof lights, windows and glass doors. A visitor in the 1870s said of it: 'I don't believe the Medici were so lodged at the height of their glory.'

The relationship between the house and its grounds was carefully considered, much in the way of an eighteenth-century ideal, though here the small flower gardens immediately outside the windows were formal and highly decorative. Indeed, initially, Mayer did not want a garden at all, though later, there would be an aviary, a range of glasshouses filled with exotic and valuable plants, vast orchards, a subtropical garden and a rose garden. Paxton continued to work on the grounds into the final years of his life, becoming great friends with the family and often staying as their guest with one or other of his unmarried daughters. After his death, Meyer's daughter, Hannah, developed the flower and fruit gardens extensively. Mentmore was the first Rothschild house in Buckinghamshire and perhaps always the grandest. Mayer's brothers and their families soon followed him, building seven more houses within lunching distance of each other and with easy access to London.

Back in Derbyshire, the Duke had proposed Paxton as well as Smithers, the agent at Buxton, to be Justices of the Peace. Despite the fact that Paxton would rather not have had the bother of it, the suggestion sparked a row with the Lord Chancellor that had Lord Granville rushing to the Duke and Paxton's support. Lord Cranworth appeared to imply that the appointments were nepotistic and the Duke was livid. Granville pointed out that the Duke's probity was unquestionable and, after a protracted correspondence, Cranworth reluctantly acceded, and Paxton's name was entered into the Commission of the Peace for Derbyshire. Given that he was to spend a diminishing amount of time there, such a prominent local position was ironic.

The new Palace was progressing well but in August 1853, a year after the first column was raised, disaster struck. Twelve men were killed when the staging for the great central transept collapsed and they fell over 100 feet. Paxton knew most of the men personally and was met at the station with the news. He sat alone that evening at Rockhills in a state of deep grief, almost driven mad by a sense of overwhelming responsibility. Fox, Henderson issued a public statement denying any defect in their arrangements, which was supported soon after by the coroner's verdict. But the accident dampened the exhilaration of their earlier successes, and less than a month later, another part of the structure gave way. This time there was no injury and no apparent harm to the building, but it was imperative to keep it a secret if confidence in their enormous undertaking was to prevail.

Eleven-year-old Annie came to stay at Rockhills to keep her father company for a while, and the Queen insisted on visiting the works, which Paxton now found rather a bore since everything came to a standstill when she graced them with her presence. The railway company were moving forward with their plans to form the crucial rail link from Sydenham station to the palace and Paxton, of course, was included among the directors. Confident of a very high volume of day trippers, the company marketed combined tickets for the journey and entrance to the palace and planned a dedicated new track parallel to the existing Brighton and South Coast line, with a spur to the palace low level station. From here, visitors were to walk up the hill, through a glass colonnade to the building itself.

Throughout 1853 and 1854, Paxton, ever alert to commercial possibilities, laboured on various other schemes for the company. He drew up plans for four large hotels at the top end of the hill, by Dulwich Wood, connected to the Palace by a glass walkway over the road. While this plan did not come to fruition, it was a century ahead of the hotel and leisure complexes with which we have become familiar.

If the company had initially hoped to open the new Crystal Palace on 1 May 1853, matching the speed of construction at Hyde Park, the massive additions and sheer scale of the enterprise made this impracticable. The date was postponed for a year. By the summer of 1853, however, the whole of the west end of the edifice had been completed, a part of the east end and the small transept roof. The foundations of the new west wing were under way, the warming apparatus progressing; the pumping machines had been made and pipes for the waterworks were being delivered weekly with the upper range almost finished and the large reservoirs in a forward state. As at Hyde Park during the winter of its construction, visitors flocked to the site to see for themselves the progress they read about in the papers. Onlookers were ordered not to speak to the workmen, not to touch anything and to keep themselves away from any potentially dangerous area. The very idea of hordes of sightseers parading around a building site was clearly not as extraordinary as it would be today, yet while they undoubtedly slowed the work at times, not one was ever injured.

Paxton had insisted that there should be no chimneys to ruin the line of the Palace's roof, so flues were constructed to take smoke from the boilers north and south to towers at each end of the building, under the supervision of the engineer Charles Wild. Wild had worked for Stephenson on the Britannia Bridge and with Digby Wyatt and Owen Jones on the original Crystal Palace, but he was increasingly absent from the work at Sydenham. Additionally, since there was no natural, high-level watercourse like those on which he had been able to rely at Chatsworth, Paxton's elaborate scheme for over 12,000 jets, fountains and cascades for the park necessitated a complex and costly system to circulate the water. A deep bore was sunk at the lowest level of the park from which water was pumped into a large reservoir; from here the water could be driven into an intermediate level lake to supply the smaller waterworks. Several large engines forced the water still higher to a feeder-reservoir situated just beside the palace itself. But to achieve the head of pressure necessary for the highest of the jets at the park, water tanks were to be situated at the very tops of Wild's chimney towers, tanks so large that they weighed 500 tons when full. In all, 120,000 gallons of water a minute would be used when all the waterworks were in play.

It is possible that Charles Wild was in the tertiary stages of syphilis.[*] His attendance was erratic and Paxton, increasingly concerned about the stability of the towers, decided to consult Brunel in September 1853, a request that put Brunel in a very awkward position with regard to Wild since he soon confirmed all Paxton's anxieties. Brunel felt that the legs of the towers were too slender to support their weight, and that the foundations were unsatisfactory to carry such load-bearing structures on the sloping clay soil. He also considered that the tanks should certainly be of wrought and not cast iron. Aware that he had been called in over Wild's head, Brunel advised Wild privately to consult with his own engineering friends, including Robert Stephenson, for a second opinion. Wild was to find no comfort there – for the most part, Stephenson agreed with Brunel.

The Crystal Palace Company, distressed at delays to the towers and to the potential profits of the company, had already decided to ask Wild to resign on grounds of his health. Brunel discovered this and went to some pains to point out as gently as possible to Wild that the decision was imminent and that he, Brunel, had played no part in it. Wild left the company and, at the end of the year, the half-built towers were demolished. Brunel started from scratch with new designs and well-prepared foundations sunk deep into the clay, stabilised with concrete and brick, capable of supporting the substantial load of tanks over twice as heavy as had initially been planned. Thirty-eight feet deep and roofed with ridge and furrow glazing, they would weigh 1,200 tons when full.

Ever a perfectionist, Brunel and his assistant F. W. Shields chivvied and bullied Fox, Henderson to ensure that the work was carried out absolutely to specification; on several occasions they insisted that it was stopped and rebuilt to a higher standard. All this meant more

[*]   Wild's death certificate shows that he died of meningitis of the brain – a contemporary euphemism for syphilis. He had been ill for six years at least.

delays, and it would take over two years to complete the construction of the towers and, therefore, the opening of the waterworks, throughout which Paxton was bombarded with long letters from Brunel on every conceivable detail. Finally, the twelve-sided towers, supported by hollow cast-iron columns at each angle and braced with wrought iron, became one of the abiding features of the palace, surviving even the catastrophic fire nearly 100 years later.

Tied to a public company, Paxton was rarely in Derbyshire, practically enslaved by his responsibilities and by the sheer scale of his imagination on the one hand and his attention to minute detail on the other. His experience at Chatsworth had taught him that the public loved elaborate schemes, and every aspect of the new palace and grounds was designed to impress and satisfy that desire for extravagance. While the directors of the company kept a watchful eye on economies they, too, wanted to create a palace and a park truly worthy of the nation, and they failed to rein in either Paxton, Digby Wyatt or Jones from their magnificent plans. A further half a million pounds of capital was raised through new shares with an additional loan from the Union Bank. Years later, Paxton would say that he warned the directors that they were creating a space many times larger than could possibly be filled regularly. But the plans and the calculations of income were based on the numbers that had flocked to Hyde Park over those six extraordinary months, the sort of numbers that could never be replicated on a regular and long-term basis.

ᔑ

By the end of 1853, the prospect of war loomed, with Britain and France joining forces against Russia in defence of Turkey. The Duke and Paxton briefly discussed the ludicrous plan of the Duke going to Russia on a peace mission to his old friend, Tsar Nicholas. At least 1854 was to start with promise – Blanche gave birth to a son in Hastings and Baron James de Rothschild asked Paxton to go to Paris with the view of designing a new mansion for him at Ferrières to rival his nephew's at Mentmore. But all the other signs were for a personally and politically disastrous year.

In the middle of January, in heavy snow, the express train on which Paxton was travelling hit a coal train. He escaped lightly but a solid box under one of the seats had been thrown into his leg, laming him badly. The rheumatism in his back returned with a vengeance and he fell out, uncharacteristically, with Digby Wyatt and Jones. By February, the British Bulldog had been let slip and was creating havoc in the Crimea, dashing the confident hopes of a peaceful world united by free trade and competitive manufacturing spirit. At Chatsworth, in mountains of snow, Sarah felt Paxton had deserted them. When he was at home, Sarah was happy, but as soon as he left, her misery would return.

He might have felt a degree of pleasure at the prospect of the planned opening of the palace that summer, and at the commission he won from James de Rothschild that March. He wrote to Sarah that this was 'a pecuniary engagement of the most perfect sort . . . in all it will amount in five years to £10,000 . . . not requiring me in Paris more than five or six times each year and that only for a day or two'. But any such pleasure was to be utterly blighted by George, who had become entirely unmanageable. Woolwich had not worked out, he had borrowed money from a lender, pawned his own rifle and Emily's watch and his 'pomposity [was] something awful'. Sarah wrote imprecisely of his 'vile habits', his 'sin and wickedness'. She would not, and could not, have him home to Barbrook.

George demanded attention that Paxton simply was not able to give. Equally, his own upbringing had been so radically different from the one enjoyed by his son that it is perhaps unsurprising that he floundered in the face of his greatest personal challenge. Born only two years after William died, perhaps George had always been spoiled by both his parents. Perhaps they just expected him to be like their dutiful daughters. If so, they could not have been more self-deluded.

In the end, Paxton agreed that George could come to live for a while at Rockhills on the understanding that he stayed away from London in the evenings. But things were made complicated when, in April, the Duke arrived unannounced to stay for ten days – beginning to treat Rockhills as one of his own several homes and taking over Paxton's own room. Not long after this, George was summoned by the police for recklessly driving his coach. Paxton quietly went to the superintendent, paid his fine and arranged for the story to be hushed up. He was firefighting on all sides.

Two days later, and with the grand royal opening of the palace only eight weeks away, George went one step too far. Paxton wrote to Sarah that their son had come home 'staggering with drink. I burst out crying to see him, he moreover went out at the Dining Room windows and exposed his private parts to make water in the most disgusting way.' An argument ensued and George was sent from

Rockhills 'disgraced and abominated as he has been everywhere else'. Paxton cried for an hour, sitting in George's bedroom and looking at his empty bed, filled with sorrow, regret, disillusion and self-reproach. To have proof now that George added drunkenness to his other scandals – gambling, womanising and running up huge debts – was insupportable to Paxton, haunted by the sight of his 17-year-old son's departing figure. He collapsed with grief and cried to Sarah, 'I am sure I have been as kind to him as it is possible for me to be . . . He has neither a sense of honour nor honesty and all he asks for is . . . to get into the lowest of the low company.'

George returned to Derbyshire for a few days, quiet and subdued, before being sent to live with a family in France, his return forbidden. Sarah was sharply ordered to desist from sending him the secret subsidies that in the past had only fuelled his temptations and mollified her own feelings of guilt and pain. Paxton fled Rockhills for Paris and a short rest at the Hôtel Meurice in the rue de Rivoli to escape the 'everlasting turmoil' of the Crystal Palace and the comfortlessness of being bound to please a merciless public. But he could not disappear for long.

CHAPTER TWENTY

In order to get the Palace ready for its royal opening, set for 10 June 1854, Paxton assumed an absolute dictatorship, overseeing everything and everybody within and around the building. He survived only in the greatest state of worry, working endlessly to ensure that the miniature world being created would astonish its audience.

The dimensions of the park echoed those of the building, worked on multiples of 8 and 24 feet. Superintended by Edward Milner, who had managed the laying out of Prince's Park in Liverpool, it flowed from the top of the hill over a grand formal terrace running the length of the Palace front, whose raised surface was designed to dry quickly after sudden showers. From here there were stupendous views over the park below and to the distant Kent hills. Granite pedestals on either side of the wide steps sweeping up to the Palace were surmounted by great crouching sphinxes and copies of fine sculpture graced the length of the lower balustrade. Below it, the wider Italian terrace was planted with an enormous quantity of massed bedding. Unlike the parks elsewhere in Britain, including his own, the open spaces of the Crystal Palace park were packed with lavish and dramatic floral displays. This was the ultimate extreme of the theory of the Gardenesque and the precursor of carpet bedding, in which low-level foliage plants were arranged to imitate the patterns of oriental carpets. The large beds were laden with a profusion of verbena, salvias and ageratums edged with scarlet geraniums, and the blaze of flowers satisfied utterly the new contemporary taste for the gaudy. Paxton remained steadfastly against the massing of flowers in public parklands, but the commercial nature of this park alone justified for him the gardenisation of the land.

Below the terraces, the park became less formal, with winding walks, groups of shrubs, enclosed areas and wide lawns. There was a boating lake with model replicas of the geological wonders of the earth, the dinosaurs, whose emerging antediluvian fossils were rocking the very basis of established religion. It was, in effect, the world's first dinosaur theme park – filled with 'hextinct hanimals' as Paxton called them, modelled to a life-sized scale by the sculptor Benjamin Waterhouse Hawkins under the direction of the palaeontologist Professor Richard Owen. Even before they were 'hexhibited' they were a sensation. A publicity stunt was engineered for New Year's Eve in which members of the press were sent invitations on drawings of the wings of pterodactyls to a dinner *inside* the model of the iguanodon. The feast was so graphically reported in the *Illustrated London News* that Owen and Hawkins were flooded with requests to visit their ambitious reconstructions.

Inside the palace, Jones and Digby Wyatt displayed the treasures of the ancient world in a series of Egyptian, Greek, Alhambra and Roman courts, with smaller courts displaying German, British, Italian and French Gothic art. There were also areas devoted to geology, ethnology, zoology and botany, each created by leading scientific figures. Osler's grand crystal fountain had been bought from the Great

Exhibition and graced the south transept. Exotic creepers wound around the slender iron columns and along the handrails of the galleries and orange trees perfumed the air. Paxton had sought donations of plants and trees from Kew and from provincial botanical gardens, from private estates and from nurseries, recreating in part the glories of the Great Stove at Chatsworth. Two tall Norfolk pines, given by the Duke of Devonshire, cast their green shade over statues in the central transept. Lemon and pomegranate trees and exotic flowers had been bought en masse from the famous nursery of Loddiges in Hackney, which was now closing. Paxton transported their most famous palm tree, over 50 feet high, upright to Sydenham in a special cart pulled by 32 horses, in the kind of operation that only he could perform with such apparent ease. Here, unlike at the Great Exhibition, he was able to form a harmonic interchange between the horticultural and the cultural, a flourishing winter garden to entice the masses.

Enormous crowds were expected for the opening, despite the fact that few even knew where Sydenham was. Road and rail routes and connections were widely published, and special trains were organised from London Bridge. The lawns were clipped, dais erected and chairs and flags set out in their hundreds. The royal procession – which included cabinet ministers, ambassadors, the Archbishop of Canterbury, the King of Portugal, the principal company employees and, bafflingly, George Paxton – was planned in detail. As an indication of just how unique this commercial venture was considered to be in terms of its national importance, it was to have all the significance and ceremonial of a state occasion.

Of all the fashionable and powerful world, only the Duke of Devonshire could not be there. A week before the planned opening, he suffered a devastating stroke at Chatsworth. He retained the movement of his left side and his speech, and immediately arranged to be taken to London. For Paxton, it was a terrible calamity. He was almost prostrate, begging Sarah to come to him immediately. When she arrived at Devonshire House in Piccadilly, she found her husband in a state of near collapse. Crippled by stomach pains and anxiety, he was pouring medicine into himself in an attempt to keep himself going at least until the opening. And the Duke would not let him out of his sight.

The building was swathed in royal red cloth. When the workmen and needlewomen withdrew from the central transept on the morning of 10 June and the doors to the palace were opened, over 30,000 season-ticket holders and invitees burst like a pent-up tide into the seemingly fragile building, sweeping aside barriers and police in their search for the very best viewpoint for the ceremony. While crowds streamed from all over London to picnic in the grounds and surrounding woods, 1,600 vocal and instrumental performers held themselves ready. At two o'clock diplomats and ministers arrived, including Lord John Russell, Disraeli and Palmerston, while the crowds, anxious for sherry and lemonade, passed notes with money over one another's heads in the hope of some refreshment being passed back.

At three o'clock the Queen arrived. The crowds erupted into thunderous applause and the living amphitheatre of singers and three military bands broke into the National Anthem. Then the rather tiresome ceremony began. Paxton, sword again at his side, presented her with the *General Handbook to the Palace*, and the crowd cheered at the marked graciousness with which the Queen received him. Each and every head of department in turn mounted the dais to present Victoria with handbooks for their sections, before retiring, backwards and with some trepidation, down the very steep steps – reaching the ground with more good fortune than skill and much to the amusement of the crowds. The dais was quite littered with books of all descriptions.

Over £1,350,000 had already been spent on the building and park. Although the water towers were built, they remained unfinished and it would be two years before the grand waterworks, the English Versailles, would thrill visitors. The park, though planted, would benefit from several more summers before its ingeniously contrived vistas would be completely evident and the galleries in the building itself remained virtually empty above the first floor. Nevertheless, every paper, including many on the continent, carried page after page of description of the delights available in the building and the glittering triumph of its opening. The publisher Routledge issued a *Guide to the Crystal Palace* which became a best-seller. The Duke signalled his pride and delight in the Paxtons by presenting Sarah with a bracelet inscribed with the words 'beloved and worthy' and by sending Paxton a vast collection of silver plate. The architectural purist, John Ruskin, was certainly in the minority when he published his own pamphlet on the opening of the Crystal Palace, sneering that it was nothing but a magnified conservatory. Even he, though, recognised that 'for the first time in the history of the world, a national museum is formed in which a whole nation is interested'.

Ruskin, however much he detested the building as a corrupting architectural influence, emphatically believed that 'it is impossible to overestimate the influence of such an institution on the minds of the working classes'. It signified a revolution in leisure, a respite from the gloom of domesticity and industrialisation in a world where provided entertainment, outside the pub or the church, was negligible. As early as the close of the Great Exhibition, newspapers like the *Morning Herald* had espoused the cause of the Sabbatarians and lobbied against a 'continental Sabbath' which included, of all things, enjoyment. As the palace had neared completion, working men's groups argued for Sunday opening, since, before the advent of a five-day working week and the invention of the weekend, Sunday was their only opportunity to visit it. Pamphlets against Sunday opening were swiftly marshalled, predominantly by the middle classes, the bishops and the clergy. Sunday observance groups were so unyielding that the palace was never opened to the paying public on Sundays, despite Paxton's belief that it would provide a great moral and intellectual advantage to the working classes. Nevertheless the crowds flocked and, that summer, numbers on the shilling days reached almost 13,000.

If the grand opening provided any catharsis for Paxton, it was not to last. Less than a month later, Sarah was again writing from Barbrook that his 'old letters' had returned – the ones that said he could not come home. George was back misbehaving and uncontrollable in Derbyshire and talking of joining the militia at Sevastopol. Sarah, flustered by George and lonely for her husband, again trembled at the size of the monthly estate bills to be paid and begged him to remember to send the cheques she needed. Then his brother, William, also suffered a stroke and died as Paxton rushed to his bedside in Bedfordshire. Even though William was 20 years older than Paxton, this focused Sarah's attention on her husband's well-being. She believed he was destroying his health for the public and sacrificing his contentment for nothing. On his 51st birthday, even Victoria (known as Toey to her parents), still unmarried and now passionate about the new technique of photography, wrote, too, that she wished his 'health may be restored to what it was before the excitement of the Crystal Palace'.

The Duke had again moved temporarily, uninvited if not unwelcomed, into Rockhills and was not to be satisfied unless Paxton spent at least three-quarters of his time in his company. He was frail and needy and, apart from his doctor, the Duke wanted only Paxton. He needed, too, his own personal comfort, and now asked for alterations to be made to Paxton's own house. Paxton was frustrated, he simply did not believe that the Duke would be staying long enough to benefit from them. The Duke, in effect, held him in an eternal state of expectation that he would be 'wanted' somewhere or other, or that he might have to drop everything and travel to Ireland again. Paxton felt himself torn in every direction. Cholera had returned to Sydenham. His only sanctuary was assailed and quite topsy-turvy. Blanche needed him, her husband Edward Ridgway had been offered a living not far from Lismore in Ireland, but the rectory at Mothel was wretched and needed plans and at least £500 of her father's money to make it habitable. It is understandable that with so much domestic frustration clouding around him, a quick decision was made to send little Laura, aged only fifteen, to a school in Switzerland as punishment for writing to a local 'jackanapes'. It was harsh, but the plan was to be swiftly effected – ironically so when compared to the endless prevarication over George's future.

After a whistle-stop trip to Lismore to check on the progress of the works at the castle, Paxton left for Paris. James de Rothschild was in a perfect outcry for yet another set of plans for the house at Ferrières and Paxton, who had been working on them with Stokes since the spring, hoped that these would be the last. Like his nephew Mayer in Buckinghamshire, James had bought the domaine of Ferrières in the late 1820s and had added parcels of land to the estate as they became available. The original house, which had been destroyed, had nestled in over 3,000 hectares of wood, pasture and farmland in an elite area famous for the Rothschilds' favourite country pursuit, hunting. The new house, which James demanded be grander than Mentmore, would, like its English precursor, provide a gilded casket for some of the finest works of European art and antiquity while emphasising the social standing and wealth of the immigrant family.

No English architect had, at that time, constructed a large private mansion in France and there was no reason why James should not have chosen one of the many notable French architects for his grand schemes. Certainly, James wanted a symbol of his wealth and power and a home for his art comparable to his nephew's but, more than that, he wished his house to exemplify the new industrial era, and there was only one man in Europe who could provide it. Paxton.

But the Baron's indecision infuriated Paxton, and their relationship was to continue to be tense. The massive house would take years to

John Lindley, 'the father of
orchidology'.

William Jackson Hooker, the first
official director of Kew.

The Royal Commissioners. Standing, left to right: Charles Wentworth Dilke, John Scott Russell, Henry Cole, Charles Fox, Joseph Paxton, Lord John Russell, Sir Robert Peel, Robert Stephenson. Seated, left to right: Richard Cobden, Charles Barry, Lord Granville, William Cubitt, Prince Albert, Lord Derby. (The painting should more properly have been titled 'Some of the Royal Commissioners' and, of course neither Paxton or Fox were members.)

The opening ceremony of the Great Exhibition, May 1, 1851. Paxton is in the front row, 2nd from the left, with Charles Fox to his left, then Owen Jones, then Henry Cole. Samuel Morton Peto stands in front of Cole, Earl Granville, also in uniform, to his left. Behind them the Duke of Wellington stands to the right of the Archbishop of Canterbury.

Lithograph of the Crystal Palace in Hyde Park, looking south to the River Thames.

Top: The elm tree in the central transept of the original Crystal Palace.
Centre: A lithograph of the Crystal Palace and Park at Sydenham at the time of its opening in 1854. The waterworks were not then in fact complete and an alternative design to Brunel's eventual water towers is shown.
Bottom: The Crystal Palace aflame, November 1936.

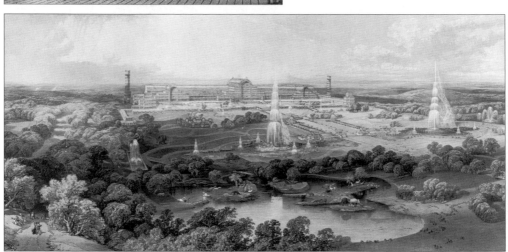

Mentmore.

Baron Meyer de Rothschild.

Ferrières.

Lismore Castle, Ireland, showing Paxton's projected north west tower, 1858.

Sectional perspective of Paxton's design for the Great Victorian Way.

Rockhills, Sydenham, c1860. Paxton is said to be the figure leaning against the urn. The Crystal Palace is visible in the top left hand corner.

construct and many of the Rothschild family believed that it would
never be finished. Finally, after the Baron had ordered alterations to
many sets of plans, he agreed on a design echoing the general shape
of Mentmore, with its four corner towers, but the central hall, also
glazed and with a first floor gallery, was far larger. The Rothschild
family wrote to each other that the architects in Paris were incensed:
'Les plans de Paxton ont enlevé tous les suffrages. Les architectes de
Paris vont nous excommunier.'* Despite professional grievances in the
background, work was started, with a team of part French and part
English labourers, whose constant in-fighting would add even further
to the delay in getting the mansion up.

Before he left France, Paxton paid a visit to the Emperor Napoleon,
who was deeply involved with his own plans for a Paris Exposition
the following year. Paxton took with him plans of the Crystal Palace
at Sydenham and may have entertained the notion of designing a
Parisian showcase building. But while the Emperor and his wife held
the new Crystal Palace in high esteem, and had visited it several times,
Paxton would not formally submit plans for a French exhibition
building until the final years of his life.

He now returned to England tired but invigorated by his several
weeks' absence from the palace, liberated by the pursuit of private
commissions rather than corporate responsibilities. And then he took
a step that would enshrine him as a servant of the people for the rest
of his days. Two years before, at the height of the debate over the
retention of the Hyde Park building, he had been invited to stand as
a Liberal candidate for Nottingham, which he had declined on the
grounds that he would be unable to give the role his complete attention. But now, on the death of Charles Geach, a deputation of businessmen from Coventry – known to him through his work on the
London Road cemetery – asked him to stand as their city's Liberal
representative. Encouraged by the increasingly frail Duke, whose
approbation he sought before answering the delegation, Paxton now
felt ready for the challenge.

Sarah was anxious that he would now be torn in four between the
Crystal Palace, Chatsworth, the Duke and Parliament. She was also unwell,
skirting around the edges of jaundice, and had not the energy to opine
as sharply as she was used to doing. With a sigh, she accepted the likelihood of his being enjoined to more time-consuming committees. But she

---

* Which, of course, would have been impossible since the Rothschilds were Jewish.

did embrace a hope that they could buy a house perhaps ten miles outside London, where they could be together more often, at least for the three month summer season. She hated Sydenham, believing that its atmosphere was unhealthy and that it was a den of vice that had played its part in encouraging George's waywardness. She clipped advertisements from papers and sent them to Paxton with her letters, pleading with him to give his opinion before the sales took place. Failing to take her hope seriously, and bound up with his own preoccupations, he rarely answered her until it was too late.

John Ellis of the Midland Railway supported Paxton's candidature but warned him that becoming a Member of Parliament would 'so add to your great labours as to interfere with . . . enjoyments of life, and shorten your days'. He knew, of course, that Paxton would continue to laugh in the face of any such advice. Paxton would stand, unopposed, since the Conservatives could find no suitable candidate, alongside Robert 'the bear' Ellice and, as the year waned, he threw himself into the cause with vigour. From Rockhills he wrote his first address, stating his belief in Liberal measures including the ballot and extended representation, the improved condition of the labouring classes and the strengthening of local government through constitutional municipal bodies. He modelled himself as a reformer, a free-trader, and an advocate of the removal of trade restrictions and any limitation of civil or religious liberty.

The last fortnight of November was consumed by nominations, speeches and canvassing, often speaking to rowdy crowds from the balcony of hotels. At public meetings he criticised the method by which Britain was conducting her war in the Crimea, stating his belief that only a watertight, permanent peace would be acceptable. He pronounced his support for the extension of the franchise to all householders rather than confining it to those earning over £5. With an eleventh hour threat of the Conservatives finding a candidate to oppose him, Paxton then set about visiting each and every member of his constituency personally. His hands were bruised from knocking at doors, his arm stiff from shaking hands nine solid hours a day. His effort, though, was rewarded, and at the start of December he was elected as joint MP for the city. He immediately went to the Duke in London to celebrate. In Edensor and Beeley the bells rang until midnight and coloured fires blazed, but the villagers celebrated his success without him. Sarah wrote wistfully that she 'knew you would go . . . so I am not disappointed, but I hope you will come home soon'.

On 18 December he took his seat in the House for the first time, returning alone to Rockhills at 2.30 in the morning to devour a box of black pudding sent by Sarah from Barbrook.

Personal tragedy continued to catch at the coat-tails of his busiest moments, delaying his return to Derbyshire still further. In Bedfordshire, his 16-year-old nephew, Jonas, was dying of heart disease and he felt obliged to go to him. Never fond of her husband's far poorer relatives, Sarah was again frustrated.

Paxton finally made it to Chatsworth for Christmas, arriving home for the first time as an elected representative of the people and a truly public figure. It was, perhaps, inevitable that he would eventually succumb to the pressure to lead a political life, like his railway friends Robert Stephenson, John Ellis, Samuel Morton Peto and Thomas Brassey before him. In many ways, it was the natural progression of his public spiritedness, and a hallmark of his success. With the innate sense of occasion and theatricality that drove all his enterprises, he asked Sarah to organise something of a stir for his return. This was the new ground that he loved. But it would mean that, over the next decade, he would pursue a thankless and unremitting schedule of committees, delegations and grand public projects. These, rather than gardens and family, would make the loudest demands for his attention and Rockhills would now welcome him in the early hours of the morning far more often than his wife at Barbrook.

PART 3

FIRE

CHAPTER TWENTY-ONE

Laura's body was brought home from Switzerland in the early days of the New Year, 1855, and buried at Edensor churchyard on 16 January. At only sixteen years old, she had been killed in an accident, possibly a fall. The speed at which the decision was taken to send her away was now particularly painful to her parents, as they followed her coffin in the snow the mile from their home to the village. Her death threw Sarah into a year of mourning. With Emily and Blanche married and Rosa and Annie away at school in Matlock, she rattled around the big house, desperately lonely.

Increasingly anxious about the escalating accounts at Chatsworth, Sarah's life became emptier as Paxton's became fuller. He had new, grand schemes to keep him company, along with his staff at Rockhills, his son-in-law and architectural partner Stokes, and Stokes' wife, his daughter Emily, who visited him regularly. Throughout the year of Laura's mourning he made flying visits to Ferrières for the laying of the foundation stone, to Lismore to superintend the work on the new tower, and to his Coventry constituency. He travelled to Paris for the opening of the French Exposition (on which trip the Emperor gave him a precious snuff-box) and went on to the Duke's house in Brighton and from there to Mentmore, which by November was looking even more magnificent. He provided plans for a new Russian cottage at Chatsworth, but he rarely made it back to Derbyshire for more than a few days. So absent was he that Sarah feared he would lose his Derbyshire magistracy.

She continued to search the papers for a summer house in or near to London, but by the autumn of that year, and after protracted negotiations, the Crystal Palace Company directors had agreed that Paxton should have use of Rockhills free for his lifetime, crushing all those dreams. Shouldering the load of his responsibilities in Derbyshire, she longed to be able to break 'fame's trumpet', begging him to return to 'this once beloved place' as soon as the waterworks at the Crystal Palace were completed. As she sent him prepared food in boxes (not that he did not have his own cook and servants), she pleaded with him to abandon 'the worthless public who have never paid you for what you have done'. The more work he took on, often declining payment, the more incensed she became.

George Paxton remained 'wild' to go to the Crimea. It was the first war to which permanent correspondents were sent by the newspapers, and detail of the humiliations inflicted on the allied armies flooded their pages, most particularly in October of the previous year when at the Charge of the Light Brigade so many British mounted forces had been massacred. Paxton was against his son going to the East, but in the meantime, George was safely installed with the 4th Light Dragoon Guards in training, out of immediate trouble of either the metropolitan or the military sort.

When Paxton made his maiden speech in the Commons, late one March evening, he chose to speak on a subject about which he was knowledgeable, in this case the question of the chaotic supply of 20,000 barrack huts to a new army camp at Aldershot. It was neither a brilliant nor a memorable speech, yet it was concise, clear and forceful. On subsequent days, he continued to raise the issue, speaking vehemently on behalf of the builders and the soldiers, who, he believed, would suffer in the poorly built, badly ventilated and dimly lit huts. It was a creditable beginning.

In London, though, it was transport that was becoming the most desperate concern. Between 1811 and 1851, the population of the capital had doubled to just under two and a half million, making it the largest city in the world. It was estimated that, every day, over 200,000 people entered the city on foot, a further 15,000 by steamboat, 7,500 by omnibus and many thousands by railway. Thoroughfares were overcrowded, main arteries and bridges were regularly blocked. There was a pressing need for comprehensive and full-scale improvement and, before the House broke for Easter, a commission was appointed, chaired by his old friend, William Jackson, MP for Birkenhead.

Paxton thought he had the answer and he was working on an entirely visionary scheme to improve the whole of the city's communications, an idea of revolutionary daring that he believed would thrill the country as the original Crystal Palace had done. At the end of March, he described it to the Duke, who was 'quite wild' about it.

In the meantime the war in the Crimea and more particularly the problems faced by an army without roads, huts or stores were far more pressing. The appalling conditions and avoidable suffering of the soldiers during the worst of the hard winter, with insufficient clothes, food or shelter, had been the cause of outrage and criticism of the government when reported back in England. The engineering contractor, Samuel Morton Peto, MP, and his partner, Edward Betts, along with the railway contractor, Thomas Brassey – all friends of Paxton – had suggested to the government that they would build a railway from the front line back to the port at Balaklava. In addition, they would supply the rolling stock and equipment for only the capital cost. Within six weeks of arriving, 20 miles of double track railway had been laid, and before the end of the siege, nearly 40 miles of rail connected the port with all fronts.

By the spring of 1855, the remaining pressure was the lack of roads, particularly the 6 miles between Balaklava and Sevastopol. Paxton had spoken in Coventry the previous October of the importance of sending navvies to assist the army in the works that had become so vital. *The Times* – and particularly his great friend there, John MacDonald, the man who coined 'the lady with the lamp' as a description of Florence Nightingale – had taken up Paxton's call and pressured the government to act. After weeks of meetings with the War Office and general lobbying for the chance to put his own ideas into action, the Minister for War, Lord Panmure, wrote to Paxton to ask for his help in forming a 'Corps of Navigators', or navvies. He believed that Paxton's own experience with the navvies at the Crystal Palace made him uniquely qualified to form this experimental Army Works Corps, the first Civil Engineers, efficiently and at speed. Paxton agreed on condition that he, too, would not be paid, but that he would have the authority to organise the work without government interference.

A new office was quickly found for Paxton at 18 New Street, Spring Gardens, near Whitehall, practically next door to the London offices of Fox, Henderson. One thousand men were to be gathered together – 800 of them navvies and the rest 'artificers' or skilled carpenters, blacksmiths and riveters. All were to be unmarried, contracted for two years, followed by a third year if the war had not abated. All would be given free passage home and a further six months' pay if disbanded early. Paxton worked intently on the details of the plan. Right from the start, he insisted that all should be paid at the rate they would receive if working in Britain and all would be promised disability pensions if wounded. No detail was left unexamined. The corps would remain a civil force under a chief engineer, William Doyne, who arrived with glowing references from Robert Stephenson. The Army Works Corps was an entirely new feature of military operations and Paxton staked his reputation and credibility on its success.

By the end of June, 800 of what Sarah called 'those dirty ill-conditioned navvies', most recruited from their work at the Palace, were camped in the lower grounds of the Crystal Palace park or gathered around the village of Penge like a time bomb waiting to explode. They drank, fought and, on one occasion, almost murdered two local policemen. Paxton, unlike Panmure, knew that these were men who would get the job done but, unaccustomed to military discipline and with too much time on their hands, it was imperative to embark them on ship as soon as possible. He wrote to Panmure that, once they landed, they must be separated from the combatant part of the army in order to avoid any similar collisions.

The new recruits were herded on to three ships including the 'floating steam factory', the *Chasseur*, and departed for the Black Sea in the middle of July, less than three months after the first call from Panmure. Better outfitted than the majority of the army, their 'uniform' consisted of good quality grey frock coats, grey waistcoats and forage caps. With them sailed Doyne, and a letter from Paxton setting out his own management plan for the men, which suggested that Doyne should 'take them as you find them and use their strengths'. As soon as they arrived, in August, they immediately set about helping with the railways, making sawmills and platforms for gun carriages, repairing carts and wagons, constructing depots and stores, improving the wharves and, most crucial of all, forming roads. Doyne wrote to Paxton immediately that they could use 5,000 more men. Paxton proposed to Panmure that he organise 1,000 each of navvies and artificers. After some delay on the part of the War Office, around 200 were sent immediately, with 1,500 to follow.

The army did not know what to make of this new civil force, and the navvies were unused to military discipline, so that rules had to be developed as they went along to avoid disorganisation and to manage the tension and unease between the two groups. Despite some criticism of the navvies' conduct, it is indisputable that the Army Works Corps radically altered the conditions of the forces in Russia, straining every nerve to avoid the horrors of the previous winter. When tools broke, Paxton had new ones dispatched from England rather than waste time with repairs.

In London, Paxton had been appointed to a parliamentary committee of inquiry into barrack accommodation for the army in Britain. Its report proposed several revolutionary changes to the men's comfort, and he campaigned tirelessly for these to be adopted. Meanwhile, in the Crimea, a quarter of the men were sick from weeks living in small, damp tents. Paxton set about designing practical, light, folding beds to prevent the men sleeping on the ground as well as a much larger tent than normal, whose central tubular pole acted as the flue for the stoves. Additionally, he applied himself to the design of high quality wood huts made up of double walls interlined with felt – heavy, waterproof structures that could be shipped, prefabricated, to Balaklava and which reduced the suffering, and sickness, of the corps.

In Parliament, Paxton did not always toe the party line, but followed his own judgement. There was a moment that summer, when he appeared to be campaigning against the Liberal government of Lord Palmerston, speaking at a meeting in Drury Lane, in concert with a group of other back-bench MPs, for administrative reform, a meeting widely reported in the press. Lord Granville took the time to write counselling him against such behaviour, believing that he would 'erect great obstacles to much future success', and stating that the right place for such petitions was Parliament itself. Sarah also recognised that he was unlikely to receive government support for his own plans if he spoke publicly against them. His typically passionate, public involvement with an issue before pausing to consider its ramifications appears to have been only momentary, as with his earlier demands for free entry to the Great Exhibition, and his Drury Lane 'theatricals' were not repeated, nor do they appear to have had any backlash. It was a clear indication, however, of his sometimes radical and tactically unmeasured ideology.

On 7 June, Paxton was finally given the opportunity to present in detail his design for a new London communication network to the select committee. He had been working on his plans for about four months and had drawn up elaborate designs that had been displayed at Devonshire House for weeks. He had also consulted widely on logistics, quantities and costs. Relying in part on earlier suggestions by Christopher Wren (after the Great Fire of London), John Nash and Sir Frederick Trench (who had suggested an embankment of the Thames as early as 1824), Paxton proposed a boulevard, or girdle around London, just over ten miles long. It would be a sophisticated system: a street, a railway and an arcade with both stopping and express trains running through the upper levels. It would cross bridges and parks on a route calculated not to destroy any important buildings, passing through elite as well as poor districts, with a mile long spur to link Piccadilly to the South Western station. With access on to all existing streets, in some sections its arcades would also include shops, cafés and hotels, and his plans included designs for the surrounding housing.

The girdle would start near the Royal Exchange, pass around the back of Moorgate and cross Cheapside, down Cannon Street to a new river crossing near Southwark Bridge. From here it would pass through Lambeth, crossing the South Western Railway and turning back over the river near Parliament. The line then followed Victoria Street, through Brompton, across Kensington Gardens to the Great Western Railway, up through Marylebone towards Oxford Street, diverging slightly to meet the London and North Western station and continuing up around Islington to its starting point. It would pass through the dense populations of Lambeth and Southwark, satisfying the urgent need for effective communication, particularly in the south west of London.

Paxton proposed that the arcade would be the same breadth as the transept in the old Crystal Palace, around 72 feet. The track would be 26 feet above it, and would provide a link between all the railway termini in the city. He suggested that only passenger carriages and omnibuses should be permitted to use it during the day, but that after nine at night it could be used for the conveyance of merchandise and coals. He detailed proposals for ventilation, pointed out its minimal maintenance costs and even presented costings for the construction of the new bridges and the most essential part of the line, from Mansion House to Victoria Street.

The Great Victorian Way would be made entirely of glass and iron with the addition of pottery tiling, creating a luminous, glittering band around the city. It was an uncanny vision of the future – radical, modern town planning. Again, he had marshalled the forces of others in advance. Granville had seen the plans and arranged for them to be presented to Prince Albert, who thought them ingenious, and showed

them to the Queen. Paxton estimated the cost of construction at
£34,000,000, to be paid for either through a national levy, a metropolitan tax or by private speculation.

Eccentrically, Paxton also believed that the covered glass way would
negate the need for the elderly and infirm to travel abroad in the
winter, that the temperature could be maintained in some parts to
approximate continental climates. But his belief in the relevance and
commercial viability of the plan was absolute. He spoke to the
committee with resolve and determination, sweeping aside any uncer-
tainties to present a complete, practical vision that, he assured them,
would make London the grandest city in the world.

Paxton may have been considered by some as an impractical
visionary, despite having already demonstrated the expediency of his
revolutionary designs with the two largest glass and iron buildings
in the world. Now London was heading towards a monstrous crisis
in its sanitation precisely because there was neither the will nor the
official body to grapple with improvements on such a scale. Along
with some smaller proposals, Paxton's plan was recommended by the
committee, despite its formidable cost, but despite continuing to lobby
the Prince Consort and Lord Granville in the spring of 1856, his plan
was doomed to languish. The new body set up by the select committee
in order to wrench some order out of the chaos of conflicting interests, the Metropolitan Board of Works, would wait for years for the
budget and the power to fulfil its mandate.

⌒

It had been a year since the Crystal Palace was opened for a second
time by the Queen with such fanfare. Paxton was still fighting to
complete the waterworks in time for their opening in May the following
year. Sitting on parliamentary business from the evening until well
into the night, he was regularly called on to escort the Queen and
European monarchs – including Napoleon, the King of Sardinia and
the King of the Belgians – around the Crystal Palace whenever the
whim took them. All this had to be balanced against the growing
demands of Brunel and the water towers. In addition, during July, the
Duke had turned up again at Rockhills, unannounced, unclear about
how long he would stay and giving Paxton the distinct and frustrating
impression that 'he wants to live here half his time'.

Music, under the direction of Mr Schaller, and contrary to Paxton's personal wishes, was becoming a feature of the Palace. Willert Beale, partner in the firm of Cramer and Co. and seeking a venue for his New Philharmonic Society, petitioned Paxton to be allowed to use the central transept for concerts on a large scale. When Paxton declined, believing the exhibition and gardens provided sufficient entertainment, Beale went over his head to the chairman and directors, who saw the obvious commercial potential in the proposition and allowed the first concert on 4 June 1855. Thereafter, August Manns began to conduct Saturday concerts of Schubert, Schumann, Brahms and Handel, to which people flocked from all over England.

The waterworks were, by October, at a standstill for want of money. Although Brunel's north tower was all but complete, severe weather that winter and ongoing construction of a new railway tunnel by the south tower had hampered the completion of that tower. There were leaks and breakages in the tanks and pipes and Brunel exhorted Paxton to begin to prove the system. He was especially anxious about the pressure effects on the pipes as the water was turned on, writing, 'I should enormously impress upon you that such columns of water are like loaded cannons or rockets, and not to be trifled with.' Paxton assured him that he had already taken great pains over this particular problem at Chatsworth in the construction of the Emperor Fountain, but Brunel was not to be appeased. He was particularly concerned at the means of filling the south tower via a 12-inch pipe linked to the north tower which ran right through the centre of the building. If the pipe failed perhaps 2,000 tons of water would discharge into the vaults. Brunel left it up to Paxton to come up with an alternative – a slight modification with which he initially disagreed, but eventually sanctioned. Perfectionist that he was, he bombarded Paxton with long detailed letters, at one point in the middle of Paxton's frantic summer schedule, lashing out at him for asking for the opinion of his assistant Shields.

Brunel was as fraught as Paxton, embroiled in the process of building his mighty steamship the *Great Eastern*. Adept at smoothing the waters, Paxton contrived to put the disagreement behind them and, by the end of the year, Brunel believed that Fox, Henderson would be able to finish in time. Paxton would then be able to renegotiate his position with the company and free himself of what was becoming, on occasions, a millstone round his neck. Meanwhile he was still dashing between brief visits to Lismore and to Paris. From Chatsworth, Sarah wrote, 'it seems an age since I saw you. When will it be different?'

CHAPTER TWENTY-TWO

Towards the end of April the following year, 1856, the Duke was once again flitting between his many houses and finding none of them satisfactory without Paxton. He announced that Rockhills, with Paxton in it, would again afford him delightful respite and a change of scene, arriving with his luggage and servants almost immediately. To his friend, it meant the sacrifice of his own room and his dining table, and a 'state of everlasting bother'. Paxton had become portly as a result of his busy dinner schedule, his evenings at *Punch*, and the hampers Sarah sent or brought from Chatsworth. Even Dickens noted this girth in a letter to the Duke that year, commenting that there must be 'something of Daniel Lambert in his family'.*

Right up to the much-postponed grand-opening of the waterworks by Victoria on 18 June, Waterloo Day, Paxton was, as usual, given no quarter in his workload. The royal family, wont to treat the park as their playground and a crucial element in the entertainment of any of their foreign relatives, continued to be distracting. He was hounded by those wanting last-minute tickets, including John Tenniel – the *Punch* contributor – for whom he arranged early entry to the Palace so that he could prepare drawings of the ceremony. With only two weeks to go, the waters were tested for the first time before an invited

---

* Fat Dan was Leicester's favourite fat man. At 52 stone, he made a living from people visiting him and died at 36 – in 1806 – of a heart attack. Although Paxton had gout, he was never portly enough to warrant such a jibe.

audience of the Royal Horticultural Society. Brunel's towers duly
provided enough pressure to make the highest jets soar to 250 feet
and minor defects in the system were perfected in time for the opening.

This was not merely a garden of jets, it was a grand system of
fountains and waterworks, cascades and basins, a Versailles set in the
undulations of an English park. Between the upper and lower terrace
there were two square and two round fountain pools, with two large
rectangular pools on either side of the central walk. In the lower park,
between the artificial mounds, winding walks, raised flower beds and
ribbons of trees, rose a large circular central fountain flanked by two
others of diminishing size. Below this, on either side of the broad path,
were water temples clearly modelled on the seventeenth-century water
temple at Chatsworth, but here they were constructed of iron. Water
was forced up through their centres to spread out over their domed
roofs, and fall in a curtain before joining the 384-feet-long cascades
which dropped gradually in wide, shallow steps over a fall of 30 feet.
The water flowed from there into two vast basins, in which the highest
of the jets played.

No one seemed to mind that a slight miscalculation in the angle
of perambulation, or a change in the direction of the wind, could drench
the ladies' silks in a moment. This was theatre. The air was filled with
rainbows as the top of the jets plumed out into spray, demanding the
wonder of the tens of thousands of pleasure seekers in the park. It
was a summer day's magic worthy of the end of the Crimean war.

The opening of the waterworks was another triumph for Paxton,
and a moment of relief. He could now shake off the sometimes suffo-
cating blanket of responsibility in a venture whose popularity was to
remain undiminished for a generation. New attractions such as the
Handel Festivals, at which the organ with its 3,500 pipes billowed out
its thunderous music to the accompaniment of massed choirs of 2,000,
had people flocking from all over England.* Some concern was felt
when part of the tunnel linking the west end railway to the low level
station, which ran close to the south tower, appeared to be collapsing
in December 1857, but once the danger had passed Paxton ensured
that the news was kept entirely quiet. While still not making a profit,
the Crystal Palace and grounds knocked attendance at London's two
most popular tourist attractions – Madame Tussaud's and the Tower

*   The first Handel Festival took place in 1857. In 1859, the concert to mark the
centenary of Handel's death included a choir that was 2,000 strong and attracted
an audience of over 18,000 people.

of London – into a cocked hat. Any failure of confidence in the stability of their structures could send them all reeling into a bankruptcy perpetually hovering in the wings.

⌒

Paxton had one less crushing responsibility to juggle and, with the park safely superintended by Edward Milner, he could again turn his attention back to his own business. In particular, he had joined forces with his friend George Wythes in his first overseas venture: Turkish Railways and lines in Smyrna and in Aiden from which he told Sarah that he expected 'some fabulous sums of profit . . . I dare not tell you what I expect, you would only laugh at me'. As a contractor, Wythes had purchased some of the land from the Crystal Palace Company for development and had fulfilled many projects for Brunel. He lived in the district and dined regularly with Paxton.

That summer, as George Myers completed Mentmore and turned his attention again to the building at Ferrières, Paxton took on three separate landscape design projects. First, he planned out Halifax Park, a gift to the city from the carpet manufacturer, Francis Crossley. It included his signature features of a small lake, winding paths and mounds to enclose the views, with an arcaded pavilion designed by Stokes. Milner was deputed to superintend the work. Next, he developed designs for a pioneering Scottish park on 45 acres of land purchased by the Glasgow corporation for the city inhabitants. In the event, Paxton's plans for Kelvingrove Park, as it was called, were substantially altered by the corporation before it was completed. Finally, he accepted a commission from the Scarborough Cliff Bridge Company to develop their spa buildings and provide plans for landscaping their precipitous grounds.

These were all relatively quick commissions and, at the end of the summer, Paxton returned to Lismore with his daughter Victoria, joining a procession of tenants and riding up over the moors with Francis Currey to meet the Duke's carriage. As usual, there were floral arches crowned with coronets to mark the Duke's return and, once installed at the castle, grand balls, private bands, dancing, fireworks and endless toasts. Throughout the following week, Paxton was sent for ten times a day by the Duke, who would allow him no peace.

The foundations of the largest tower, named the Carlisle, which was to rise 140 feet to the battlements, surmounted by 30-foot turrets, were now complete and the Duke had laid the first stone. Paxton was irritated by his rheumatism and the onset of gout and infuriated by Victoria's obstinate and unexplained refusal to go to the Duke's dinners. Then Blanche drove over from Mothel to visit with her youngest son, causing Paxton such a pang that he wrote to Sarah that the child 'was so like what poor William was at his age that it almost gave me pain to see it – you never saw a prettier child'. Twenty-one years after the death of his first son and now a different man, with all too little time for self-reflection, that wound was still tender, kept open, in some respects, by the extravagant dishonesty of his only remaining son.

It was impossible for him to languish in Ireland, much as the Duke pressed him to stay. What he called 'the Russian affair' demanded his return. In April 1856, only one month before the men were discharged, questions were asked by the War Office about discipline within the Army Works Corps – Panmure, in particular, held a rancorous dislike for them as did the army chiefs – and Paxton was strongly censured about their conduct. He replied in his usually vigorous manner. It was hard, he said, to maintain order when they were not fully employed, when the great pressure of the work had passed, especially as they were not under the stricture of military regulations, and he exhorted the War Office to recognise the extraordinary service they had performed. MacDonald at *The Times* supported him.

Although the 3,700 men had ultimately cost the country almost £400,000, their 'immense amount of useful work' was praised generally. But the War Office neither consented to recognise the navvies by casting a medal for their service, nor officially bothered to acknowledge the mountain of labour undertaken by Paxton in order to turn a vision into reality. From the moment the men had landed – all having been paid during the voyage home – they were formally discharged and issued with a written receipt by Paxton's office. By July, however, around 400 of the men were protesting that since they had not received an official discharge they were prevented from obtaining work elsewhere and claiming for wages to be continued until a certificate of discharge was issued. Questions were asked in Parliament. Paxton investigated every one of the claims and found each one to be spurious, but the men, each scenting gratuity, would not back down. Since Paxton was adamant that the claims should not be tolerated, the argument would rage for the next three years until one petitioner was singled out for a test case. Only then did the War Office agree that the government should refund William Currey's expenses as solicitor acting for Paxton.

In a disconcerting parallel to the treatment of Fox, Henderson after the Great Exhibition, Paxton was also dogged for months with demands to submit final accounts to Panmure's office to show his expenditure on the formation of the Army Works Corps against the money advanced. He was repeatedly asked to justify the continuation of the salaries of the office staff at Spring Gardens and, by December, in some frustration, Panmure ordered him to vacate the rooms there. The accounting fiasco, which amounted to the reconciliation of only several hundred pounds, rumbled on interminably, letters coursing between Rockhills and Westminster. In the end Paxton – never noted for the diligence of his accountancy, brought up as he was in the school of the 6th Duke's profligacy – threw up his hands at the whole affair. He retorted that since the War Office now held all the vouchers and receipts, the task was impossible, an argument which finally closed the issue.

George Paxton had missed the front lines of the Crimean war narrowly. Back in England in the spring before the end of the war, he had joined the Dragoon Guards and, after training, was called up. He had been fully outfitted for war and was on the verge of departure when peace came. Paxton, busy in committee, did not attend his son's presentation at Court and he swiftly fell back into his old ways. He lived with an extravagance at which his parents could only wonder – in one year, for example, he got through 21 pairs of boots, as many as Paxton had had in seven years. He, or a writ in his stead, arrived at their doors continually, hounded by his beastly bills – debts for which, because he was still in his minority, they were liable.

Sarah at last saw sense and begged her husband not to pay, but to have their son declared bankrupt and sent as far away as possible. Paxton, though, could neither stop his kindness nor his hope and, once all George's own property had been sold, he regularly came to the rescue. George, to his credit, asked to be sent far away, to America, India or Canada, but, before any plan could be made, he fell in love with a woman about whom almost nothing is known but whom Sarah considered to be a 'beast in human shape' and a 'female snake'. George eloped with her to London, taking with him his parents' peace of mind. On the strength of being married to the son of a knight, the girl embroidered coronets on their handkerchiefs. Sarah, rheumatic now in her arms and suffering regularly from bad teeth which made her face swell painfully, began to wonder whether they might not be better off if he were dead. She had finally given up on him.

Rosa was the only child left at Barbrook to keep Sarah company and even she was away at school in Matlock most of the time, leaving her mother in silence and suspense. At fourteen, Annie had moved to a school in Finchley Road in London and Victoria, nearing her mid-twenties, had finally become engaged to the younger son of Paxton's friend John Allcard, for whom he had built Burton Closes. Toey and George Allcard were married on 22 January 1857, five years to the day after her livelier sister Blanche's own wedding. She became ill almost immediately and for weeks she could not get out of bed, wracked with pains in her liver. For years she continued to languish on a sofa in the drawing room, from where not even her passion for photography could lure her. As her father had done for all his children, Paxton gave her £3,000, a tidy sum from which she could draw a regular income.

Politically, Paxton again demonstrated his independence of spirit when he joined sixteen Liberal MPs led by Cobden in a revolt against Palmerston's bombardment of Canton, forcing a General Election. Sarah hated her husband voting again with the 'dirty Radicals' and she loathed 'the scum of Coventry' with a passion. With the election looming, she dreaded the details of George's misdemeanours being paraded before the electorate. More than once on the hustings Paxton had to defend his stance against the government, declaring to his constituents that he was no pacifist, but he could not agree with the barrage of an undefended city, nor with Britain's involvement with the opium trade. Once again, the General Election passed off without undue incident and the Liberals repeated their defeat of the rascally Tories. Paxton took his place again in the House.

As an MP, Paxton attended regularly, spoke with conviction on issues about which he had experience, and voted conscientiously. Director of many railway companies, and now of the Union Commercial Bank – the company building Brunel's steamship, the *Great Eastern* – he had little time to spare. What he had was often spent with the Duke, acting as deputed host to his many guests.

⌒

In mid-January 1858, Paxton found himself at the Duke's Elizabethan fortress, Hardwick Hall, with the Duke, John Cottingham, Dr Condell and Coote. They visited the Duke of Newcastle together at Clumber for a shooting party. Someone shot a swan. This was the kind of thing the Duke loved and, though he was frail, crippled and nearing seventy he invited several local gentlemen back to Hardwick to share the swan with him. One guest failed to arrive and, much to Paxton's horror, thirteen guests assembled for dinner. He had a strong prejudice against sitting in a group of thirteen and, coupled with the symbolism of the rare dish they were about to eat, the dinner seemed inauspicious. Thinking that this was what was on his mind, Paxton noticed throughout the evening that the Duke appeared to be gazing at him, and he often caught his eye.

The next day, before leaving for Bolton Abbey, Paxton sat with the Duke in his private room, listening to him talk about his family. Having heard it many times before, he was not particularly perturbed when the Duke said that he would probably be dead by the time Paxton returned. As he left the room, the Duke called him back to show him a cartoon in the copy of *Punch* which he had been reading. In it, two old gossips were talking about superstition and one of them said 'well, thank God I'm not superstitious, but I don't like thirteen to dinner'. Paxton laughed, and left. William Condell helped the Duke with his letters that evening, the last he dictated was to Paxton. Then the Duke sat quietly in the still evening of the great house and listened to Coote at the piano. Just before seven o'clock the following morning, Monday, 18 January, the Duke's footman, Charles Harris, found him dead in his bed.

It emerged that the Duke had only a few days before asked John Cottingham to move his portrait from the gallery to the dining room to hang by Gainsborough's famous portrait of his mother, Georgiana. Lord Burlington, now the 7th Duke of Devonshire, arrived the following day to find Paxton 'dreadfully upset and I have no doubt miserable in the extreme'. Paxton wanted to record every detail of his master's final days and he sat up late to take statements from all the staff in his own hand. He noted with some sorrow that the Duke had latterly tried to make his health appear better than it really was, whereas formerly he had always made himself out to be worse.

Two days later, as the evening closed in, he accompanied the Duke's body across the dark moors on its slow four-hour drive home to Chatsworth. The red velvet coffin was left to rest in the private chapel, which had been hung with black crape. Since no directions for his funeral could be found, it was decided that he would be buried in the churchyard at Edensor. Paxton, Cottingham and Cavendish took over most of the arrangements. Shattered and inconsolable at Barbrook,

Paxton wrote and received many hundreds of letters in the five days between bringing the Duke home and laying him finally to rest. He turned to Granville, in particular, and wrote letters to all the Duke's family with details of the funeral.

There were endless condolences addressed to him personally. From the Duke's aristocratic friends who had taken him to their hearts, from his family who viewed him as part of theirs* and from the men of his own world, all of whom understood how extraordinary a relationship had existed between the two men. There were letters from Frederick Evans, William Bradbury, from John Ellis at the Midland Railway and William Currey in London, from Lord Carlisle, Ridgway, Mark Lemon at *Punch* and the Baroness Mayendorff. The Duchess of Sutherland wrote in sympathy at his wretched grief: 'I knew and saw your devoted love for him. I am sure he knew it too – it was so penetrating and effective. Think of this with comfort, dear sir. It is so pleasant to be loved and to know one is.' John Gregory Crace wrote less sympathetically, asking what he should do about the decorations at Chiswick.

On a cold, bright morning, the Duke was buried in Edensor in sight of the immense buildings and works in which he and Paxton had taken so much pride. Great crowds filled the park to watch the long procession of family, friends, mourners and tenants from the house to the small graveyard. The 7th Duke later wrote that, while several were quite affected at the graveside, none was more so than Paxton, whose emotions were so strong that he thought he would not get through it.

Back at Chatsworth directly after the service, the will was read in the company of Cavendish, Currey, Granville and Paxton among others.† When they had all left, Currey told the new Duke the state of affairs in his inheritance. It was far worse than he had anticipated. Most of the large income was again being eaten away by interest

---

* When the Duke's sister, Lady Granville, died in April 1863, attendance at her funeral was confined to her children, grandchildren and her nephew. Only one exception was made – for Paxton; Richard Cavendish wrote, 'we all feel towards you so entirely as if you were one of the family' and invited him to attend, while acknowledging that to come would revive memories of the intense suffering he had experienced on the death of the Duke.

† George Paxton was quick off the mark, writing to Sarah to ask about the contents of the will in a vain hope that the Duke would have left him £4,000. He also exhorted his mother 'for God's sake' not to continue to work for the new Duke as she had for the last: 'don't do it at any price'.

payments. With the enormous economies that were needed, the Duke confided in Currey that he felt Paxton was not the man to be asked to undo much of what he had himself built up and he thought it impossible that Paxton could remain in his position as agent. Currey was surprised. Paxton was an institution at Chatsworth and had been known to the 7th Duke for decades.

A meeting between Paxton and the new Duke was arranged for the following morning. The Duke was 'more nervous about the interview than I ever recollect being' but Paxton was prepared, and arrived with his letter signed and sealed. He resigned to spare the Duke any possible embarrassment with regard to himself, writing: 'you will readily believe that it is not without a feeling of great sorrow that I make this communication. My close and intimate relations with Chatsworth and the late Duke for a period upwards of thirty years, cannot be severed without a pang; but my other engagements are now so varied and important that I feel it a duty to both Your Grace and myself to make this proposal.'

Whatever Paxton felt about losing both his patron and closest friend and, in the same week, the position at Chatsworth that had been his gift, he now acted with great grace. The new Duke was, he said, deeply touched. He knew that the course Paxton had chosen to adopt caused him a more bitter wrench than many men would ever experience. Both men picked their way carefully through the grief and duty they each felt. Fully aware of the remarkable connection between servant and master, the 7th Duke gave Barbrook to him for life and allowed him to make and carry out his own plan for laying off the great quantities of staff necessary for the economies needed. Sarah must have been relieved that her home was not to be taken away from her at least until her own husband died. Lord Granville wrote to Paxton to reassure him of the rightness of his resignation. He also mentioned, as did several other correspondents at the time, that the Duke had wished to erect a monument to him at Chatsworth. In fact, the gardens themselves, the glasshouses and kitchen garden, the rockery, the arboretum and pinetum, the Emperor Fountain and the Great Stove were monuments enough to the extraordinarily productive friendship between the two men, and the magic Paxton had wrought there.

CHAPTER TWENTY-THREE

Under the new regime of the businesslike 7th Duke, things changed fast. William Currey found that his services were no longer needed and Sarah's cousin, John Cottingham, succeeded Paxton as agent. Kemp Town in Brighton was sold and, at Chatsworth, Paxton drew up the plans for hundreds of staff to be laid off in the house and gardens. Andrew Stewart now took over the tiresome business of the pay from Sarah. She noted by the spring that he was 'getting tired already, and wonders how I have done it for so long. I could have told him my hatred of it for years, and loss of health into the bargain.' Paxton collected his things from Devonshire House but, unable to cut himself off completely from his past, he proposed to the 7th Duke that he should retain some connection with his affairs and the Duke agreed to consult him occasionally. The following year, unexpectedly, the Duke settled £500 a year on Paxton for life.

With the death of his patron and friend, and his duties at Chatsworth over, Paxton found himself initially a freer man, able to focus entirely on his own business and that of Westminster. In June, portable glasshouses – or Hothouses for the Millions as they were advertised – were born. Designed for those more modest in their horticultural passions than the 6th Duke at Chatsworth, the middle classes in their suburban villas, they were, in effect, simple wooden hinged frames which could be shipped flat, unfolded and glazed, a relation to the huts he had developed for the Crimea. Mass-produced and marketed through the means of horticultural magazines and nurseries throughout Britain, Paxton's long-term

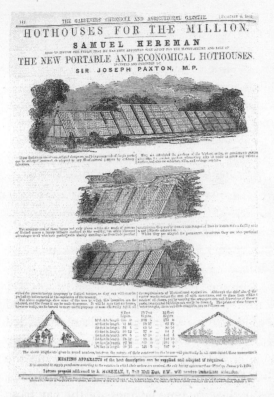

and self-effacing secretary, Samuel Hereman, wrote the do-it-yourself construction manuals and ran the business, acting as sole agent, from Paxton's new London offices close to Parliament in Pall Mall East.

That summer, as temperatures soared, the stink in London, not least in the poorly ventilated Palace of Westminster where the smell was pushed up through the building from the basement levels by the fans, was focusing everyone's minds. It was the summer of the 'Great Stink of London' and the ninety million gallons of raw sewage estimated to be pouring into the Thames daily, making up a quarter of its volume, were getting, quite literally, up the noses of the people's representatives. Bubbling past their very windows, the stinking water forced Parliament to consider decamping down river to Henley, below the tidal flow. The curtains in both Houses were drenched with chloride of lime and it was also poured into the river in bulk in a desperate effort to deodorise the water, killing any remaining fish.

Ten years earlier, the Metropolitan Sewers Commission had been established in recognition of the growing problem created by the vast population in the world's largest city. The individual cesspools in houses were overflowing – as the city expanded and the distance to the fields on which their contents could be used increased, the collection of night-soil became preventatively expensive for many householders, who simply allowed the cellars to overflow on to the streets and into their neighbours' houses. The problem was compounded by the rise of the domestic flushing toilet and the consequent multiplication of the amount of water being poured into the already crippled system. In newly-built houses, the Sewers Commission had made mandatory the connection of all drains and cesspools to the sewers, and thus effluent poured into the valley of the Thames and into the river.

Six different, short-lived and underfunded commissions sat in the following seven years, each without the authority to resolve the issue. Cholera rampaged around London – its third epidemic in the winter of 1853 had killed almost 11,000 people. Yet appreciation of its water-borne nature was still years away. Few doubted that the great mass of ordure floating around the city was to blame, but most believed still in the 'miasmic' theory. Because of the lack of scientific connection between contaminated water and death, delays extended across the years.

Now, as temperatures rose to over 80°F, the smell was becoming unbearable, particularly around Westminster. A motion was proposed, seconded by Paxton, that the government act decisively in making permanent the Thames Committee, joining it with the Thames Conservancy Board and the Commission of Works to improve the banks of the river and deal with the mouths of the existing sewers. He reminded Parliament that his own extensive drainage work at Birkenhead, undertaken in parallel to the construction of the new town's sewer system, gave him particular experience in these matters. On all sides there were calls for a permanent scheme not to be delayed. In July, Disraeli, the new Chancellor of the Exchequer, introduced a bill which was passed into an act within days, finally providing the 3-year-old Metropolitan Board of Works with the power to borrow three million pounds to execute a new system of mains drainage for London.

⤳

As the summer ended, Paxton's desk once again became a battleground. Letters were still regularly, if temporarily, mislaid. Underpinned by his significantly successful investments in British Railways – he owned around £63,000 of shares – he threw his energies into several unsuccessful enterprises including the Thames Graving Dock in London and, in partnership with Thomas Brassey, foreign railway lines.

The first was the East Bengal Railway running over 100 miles north from Calcutta and engineered by Brunel. Though he had calculated a profit of £12,000, the rising cost of labour and materials in India after the Mutiny of 1857 ensured that the line, in fact, made a significant loss. The second was a 60-mile track in northern Spain for the Bilbao to Miranda Railway, passing through tortuously rocky

mountains where the work was hampered by heavy snow falls or under-
mined by constant rain. The railway line was completed, but all those
involved sustained heavy losses.

At Ferrières, Baron James de Rothschild prevaricated again over
the final design of the house, consulting a French architect and
demanding a further set of plans from Paxton and Stokes, which
included moderate alterations to the main fronts and the addition of
sweeping staircases. It remained a giant, theatrical mansion, a stage
for James' role as the head of the Rothschilds and a backdrop for his
political aspirations. But it was not 'opened' by Napoleon III for more
than three years. At the same time, Paxton, now almost the Rothschild
family architect, was given another commission. Baron Adolphe wanted
a grand mansion built on the hills above Lake Geneva, outside
Lausanne. This house, Prégny, would be entirely designed by George
Stokes while Paxton concentrated on the landscaping of the parks and
gardens both here and at Ferrières. Both included great ranges of
glasshouses to contain the Rothschild passion for exotic species.

The following spring, a number of back-bench MPs, including
Paxton, again forced a General Election by voting against Palmerston's
'dirty' Electoral Reform Bill which, Paxton calculated, would deprive
at least 700 people of the vote in Coventry alone. This time he faced
opposition on the hustings from a third Liberal candidate and from
two Conservative hopefuls. Five candidates for two seats meant the
most hotly contested of any election he had had to fight – endless
meetings in pubs and hotels to receive deputations, tens of speeches
in unruly town halls and interminable visits to constituents. Ultimately,
Paxton and Ellice both roared to a Liberal victory.

Returning to Westminster that summer, Paxton's political attention was caught by landscape issues. He spoke passionately against the
'gardenisation' of the royal parks and criticised Kew for becoming a
flower garden rather than a botanical institution, posing unfair competition to commercial enterprises like the Crystal Palace since it was
open on Sundays. Then he found himself in amicable, though forceful,
disagreement with his old friend Robert Stephenson. Stephenson and
Peto backed a plan by the engineer Hawksley to clean the stinking
Serpentine, the body of ornamental water in Hyde Park that was regularly polluted by sewage outfall during heavy rain. Paxton was utterly
opposed to Hawksley's proposed filtration beds, which, he said, would
be unsightly and offensive and would not, in any case, remove the evil
entirely. Although Paxton lost the first round, and funds were voted

for the scheme, he won the second. Both he and Peto sat on a select committee to inquire into the work the following February, and his arguments held sway. The committee recommended that Hawksley's plan be abandoned. Only the pumping house, never used, remains to this day as witness to the argument between engineer and gardener.

Paxton's son George had a boy, also called George, in the summer of 1859 and, in the hopes that this might encourage him to think of the future and reform his ways, Paxton agreed to take him to Paris and on to Madrid to inspect another prospective railway line. They were to meet with Brassey and William Jackson. Before they left, on 15 September, Isambard Kingdom Brunel died, aged 53. Less than a month later, while Paxton was walking mile upon mile of line, Robert Stephenson, with whom he had planned to visit Egypt the following month, also died, in his 56th year. Two of the greatest British engineers of all time had vanished. Stephenson's body was taken to Westminster Abbey. Paxton wrote to *The Times* from Spain in memory of his intimate friend.

For Paxton, entering his 57th year, the work on the railway from Madrid to Toledo was a terrible strain, travelling all night and walking the lines by day, with only wretched food to sustain them. George's company was barely tolerable. His habit of putting himself forward and his forceful, often misguided opinions irritated not only his father but the rest of the company. It was a relief, therefore, to return to England.

In November, Paxton made the journey to Lismore, for the first time without the Duke. The place wore a melancholy air. This was a different Lismore, shrouded in mourning for the man who had loved to party there, and Paxton cut a melancholy figure as he walked through its gardens and great rooms, accompanied by the swirling memories of quite different days. With the works halted, two towers were still covered in scaffolding. The tower in the north-west corner remained incomplete, a memorial to a Victorian ideal.

CHAPTER TWENTY-FOUR

Rockhills, despite Sarah's hatred of and absence from it, had become Paxton's real home. By 1860, the elegant Victorian house on the high corner of the Crystal Palace park, extensively altered and renovated to suit the Duke, who had died as it was completed, boasted ceilings with gilded centre roses, painted cherubs and floral patterns. Set over three storeys and with five main bedrooms, it was lavishly furnished and decorated. The gates and their posts were said to have been a present from the Queen herself. The housekeeper, cook, housemaids and menservants had their own rooms, the wine cellar was full and the larder, lined with zinc and including a heavy marble pastry slab, was laden with meat on hooks.

A wide, glazed and paved veranda stretched along the garden front of the house, where an American rocking chair and three wicker garden chairs waited to be occupied in rare moments of peace. The columns were planted with climbers, with wisteria, camellias, passion flowers, jasmine and forsythia trained on to trellises. Raised circular beds, massed with blue hydrangeas, flanked a gravel walk, and smaller beds were cut into the lawn for displays of bright compact and variegated geraniums. Driven by the taste of the age, and like the magnificent Crystal Palace park, the garden was filled with labour intensive pattern planting which, though it went quickly out of fashion, was the finest of its type.

Out of sight of the house, below the rhododendrons, ran a terrace walk with a crystal palace summer house at each end. To the side lay a kitchen garden filled with a large variety of portable Hothouses for the Millions, each crowded with plants that had wintered in pots ready for 'bedding out'. There were tens of varieties of fruit and vegetables, including forced strawberries, early potatoes, kidney beans and melon. In this garden, as he had at Chatsworth, Paxton proved himself the greatest garden authority of his time.

He attacked the first years of the new decade with much of his old vigour. Railway business up and down the country, and indeed out of it, claimed much of his attention. He presided over the amalgamation of the Lancashire and Midland Railway, chaired the new Dublin and Meath Railway, kept an eye on progress with the East Bengal and visited his lines in Spain regularly, wearing his boots to ribbons as he walked down the lines. He traded regularly in large amounts of shares, his deals often driven by inside knowledge of the companies' business – a practice considered entirely above board at that time. He dined regularly at the *Punch* table, where his affability and tendency to drink large amounts of champagne while retaining his ability for straight talking was coveted. On one riotous occasion he firmly put a stop to any notion of 'spirit rapping' by planting his feet firmly on the stretcher under the table, on another they drank Sarah's health – for he had said that it was impossible to succeed without a good wife.

The company of these intelligent men and the memory of their friendships with the Duke when he was alive, gave Paxton great joy and among them he was loved and respected. He dined regularly, too, at the Reform Club, with men like Dickens – through whom he met Wilkie Collins on the eve of publication of *The Woman in White* in 1860 – and his friends, Gladstone, Palmerston and Thackeray. He was a regular guest, accompanied by Annie rather than Sarah, of the Rothschilds at Mentmore, where the parties were always merry and Annie's pealing laughter and ready wit were appreciated by the Baroness and all her children.

The house where he had taken up his first gardening job as a young boy was now in ruins, and he had been commissioned by Sir Edward Page Turner, son of the insane Gregory, to provide designs to rebuild it. Along with Stokes, he, therefore, returned to Battlesden, to the lake he had created there, the churchyard where his parents were buried and the crowding memories of his family and of visits to Woburn on behalf of the Duke. Stokes was to take charge of the designs once the commission was won – as he had for Baron de Rothschild at Prégny.

Over the next few years Paxton provided plans for a moderate but romantic building with soaring French Gothic spires that the *Building News* would later dub 'one of his happiest efforts'.

His work schedule remained punishing. Over two days in March 1860 he went to Battlesden with George Stokes, on to Oxford to survey a plan for Jesus College, rushed back to London for a 9 a.m. meeting of the Midland Board, met the 7th Duke at 11 a.m., joined the Serpentine Committee at midday, the Graving Dock Board at 4 p.m. and finished at the Speaker's levee at 10 p.m., remembering to send his daughter Blanche money for alterations to her house and overseeing orders for the portable hothouses at the same time.

On visits to Glasgow, Paxton was as lionised with lavish dinners as he had been in Liverpool and Birkenhead in the 1840s, though he complained in letters to Sarah that Stokes was so shy and retiring that he had great difficulty in bringing him out of himself. Three years earlier he had been asked by the Glasgow Corporation to advise on the formation of a second, far larger, city park: Queen's Park. Although he had furnished plans including, in 1860, designs for a winter garden as an essential feature of its 143 acres, these were much altered by the City's own planners and the park as constructed contained neither a glass building nor many of Paxton's original ideas. In Dundee, he had also been commissioned to design Baxter Park and, a little later, he would be asked to provide plans for a park in Dunfermline. At around the same time, he also agreed to lay out Shepperton Park on land around the terminus of the new Thames Valley Railway. He remained in demand as a landscape designer, but the thrill of working on his ground-breaking parks in Liverpool and Birkenhead was replaced by a business-like efficiency – now he provided only the plans which were realised by those who owned the land. No doubt the prestige of having a 'Paxton' design encouraged the subscription and investment necessary to see them through.

In London, the two main preoccupations of the day, communication and sanitation, had now converged and it was his responsibilities as an MP that claimed the greater part of his attention. There had been many plans, including Paxton's own for the Great Victorian Way, designed to improve the condition of communications in London and ease the traffic jams that paralysed its thoroughfares. At the same time, the Metropolitan Board of Works (MBW) had been pressing on with the biggest civil engineering project of the age to provide a modern drainage system for the city. As its 22,000 labourers dug up streets and parks to build sewers, the problem of traffic was compounded. Once again, pressure grew to find a solution.

Chief engineer to the MBW, Joseph Bazalgette's original plan had been to run the new low-level sewer along the north bank of the River Thames, within an embankment that would also provide a major new road from Parliament to Blackfriars. The plan had, however, been amended so that the sewer was now to run in a line under the Strand and the work was creating traffic havoc as people continued to pour into the city daily from the London stations. In addition, there was a lack of consensus over how to pay for any scheme to embank the river. Some said London should pay, others that it was a scheme of national importance and that national taxes should finance the work. As the debate raged, nothing was done. At the beginning of May, infuriated by the prevarication, Paxton moved in Parliament for a final decision to be made on the embankment of the Thames. The Prime Minister, Palmerston, backed his call for a select committee to inquire, in partic- ular, into the method of payment for the proposed scheme. Paxton not only got his committee, but was appointed its chairman.

One of the evils of the drainage system as it existed, as Londoners had discovered during the Great Stink of July 1858, was that it discharged sewage into the river at low water, because the high tides effectively closed off the mouths of the outfalls. In consequence, not only did the sewage in the drains back up and overflow whenever it rained heavily, but by allowing the effluent to pour into the river at low tide, it was naturally carried *up* stream as the tide turned, washing back down again as it ebbed. Bazalgette wanted to pump the water into the high-level sewers and discharge it at Barking, some 14 miles below London Bridge, at high water when it would be carried down river and out to sea as the tide turned.

Paxton's committee was extraordinarily thorough, sitting every few days for ten weeks, and examining tens of experts, civil engi- neers and wharfingers – the men who made their business along the banks of the Thames. It investigated the tidal flow of the river, the duties on cabs and coal, and the foundations of St Paul's Cathedral which were said to be under threat from the new sewer. At the end of July, Paxton finalised his report. The committee had resolved that an embankment of the north side of the Thames from Westminister Bridge almost to Southwark Bridge would improve the banks and beds of the river while assisting the construction of Bazalgette's low- level sewer and providing a much needed new road and railway. They estimated the probable cost, including the sewer, at a maximum of £1,500,000, recommended a tax on coal and wine for the purpose and proposed that the entire works be put in the hands of the MBW and that a scheme for the embankment of the south side of the river should be considered for the future. Despite the fact that the MBW and all those in favour of the embankment felt strongly that Paxton's committee had shown the way forward, Parliament dithered and the proposed costs soared. Then, just when it appeared nothing would ever be done, an act of 1862 gave the go-ahead, at last, to the Victoria Embankment on the north side of the river, and to the Albert Embankment on the south.

Paxton would never see the realisation of the great work. While it fell short, in terms of innovation of design, of his great plans for a crystal boulevard around London, it did, as he had envisaged, provide a subway, sewer, road, railway and footpaths all created on a solid embankment built on land reclaimed from the river. It opened in 1870, forming a grand new thoroughfare from Parliament to the centre of the city. He would have loved it. He would have enjoyed the sheer scale of its creation – 65,000 cubic feet of granite, 140,000 cubic yards of concrete, one million cubic yards of earth – and its ornamental mouldings, cast-iron lamps, bronze lion-head mooring rings and recesses for pontoons and landing stages. The embankment enabled the completion of a sewer system which still serves a London population that has mushroomed in size and which effectively eradicated the great threat of cholera from the city.

⌒

On 21 February 1861, disaster struck the Crystal Palace for the first time. Strong gales had raged all day, exerting several thousand tons of pressure on the glass, but it seemed to be bearing up. Then, at half-past seven in the evening, a great gust swept over the hill. Some carpenters working late heard the smash of glass and rushed outside. Only a minute later the tower at the end of the north wing toppled, crashing down into the trees. As they watched in horror, over the next several minutes the rest of the wing began to collapse like dominoes, 30 or 40 yards at a time, until the whole length of over 100 yards lay in splinters of wood, glass and iron. The gallery in which Paxton and Sarah had dined, the tower in which they had danced, were nothing but a heap of ruins.

Paxton was devastated. The timing could not have been worse. A shareholders' meeting had been called for two days hence to investigate allegations of share-fraud by the chairman, Laing. So ill that he could 'scarcely crawl about', Paxton supported Laing, who fled to Calcutta soon after the meeting, demanding an investigation by which he was later cleared. But with its finances in tatters, the company was unable ever to rebuild the north wing of the palace.

Two million visitors came each year, drawn by unique popular entertainments that catered to almost every taste, but it still made no profit. There were zoological exhibits, flower shows and music festivals and concerts, there were even mass evangelical meetings.[*] Three years hence, Mr Brock would begin his 'benefits' – weekly firework shows on a grand scale where ship battles were fought in the sky and Queen Victoria's face appeared. Later still, there were circuses and strongmen, winter concerts and, in 1871, an aquarium 400 feet long was built and stocked with tropical species to the delight of visitors. In the early part of the twentieth century, Leonora Dare made world-renowned balloon descents hanging by her teeth; the Cup Final was played in the stadium at the foot of the park until 1913 when Wembley was built. Now, though, the most popular entertainment was provided by Blondin, the tightrope 'hero of Niagara', who staged daring shows, wheeling a barrow across a rope strung high, with a sack over his head and, sometimes, a child in the barrow. On the last day of October, Paxton took Emily and Annie to see one of his performances by firelight. Blondin slipped and a roar went up from the crowd as, by a miraculous effort, he caught the rope as he fell. Blondin later admitted to Paxton that he had never had such a narrow escape.

[*]   The Revd Charles H. Spurgeon preached to 43,000 people there on 7 October 1861.

CHAPTER TWENTY-FIVE

Often sitting in Westminster until three in the morning, Paxton petitioned Parliament to repeal the taxes destroying the Coventry silk industry. With America tottering on the verge of civil war and particularly poor British harvests, distress blanketed the city where thousands were out of work. Years ahead of his time, he organised for the men to be given work to clear ground for a common, but there was not a great deal he could do further for his constituents. As an MP, he also argued vociferously in favour of the navy replacing its wooden ships with iron. But the full force of his argument that year was often directed against the planned exhibition of 1862 and the expenditure of half a million pounds of public money on a temporary building. For a while, he and Thomas Brassey considered joining the competition to provide a design. Thoroughly disillusioned by the tendering process, ultimately they chose not to submit a plan.

At the start of May 1862, Paxton was called to give evidence at a select committee inquiry into how to dispose of town sewage. This was another debate that had rumbled backwards and forwards for years. While plans were now in place for London, other towns across Britain were still labouring under the difficulty of what to do with their sewage. Towns and cities were growing, and it was becoming increasingly expensive to transport sewage out to the fields for agricultural use. At the same time, chemical science was advancing to such a degree that it was beginning to provide its own fertilisers for land, while guano from South America provided yet another alternative to human sewage and was being imported by farmers in greater and greater quantities.

From a horticultural point of view, this problem had interested Paxton for years. He told the committee that, as early as 1849, he had made experiments at Chatsworth in which all the sewage from Barbrook had been recycled, to be used, in liquid form, on the land. In particular, he had experimented with a bamboo plant to see how fast he could make it grow under different conditions, and had found that he could force it up 1 inch a day for 20 days by using human manure as feed. He explained that at the Crystal Palace a similar use was made of sewage, which was stored in ventilated tanks in front of the transepts, from where it was used to water the scarlet geraniums at 4 a.m. each morning. He had five times as much as he needed, he said, but, always with an eye to practicality, he refused to apply it to the grass, since it would only make it grow with such subsequent luxury that it would need to be mowed more frequently.

The country was at a point where it was desperate for solutions to the problem of sewage disposal, but public opinion was hard to manoeuvre. Paxton admitted that the directors of the Crystal Palace Company had been outraged when he had put forward his plans for the sewage tanks there, but that their success had borne out his faith in the system. He admitted that his trials at Chatsworth had been on a small scale, but he had also become convinced, through his own experiments, that 6 feet of sand could filter water to an almost pure state.[*] It would have been uncharacteristic of him not to have considered the subject in all its lights and come up with an avant-garde and yet eminently sensible solution. He believed that there would be a day when two systems of sewerage would apply that would separate water-closet waste from general water or rain. He could see a time, and believed he could devise it if he gave it his entire attention, when domestic sewage would be held in cellar tanks, with a pipe leading to the street and a tap, so that they could be emptied easily into large municipal vehicles.

There were still regular trips to Ireland on railway business, to see Blanche and to take up offers of shooting and, in Paris, the promise of a very grand scheme was hovering. There were early plans for an exhibition to be held there in 1867 and much talk of who would provide designs for a permanent building to be built at St-Cloud. Since Paxton's fame made him the notional father of all such plans, it is not surprising that he began to dream of a great palace of glass in Paris. Initially,

---

[*]   He would later be proved right in this.

there was some discussion with William Jackson and Baron Rothschild about forming a Palace Company, with Paxton as the designer, and throughout 1862 and 1863 the idea seemed to be gaining strength. In October 1863, Charlotte de Rothschild wrote to her sons that she had been with the talkative and cheerful Paxton, who had confided a great secret to her, namely that the Emperor of France wanted him to build 'the most marvellous Crystal Palace ever beheld. It ought to be called the diamond palace, so dazzling is it to be – His Majesty wishes it to face the Champs de Mars and to harbour the great International Exhibition of 1867 – but never to be removed.'

Paxton provided a design, and it was sublime. Longer than the Palace in Hyde Park, the glass building was to cover over 100,000 square feet but its great beauty lay in its one vast, central, tapered Moorish dome which rose to a height of 328 feet. This was flanked by two smaller domes, each 250 feet high. He proposed that the building would be surrounded by a small landscaped park, with terracing and formal bedding arrangements. But it was never to be. A cheaper alternative was ultimately sought and built, though it fell foul of high winds almost as soon as it was constructed.

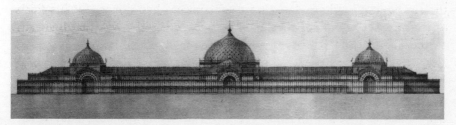

Although he had outlived several of his great contemporaries and was far from old, Paxton was not well. 'Infernal business' had for years prevented him from taking his own health seriously, and now it began to fail him more regularly. As he waited to hear whether the 'infernal French affair' would come off, and as George's swindling activities piled worry on to exhaustion, he managed short trips to Ireland and to Westminster, but he was 'quite knocked up' and relying increasingly on medicine which he detested. By March 1863, his doctor was advising him to stay indoors and take total rest, though he could not quite refrain from renting a room at the Westminster Palace Hotel, from which he could watch the processions for the marriage of the Prince of Wales. Weak and short-winded, it was now Emily rather than his wife who was unrelenting in her care and attention.

In April 1863 Lady Granville, the 6th Duke's sister, died, and with her death came the memory of his own friend's. Two months later, Dr Condell died. With the demise of so much of his old life, Paxton thought it was time to leave the country. His last unmarried daughter was engaged and when Annie's wedding to George Wayte was over in August, he decided to travel to Carlsbad to take the waters in the company of his friend, the Duke's former steward, George Ridgway. The hottest spring, he wrote to Sarah, could boil spinach in a few minutes and he was avoiding it. At a house party at Mentmore in November the following year, Charlotte de Rothschild noted how ill he was looking. He had, indeed, just come from Currey's where he had finally settled and signed a new will. He admitted to Sarah that he was not 'over grand' but he had begun at last to take things easier. He walked in the Crystal Palace grounds, he kept up with his railway interests abroad, he dined at *Punch* and he continued to attend Parliament and the meetings of another select committee on sewerage. He spoke out on issues covering railways, paper duties and the 'gardeni-sation' of parks, even though his Crystal Palace was the epitome of the style. He had witnessed the decline of the Horticultural Society's gardens at Chiswick and their removal to a smaller parcel of land leased in Kensington. Now he felt moved to criticise publicly their shows, sending a copy of his letter to the society to *The Times*.

Times were changing. In the heyday of the Horticultural Society shows at Chiswick, regularly attended by both Paxton and the Duke, he felt that a medal had been worth winning, prized highly and ensuring the commercial success of any plant which received it. He no doubt remembered the acute pride that the winning of his own medals had inspired in the Duke, and the respect of the horticultural world that came with each medal won. Now he felt that shows at the society – now the Royal Horticultural Society – had become too competitive, forgetful of what a true garden was for, with plants forced only for the benefit of the prize and not for the greater good of the gardening world, and sold to the detriment of legitimate nursery businesses. He was perhaps baffled and certainly saddened by the loss of the old values. These had held that the object of horticulture should be to increase enjoyment in gardening, diffuse knowledge widely and make as broadly available as possible the greatest number of fruit, flowers and veget-ables in the greatest quantity, throughout the year and at affordable prices. The generous passions of practical yet adventurous men and women, passions that had driven the science for the first 60 years of the century, appeared to him to have evaporated in the pursuit of profit.

Letters from Annie, who had emigrated to Australia, almost broke his heart, unable as she was to mask the unhappiness of her marriage. In December, his housemaid took it upon herself to go to George Paxton's house and bring little George to see his grandfather. Paxton was charmed by the small boy, whose father was abroad and whose mother was by now very ill with asthma and bronchitis. The weak condition of the 7-year-old reminded him piercingly of his own son, William, before he died. He sent the maid to Emily to buy the child new winter clothes to replace the summer costume he was wearing, and planned to take him to Chatsworth, and to Sarah, for Christmas.

Throughout his 62nd year, Paxton fought to control the undefined illness which was overtaking him. Blanche came from Ireland. Emily and Toey were constantly in attendance at Rockhills. He determined to keep indoors during the cold weather, to accept the doctors' recommendation of entire repose. He moved on to the large sofa in Sarah's sitting room, receiving streams of visitors as the doctors consulted over him and argued over his rheumatism, his heart and his liver. By March, he was hopeful that he was on the road to recovery, though he recognised that he could no longer play a full parliamentary role and he wrote to his Coventry agent in April announcing his intention to retire at the next election.

Joseph Paxton died at Rockhills sooner than anyone expected, at eight o'clock in the morning, on 8 June 1865. He was 61. Doctors recorded the cause of death as heart and liver failure. Henry Silver from *Punch* wrote in his diary 'more fatal overwork!'

The death of this extraordinary man occasioned a public outpouring of regard. His friends at *Punch* put aside political satire to pay tribute to the only 'outsider' to have regularly joined them at table and whose public life they had supported in their pages since his daughter, Annie, stood on the lily leaf in 1849. Obituaries filled the pages of the national press and horticultural journals. The *Gardener's Chronicle* called him 'The Prince of Gardeners' and it spoke of an aspect of his character universally appreciated, his 'kind and generous disposition' and his large and liberal heart. *The Builder* listed his achievements, though, to the end, they refused to consider him an architect, adamant that it would be absurd to compare him to Wren and regrettable to rank him as equal with Barry. Only somewhat grudgingly they acknowledged that he deserved a place in the company of architects, if not as one of them.

Icons of unfettered material progress and technological advance, quintessentially 'Victorian', the Crystal Palaces did not immediately

revolutionise architecture, but his visionary uses of materials in a radically new way unquestionably prepared the way for 'modern' concepts
and construction techniques. Ferrières is, perhaps, the most significant
nineteenth-century chateau in France and Edensor one of the best-
preserved model villages of its kind. Dominating Victorian park design,
his students, Milner, Gibson and Kemp, became the most successful
of the second generation landscape designers of the age.

If professional architects had never truly embraced Paxton, he had
been one of the most popular figures in the hearts of the public. The day
after his death, *The Times* called him 'the greatest gardener of his time,
the founder of a new style of architecture and a man of genius'. But it
reserved its most fulsome praise for his vigorous, kindly and sensitive
disposition, for his lack of pretensions, for a man who cultivated friendship wherever it would grow. Catherine Gladstone wrote to Sarah that
her husband 'Mr Gladstone valued him not only for his power of mind,
but for the more quiet qualities which are more precious. And there was
something about him which we do feel made him loved <u>peculiarly</u>.'

Entrepreneurial, sharp-minded, convivial and madly driven, Paxton
left a vast estate valued at around £180,000 – about £8,500,000 in
modern terms – primarily made up of investments in railway companies in Britain and abroad. Sarah was left an annuity of £2,000 and
ownership of all their property in Derbyshire until her death six years
later. She left Barbrook, and Rockhills was returned to the ownership
of the Crystal Palace Company.

～

The day before he died, the gardens at Chatsworth had been filled
with a great party – a grand fête for the Derbyshire Yeomanry and
volunteers. When he heard the news of his death, the 7th Duke wrote
in his diary that 'the place owes very much to him, he was almost as
much attached to it as any of the family'. Indeed, Chatsworth was
Paxton's true spiritual home.

His body was sent back there by special coach. Sarah and her daughters Emily, Victoria, Blanche and Rosa followed by train. Annie was
still in Australia and George was somewhere on the continent. The
decorator, John Gregory Crace, organised the private funeral, to be
held at Edensor Churchyard. At two o'clock, exactly a week after his
death and as a performance of mournful music at the Crystal Palace
began, his cortège left Barbrook in glorious summer weather, the

rumble of 6 mourning coaches and 30 private carriages breaking the quietude of the park. From over the hills, the muffled peal of the church bell at Baslow was heard measuring the minutes. A hundred and fifty workmen from the estate and several hundred locals lined the carriage drive from the great house as the procession turned away from Chatsworth's glinting windows and gilded casements and the wide sweep of the Derwent, towards the village.

Behind them, the gardens and pleasure grounds stood silent. There, Paxton had pioneered the exposure of half-hardy plants, built up the most valuable collection of orchids in the country and had evolved 'modern' horticultural practice through his experiments with temperature, light and food and the replication of native environments. Here were the monuments to his work, garden features developed to the highest possible perfection: the pinetum and arboretum, now well established over three decades, the rockery and the Emperor Fountain, the Great Stove, the conservative wall and the lily house and forcing houses in the kitchen garden, witnesses to a horticultural vision spanning almost 40 years.

Arriving at Edensor, Paxton's closest friends, including Brassey, Lemon and Jackson, carried his polished oak coffin to the graveside, where Sarah and the girls, surrounded by engineers, contractors, authors, artists, scientific men, aristocrats and Members of Parliament, waited. At three o'clock, he was buried within yards of the Duke he loved.

Joseph Paxton circa 1865

APPENDIX

Bear him hopefully and humbly, through the genial summer
    weather,
To Quiet E'nsor graveyard, where the dead have flowers around
    them;
While titled and untitled, Lords and lowly, weep together –
Hearts with scarce a common tie but the love of him that bound
    them.

Needs but a simple tomb stone, with birth and death carved neatly,
And no hollow sounding praises of him whose work is past.
His monument is elsewhere – in those Chatsworth gardens stately,
In the far-off Crystal Palace, where the world looked on him at last.

The Yeoman's son, the gardener's boy – still true to his vocation –
He won a worthy master, who prized him at his worth:
For grand design that came to him he found, or made occasion;
And lived to sit at great men's feasts, but ne'er blushed for his
    birth.

Let him sleep almost in hearing of the many voiced fountains
He loved to turn and tame, and make his fancy's bidding do:
Now dancing crowned with rainbow, now adown the mimic
    mountains
Dashing in crests of foam, now wreathed in figures quaint and new.

Let him sleep almost in breathing of the many coloured flowers
He loved to tend and trim and train – a gladness to the sight;
On his grave still warm and wooingly drop down the summer
    showers;
Bloom, field-flowers, bright around him, in the pleasant summer
    light.

No gentler life, no truer heart, no quicker, keener brain
E'er closed, or ceased from labour, than his that lieth here:
Long they'll talk of the 'Grand Gardener' round Chatsworth's fair
   demesne
And many a hard hand, at his name, will wipe a well-earned tear.

(*Punch*, 24 June 1865)

NOTES

_____

Note about Chatsworth sources: the many quotations taken from the Paxton Mss, from the diaries of the 6th and 7th Dukes of Devonshire and from other Chatsworth sources are so numerous that they have not been listed separately in these chapter notes. For anyone interested in tracing the exact source of any of these references, an annotated manuscript has been lodged at Chatsworth and may be viewed on application to the archivist.

Source Abbreviations:
GM – *Gardener's Magazine,* ed. J. O. L. Loudon
HR – *Horticultural Register,* ed. J. Paxton
MB – *Magazine of Botany,* ed. J. Paxton
GC – *Gardener's Chronicle,* ed. J. Paxton and J. Lindley
ILN – *Illustrated London News*
CRO – County Record Office
PRO – Public Records Office, Kew
1851 Dir. – The 1851 Commission, Director's Correspondence
1851 Win. – Windsor Archive on loan to The 1851 Commission
Kew – Royal Botanic Gardens, Kew, Directors' Correspondence
Hort. Soc. – Royal Horticultural Society

PROLOGUE

The hiring of field glasses: reported in the *Daily Mirror,* 1 Dec. 1936.
Report of streams of molten glass: *Daily Telegraph,* 1 Dec. 1936.
The fish perished: some newspaper reports, including the *Daily Sketch,* suggest that, in fact, the fish survived, but turned black.
The biggest blaze in living memory: only a week after the opening of the Great Exhibition in Hyde Park in 1851, a small fire had broken out in the Canadian section. At that time it was thought that it was caused by a burning paper from a stove in the contractor's office being blown along a vent to an outlet near the stand. The contractors were forbidden henceforth from lighting their stove.

'The very genius of December': *The Observer*, 6 Dec. 1936.
'one could go there': Le Corbusier, 'The Crystal Palace: A Tribute', p. 72.
'Colossal crinolined birdcage': P. Morton Shand, 'The Crystal Palace as Structure and Precedent, p 65.
'Queen Victoria is dead at last': reported in the *Daily Sketch*, 2 Dec. 1936.

CHAPTER 1

'You never know how much nourishment': Markham, *Paxton and the Bachelor Duke*, p. 5.
Rent books for the Woburn Estates: The Russell Papers, Bedfordshire CRO.
The price of bread: according to Edward Arpin, parish clerk of Felmersham, reported in Godber's *History of Bedfordshire*. Bread was 1s 1d a peck in 1763 and 16s 8d for the same amount in 1816.
More people and less food: for more about the village labourers' plight see Hammond, *The Village Labourer*, also Thompson, *English Landed Society in the Nineteenth Century*, pp. 213–20. The number of enclosure acts rose from an average of 25 in the 1780s to 58 in the 1790s, climbing to 133 in 1811. At the same time the rental price of land almost doubled.
No school in Milton Bryant: Sir Hugh Inglis made an endowment for the formation of a local free school for 95 students in 1853. *Victoria History of the Counties of England: Bedfordshire*.
Education did not become a requirement: however, Forster's Elementary Education Act of 1870 did empower local authorities to make compulsory education available to 13-year-olds if they so wanted.
'Large, of stone': description of the Woburn school from Dodd, *An Account of the Town of Woburn*.
'Few could do more than write their names': in 1845, 75 per cent of the children leaving 176 Midland schools after an average attendance of a year and a half were still unable to read. Altick, *Victorian People and Ideas*.
Bedford's report on the Woburn school sent to Whitbread: Russell Papers, Beds. CRO, 10 April 1808.
The Battlesden fruit garden: description from the Battlesden Papers at Beds. CRO.

William Griffin: Paxton worked with Griffin according to his own account in the records of the Hort. Soc. – 'Book of Handwriting of Undergardeners', Lindley Library, RHS. See also Griffin obituary in *GM* 14 (1838), p. 111.

Author of a treatise . . . on the management of grapes in vineries: Griffin's treatise was published in the Hort. Soc. *Transactions*, vol. 1.

Paxton at Wimbledon House?: see the *Telegraph* obituary of Paxton, 9 June 1865.

Brother James at Wimbledon House: see Paxton Group, Chatsworth, no. 1767, 9 Jan. 1901. Also a letter from the Duke to Paxton about his brother, no. 37 in the Paxton Group.

Paxton at Lee and Kennedy?: see *The Builder*, obituary, 17 June 1865, no. 1167, pp. 421–3.

CHAPTER 2

Paxton entered the Horticultural Society's gardens: frustratingly, no mention of him is made in the report for that year despite the fact that all new employees were generally listed.

The fourth, garden revolution: Thomas, *Man and the Natural World*. Thomas argues that the eighteenth and nineteenth centuries saw a 'gardening revolution' comparable to other revolutions of the early modern period

The Botanical Magazine: for more, see Desmond, 'Victorian Gardening Magazines'.

Lilium tigrinum: distribution noted in *Inwards Books, Plants and Seeds Received* 1804–1826, Kew.

The great age of English periodicals: Altick, *Victorian People and Ideas*.

'Examples of the human species': Hort. Soc., *Transactions*, vol. 2.

Hart is 'improving Chiswick': 19 Oct. 1820 and 13 Nov. 1820, *Letters of Harriet, Countess Granville*, vol. 1.

'A picture of Watteau': Scott's diaries, 17 May 1828.

'Subjected to various modes of treatment': *First Reports of the Garden Committee 1822–27* (1823 Report), Hort. Soc. Lindley Library.

Patrick Daly and other entrants: *Council Meeting Notebooks*, 6 (1823–4), Hort. Soc., Lindley Library.

Early experiments with greenhouses and stoves: for more, see also Taylor, *Some Nineteenth Century Gardeners*, and Quest-Ritson, *The English Garden: A Social History*.

Loudon's remarks on the conservatory at Chiswick: Loudon, *Encyclopaedia of Gardening*, 2nd ed. (1824), p. 510. A system of hot water heating is described by T. A. Knight in *Transactions* of the Hort. Soc. vol. 2 (1813) – this is still the normal method of heating modern homes.
Douglas fir: *Picea sitchensis.*
Loudon calculated: more on statistics of plant introduction can be found in Thomas, *Man and the Natural World.* Johnson, *A History of English Gardening*, p. 359, calculates the numbers of plants under cultivation in England in 1829 as 1,800 stove plants, 3,000 garden plants and nearly 4,000 hardy trees and shrubs 'whereas Mr Loudon makes the number of plants cultivated by gardeners at present amount to 13,140'. See also Harvey, *Early Nurserymen.* Loudon's calculations of tree introductions are found in his *Arboretum et Fructum Britannicum.*
Paxton's catalogue of dahlias at the Hort. Soc.: was completed by William Smith after Paxton had left. *Transactions*, 19 (1830), paper 14.
'Gardener's Magazine . . . to raise the intellect': preface to first edition *GM*, 1826.
'On 22 April Joseph Paxton . . . left, recommended a place': Hort. Soc. *Notes of the Council Meetings*, vol. 6. This was good timing, under the autocratic management of Joseph Sabine, the society's finances were failing and its administration was beginning to be severely criticised in the press, not least by Loudon. Sabine resigned in 1830.
'Sweet disposition': Lees-Milne, *The Bachelor Duke.*
Puckler-Muskau: reported in Cornforth's article on Devonshire House, *Country Life*, 13 Nov. 1980, pp. 1,750ff.
The Duke's inheritance: Levenson-Gower, *Bygone Years*, p. 41.
Fifty years of neglect: Paxton's immediate predecessor as head of the gardens at Chatsworth was the appropriately named Andrew Grubb. (Chatsworth Household Accounts, uncatalogued.)

CHAPTER 3

'I left London by the Comet Coach': Paxton's account of his arrival printed in Cavendish, *Handbook to Chatsworth*, pp. 111–112.
The Chatsworth garden – for a complete history see Devonshire, *The Garden at Chatsworth.* General information about the history of garden styles is usefully discussed in Hadfield, *Pioneers in Gardening*, and Quest-Ritson, *The English Garden: A Social History.*

Sycamore, poplar and birch . . . all planted four feet apart: recorded in Phillips, *Sylva Florifera*.

'First great hit out of doors': Cavendish, *Handbook to Chatsworth*, p. 160.

'At the kitchen garden': Cavendish, *Handbook to Chatsworth*, p. 112.

'Being young this gave him the authority': Henry Silver's unpublished diaries of the Wednesday night dinners at *Punch*, notes for 9 May 1860. The Punch Cartoon Library and Archives.

As head of the gardens . . . one of the highest paid members of the estate: when the 6th Duke inherited in 1811, he reviewed the pay of all his staff and the London establishments, being more important, received higher pay, so that the gardener at Chiswick, Robert Clues, was paid £100 a year. Hannah Gregory's wages remained unchanged until her death in 1843 after four decades of faithful service.

CHAPTER 4

Rules and regulations: these are taken from Chatsworth, unpublished notebook and accounts of James White, 1837–45. White was an under-gardener at Chatsworth.

'If anyone feales himself greaved': James White, Chatsworth, unpublished notebook and accounts 1837–45.

'Bit by gardening': Cavendish, *Handbook on Chatsworth*, p. 106. The orange trees, altinga and rhododendron were widely admired and, as a result, the altinga, in particular, began to be introduced into England in greater numbers than ever before.

'I first turned my attention to the building and improvement of glass structures': 'The Industrial Palace in the Park, Mr Paxton's Lecture at the Society of Arts', reported in the *ILN*, 10 Nov. 1850.

8 acres of the south park were given over to the plan: Wyatville Account Books, Chatsworth.

Seeds of the Douglas fir . . . in his own hat: Cavendish, *Handbook to Chatsworth*, pp.170–1. Fifty years later, it was already 35 feet high. The Norfolk pine costs and expenses of its transportation are noted in the Green Vellum Account Books at Chatsworth for 1830 and 1831.

'No two of a party take the same view of it': Cavendish, *Handbook to Chatsworth*, pp. 170–1.

Paxton's views on pineta: see *MB* (9), 1841, article on the grouping of ornamental plants.

Increasing expenditure on the gardens: Chatsworth, Accounts C165a and C165c (Household Accounts 1824–8 and 1829–33).
Removal of the weeping ash: see the *Leicester Journal*, 15 April 1830, and *MB* (1), 1834, pp. 46–8.
Henry Steuart's letter to the Duke: Chatsworth, 6th Duke's Group, no. 1939, 27 April 1830.
A useful description of the kitchen garden in 1850 is found in Adams, *Gem of the Peak*.

CHAPTER 5

Chatsworth had become . . . 'delicious': In his *Handbook*, p. 113, the Duke declared 'not till 32 did I take to caring for my plants in earnest', but it is clear that the seeds of the love affair had germinated a good year earlier.
Lady Newburgh's letter to Blanche: Chatsworth, 6th Duke's Group, no. 2406, 10 Nov. 1831.
Plantsmen, eager for information: The best source for the history of gardening magazines of this period is Desmond, 'Victorian Gardening Magazines', pp. 47–66.
'Embrace everything useful and valuable': Introduction, *HR* 1 (1), 1 July 1831.
A stinging criticism of Chatsworth: *GM* 7 (1831), pp. 395ff.
His reply to Loudon was no less vigorous: *HR* 1 (3), 1 Sept. 1831.
Harrison quit the magazine: See *HR* 2 (1833), Paxton's introduction. Harrison ushered in an era of really cheap gardening periodicals with his new magazine *The Floricultural Cabinet and Florists Magazine*. In 1837 he left Lord Wharncliffe to set up as a florist in Norfolk and continued to edit magazines until his death. Over a century later, *GM* profiled him in 128 (1950), p. 6.
Requirements of heat, soil and nutrition: see Paxton's introduction, *HR* (3), 1834.
Paxton concentrated on the . . . old stone greenhouse: *MB* 2 (1835), pp. 105 ff.
A new parterre to be laid out in front of it: *HR* 4 (1835), pp. 57 ff.
Fireworks, of course, had been a part of great national celebrations, military victories and royal births for centuries, though their popularity would reach unimagined heights in the late 1840s; Bengal lights were burned in open pans, generally placed in trees or by water.

CHAPTER 6

Private maths lessons: supposedly, from a master called William Birks in Stoney Middleton. Reported in *Birks' Family Memorials*, p. 8, 'I owe everything to that man, and whatever success in life I have achieved is due to his friendly influence and advice when I was at school and in his classes'.

Sending to Birmingham and Sheffield for estimates: 'The Industrial Palace in the Park', *ILN*, 10 Nov. 1850.

'I at once set about calculating': ibid.

The greatest possible amount of light would be admitted in the morning: Paxton set out the principles behind his decision to construct roofs on the ridge and furrow design in evidence given to the House of Commons Sessional Papers: Commissioners Appointed to Inquire into the Cost and Applicability of the Exhibition Building in Hyde Park, his evidence given 28 Jan. 1852.

Loudon's nascent principle: in noting the improved ridge and furrow roofs at Chatsworth in his article in *GM*, August 1839, Loudon complimented them and reminded his readers that he had first published the idea in his *Encyclopaedia of Gardening* (pp. 343 and 358) as well as in his *Remarks on the Construction of Hot Houses*. Paxton's 'Observations on the Construction of Hot House Roofs' was printed in *MB 2* (1835), pp. 80–85.

The new house was to be 97 feet 6 inches long and 26 feet wide: details on construction of the orchid house see *MB*, 2 (1835), p. 80 and 'The Industrial Palace in the Park', *ILN*, 10 Nov. 1850.

He was not working in isolation: two remarkable histories of the evolution and design of the glasshouse are by Koppelkamm, *Glasshouses and Wintergardens of the Nineteenth Century*, translated by Kathrine Talbot, and Hix, *The Glasshouse*.

Birmingham Horticultural Gardens: Loudon's plans were published in *GM* 8 (1832). The building would have included novel heating, ventilation and rain-making equipment, but lack of finances and a refusal to open the gardens to the public meant that the scheme was doomed.

'To botanists it is of no use': Loudon's review of the *Magazine of Botany*, printed in *GM* 10 (1834), p. 232.

Plagiarism: for examples see *HR* 3 (1834), p. 405, and *GM* 10 (1834), p. 232.

'With the greatest respect and gratitude': Paxton's dedication of the *MB* to the Duke, 1 (1834).

'I cannot tell you what delight it gives me': Chatsworth, 6th Duke's Group, Sir William Hooker to the Duke of Devonshire, 7 Nov. 1834.

Paxton's ideas on arboreta are found in his article 'Remarks on Arboretums', *MB* 8 (1841), p. 41. The Duke's reaction is found in Cavandish, *Handbook*, p. 168.

'The idea of an arboretum on a large and comprehensive scale': Paxton's article in *GM* 11 (1835), p. 385.

Loudon's praise for Chatsworth in *GM* 15 (1839), p. 451.

Bateman . . . finest collection of orchidaceous plants: according to Dr Daniel Rock in letter to the Duke, Chatsworth, 6th Duke's Group, 2 Dec. 1834. The orchid genus *Batemania* was named after him.

The butterfly orchid: *Oncidium papilio Lindl.*, introduced from Trinidad and described by Lindley in 1825.

By the 1760s 24 species of orchid: Aiton, *Hortus Kewensis*.

Paxton experimented with temperature and humidity: see Paxton's article on the management of epiphytes in *MB* 2 (Dec. 1835).

Huntley's opinion of Paxton: Chatsworth, 6th Duke's Group, Huntley to the Duke, 5 and 10 March 1835.

Victoria, his third daughter: I am indebted to Eddie Richardson for help in substantiating Victoria's birthdate. Markham suggests that she was born immediately after the visit of Princess Victoria to Chatsworth. Here her birthdate is predicated on her age at the 1851 census.

'You and Paxton, sitting under a red Rhododendron': Lees-Milne, *The Bachelor Duke*, p. 115.

CHAPTER 7

'The flowers are often remarkable for their grotesque configuration': John Lindley in Loudon's *Encyclopaedia of Plants* (1829).

Gibson 'has a good knowledge of plants': Chatsworth, 6th Duke's Group, Paxton to the Duke, 19 March 1835.

Gibson's article was published in *HR* 2 (Oct. 1832), p. 27. Paxton notes that Gibson was sent to Joseph Cooper in a testimonial he wrote for Gibson, part of the Paxton Group, 4 April 1845. For more on Gibson see *GC and Agricultural Gazette*, 1872, p. 865.

Botanical Garden in Calcutta . . . something of a clearing house: noted by Elliott in *Flora*. Wallich had a strain of Chinese rose known as Bengal rose named after him.

Plant cases: see *HR* 5 (1835), in particular, for articles about the many new designs for transportation of plants from abroad.

'Sea of glass': Adams, *Gem of the Peak.*

A century earlier: noted by Chadwick, 'The Great Stove at Chatsworth'.

'The curve is much depressed': Paxton's article on the Great Stove, *MB* 8 (1841), pp. 183 and 255. Further description of the Stove in construction is found in Paxton's 'The Industrial Palace in the Park', *ILN*, 10 Nov. 1850.

A scale model: Chatsworth Green Vellum Accounts, 12 Jan. 1836, John Marples – for making the model – £38 5s. A colossal amount, suggesting a large and intricate construction.

Glasshouses should be conspicuous: *MB* 8 (1841), pp. 183 and 255.

Hand-painted Chinese wallpaper: which remains to be seen in the Wellington Room at Chatsworth, where Granny Evie's bed had hidden it from view for the best part of the early twentieth century.

'Plenty of water, rich loam soil and well-rotted dung': *GM* 13 (1837), p. 141.

Ensured that the news was widely circulated: *MB* 3 (1837), p. 51, and *GM* 13 (1837), p. 141.

The odd rumbling noises could be overcome: Chadwick, *The Works of Sir J. Paxton 1803–1865*, p. 77, notes that the new fangled steam engine at first worked irregularly and 'makes a rumbling noise which we do not understand'. Over the next two years, Paxton's experiments with the cutter led to its producing the sections as required.

Princely cargo . . . at least 300 were new: Kew, Paxton to William Hooker, 9 Dec. 1837.

Dendrobium paxtonii, named in his honour by John Lindley: *MB* 6 (1839), p. 169. *Dendrobium paxtonii* was proposed twice in 1839. The modern names are *D. paxtoni Lindl*, a synonym of *D. chrysanthum Lindl*, and *D. paxtoni Paxt.*, a synonym of *D. fimbriatum Hook.*

The Duke, with Paxton, was getting into his spending stride: noted by Cannadine, *Aspects of Aristocracy*, in his wonderful chapter on the Duke's debts in 1840s, p. 162. It should be noted here, too, that the accounts for the construction of the Great Stove were maintained separately from Paxton's garden account as part of the estate balance signed by the agent Smithers. It may have been considered a capital cost deserving separate attention, but it was certainly more than Paxton could afford to sustain in his more modest accounts.

CHAPTER 8

Paxton experimented and practised with the orchids at Chatsworth: *MB* 3 (1836) and 4 (1837), in particular, for multiple articles on the subject and the sharing of information between orchidists. However as early as December 1835 (vol. 2), Paxton published an article on the management of orchidaceous epiphytes. See also '*The Culture of Orchids*', *MB* 14 (1847). Rcinikka, *A History of the Orchid*, also discusses Paxton's standardisation of orchid culture.

The potential criticism that this was his personal, unbounded particularity: Kew, Paxton to Hooker, 20 Dec. 1837.

On a cold Monday . . . the three men assembled . . . to formulate their schedule: PRO, T190, Minutes of the Proceedings. Item 6 discusses the heavy snowfall at Kensington.

The Duke increased his salary by £50: Chatsworth, Green Vellum Account Books, 1838.

'We are irresistibly drawn to the conclusion that the Royal Gardens have been badly managed': PRO, T90, item 2, Lindley's observations.

Aiton was found wanting and derelict in his duty, the gardens were a dead weight on the civil list: PRO, T90, item 4, Report on the Present Condition of the Royal Botanical Garden at Kew.

'They asked £28,000 for an entirely new garden at Windsor': Queen Victoria's journal, 30 April 1838, quoted in Guy Meynell, 'Kew and the Royal Gardens Committee 1838', *Archives of Natural History*, 10(3) (1982), pp. 469–77.

Frogmore . . . perhaps the most perfect garden of its kind in Europe: described in Paxton's *GC* 1849 and quoted in Susan Campbell, 'The Genesis of Queen Victoria's Great New Kitchen Garden'.

The Great Stove rises: for details on the workings and cost savings of the sash bar machine, see Paxton's 'The Industrial Palace in the Park', *ILN*, 10 Nov. 1850. His requests for quotations for heating are found in a letter to John Walker, uncatalogued material at Chatsworth dated 30 April 1838, including sketches.

Two ornate lodges at the entrance to what would be the new village: Wyatville designed these in 1837 and they were complete by 1839.

Edensor: it has been suggested widely that the rebuilding of Edensor was planned in order to move the village wholesale out of sight of the house. While this was not entirely unusual on large estates, it is unlikely to have been the motivating force at Chatsworth. Many of the houses were already derelict and the natural landscaping on the other side of the road allowed the new cottages to be seen to far greater advantage. Only one of the original cottages remains on the north side of the road. Work on the village can be charted through Chatsworth, Green Vellum Account Books, 1836–42.

CHAPTER 9

Those trippers that Byron reviled as 'a parcel of staring Boobies': noted in Chapman and Dormer, *Elizabeth and Georgiana*, p. 246.

News of the failure of the expedition was also circulated among the gardeners: a copy of the circular forms part of James White's notebook and diary at Chatsworth. See also *MB* 6 (1839).

The theatrical ruin: the Duke on the aqueduct see Cavendish, *Handbook*, p. 172.

A new heated wall, or 'conservative wall': noted by Loudon in *GM*, Aug. 1839, p. 451. Full structural measurements in Chadwick, *Works*, p. 100. The Duke's comments in Cavendish, *Handbook*, p. 160, and Paxton's own article in *MB* 9 (1842), pp. 60–65.

CHAPTER 10

Footnote: Burton's letter to the Duke is part of Chatsworth, 6th Duke's Group, 17 Nov. 1843. The Duke's reply is found in the Cavendish, *Handbook*, p. 179. It is worth also noting Paxton's own comments in *MB* 8 (1841), p. 107, where he notes the need for the assistance of an architect where works of great magnitude are to be undertaken. Further reading on the claims of Decimus Burton is found in an article by Francis Thompson in *Derbyshire Countryside*, Aug. 1956, p. 12. Several modern dictionaries of architecture still incorrectly credit Burton as the co-designer of the Great Stove.

By the start of 1840 . . . the Great Stove was ready to be glazed: by Messrs Drake of the Edgware Road in London, at the rate of 16*d* per square foot – *GM* 16 (1840), p. 570.

Glazing wagon: Granville, *The Spas of England*, vol. 2, pp. 66–8 describes the glazing 'contraption' which is likely to have been a predecessor of the glazing wagons used in Hyde Park years later.

Cost of the Stove: £33,099 10s 11d, or around a tenth of the Duke's entire expenditure in the 28 years 1820–48 – see Chadwick, 'The Great Stove at Chatsworth.'

The silver medal for design and innovation: *Transactions of the Society of Arts*, 53 (1) (1839–41), pp. 97–102.

Pocket Botanical Dictionary: Paxton printed a review in his own paper, *GC*, No. 1, 2 Jan. 1841, p. 7. In his introduction to the book, Paxton eulogised the printers, Bradbury and Evans, for devising a new and beautiful typeface that allowed them to print the text very small while it remained readable. The dictionary drew heavily on Loudon's own magnum opus *Arboretum*, published two years earlier.

Glenny's *Gardener's Gazette* **. . . a disgrace to gardeners and the profession:** Paxton letter to William Baxter, curator of Oxford Botanic Gardens, 9 May 1840 – quoted in Desmond, 'Victorian Gardening Magazines'.

Tankerville palms: Household and garden accounts in Paxton's own hand, which came to light as the book went to press, show that the total amount spent on the removal of the Tankerville palms amounted to an astonishing £726 18s. This included payment for repairs to broken carts, the dismantling and rebuilding of the original Tankerville greenhouses and some walls en route and the laborious preparation and packing by ten labourers over 24 days. The expense of dismantling the glasshouse alone was almost £400.

The 35,000 feet of ground space: Paxton's article on planting practice in stoves, *MB* 9, (1844), p. 13ff.

'Transported with delight . . . Art beats nature altogether there': Charles Darwin to J. S. Henslow, 28 Oct. 1845, published in *The Correspondence of Charles Darwin*, ed. Frederick Burkhardt and Sydney Smith, vol. 3, *1844–46*, pp. 259–60. Original letter is part of MS 405A (Charles Darwin Papers) in the special collections department of the Smithsonian Institution Libraries, NMAH 5016, stop 630, Washington, DC, USA.

CHAPTER 11

'A full and comprehensive record of facts only': *GC* (1) (1841).

Mrs Lawrence had a considerable reputation: *GM* 14 (1838), p. 305, description of Mrs Lawrence's garden.

Paxton was regularly invited into this exclusive group: Patrick Leary at the University of Indiana has transcribed the unpublished diaries of Henry Silver, Punch Cartoon Library and Archives, and I am grateful to him for this information.

'The worst kind of English architecture': Pugin, *Contrasts*.

He was at pains to point out to Chadwick: clear from the Chadwick correspondence at University College London, letter from Paxton, 30 Sept. 1842.

The new house . . . was . . . paid for by the Duke entirely from his private accounts: Chatsworth, 6th Duke's Diaries, 25 Oct. 1843: 'Drew Cheques for Paxton to an immense sum to pay at distant dates what he spends now and to be secret between him and me.' When Barbrook was enlarged further in 1851, a similar note is found: (25 March 1851) 'gave Paxton £1000 towards house and offices for his innumerable benefits to me. Enchanted with Paxton.' See also Chadwick, *Works*, p. 168.

An elaborate rockery: Paxton's own opinions about their formation are articulated in *MB* 5 (1838), p. 227, also 8 (1841), pp. 135–7 and 12 (1845), pp. 86–90. John Oliver, the comptroller at Chatsworth, deduced that the rocks undoubtedly came from Dob Edge.

'The spirit of some Druid seems to animate Mr Paxton': Cavendish, *Handbook*, p. 173.

Parliament took the first faltering steps towards securing Battersea as a public park: for more on the history of public parks see Conway, *Public Parks*.

Formation of Subscription Gardens in the Vicinity of Large Towns: *HR* 1, p. 58.

'The removal of large full grown trees:' *Liverpool Mercury*, 23 Dec. 1842, p. 418; see also 24 March 1843, p. 98.

CHAPTER 12

The £800 fee offered: Wirral Archives, B008.1. Birkenhead Improvement Committee Minutes 1843–8, minutes of meeting 12 Aug. 1843. Also Chatsworth Group, Paxton no. 141.

Kemp left a clear indication of the kinds of trees used: *How to Lay Out a Small Garden* (1850).

'Pray don't visit Chatsworth at present': Chatsworth, Duke's Scrapbook, Ridgway to Duke, 12 Nov. 1843.

One thousand three hundred and eighty oil lamps: Chatsworth, Green Vellum Account Books, 1843, cost £227 8s 4d and *Derbyshire Courier*, 2 Dec. 1843.

'Acknowledging [this] courtesy': source unknown, clipping in Chatsworth, Duke's *Scrapbook*.

The cascade was lit with coloured Bengal lights: Mundy, *The Journal of Mary Frampton*, 6 Dec. 1843, letter to Mrs Mundy.

'I have travelled Europe through and through': Wellington is quoted in the *ILN* report 8 Dec. 1843.

'I hope it won't turn his head – but I believe nothing can': quoted in Lees-Milne, *Bachelor Duke*, p. 157.

CHAPTER 13

Paxton was investing fortunes: see Chadwick, *Works*, p. 239 – amounts drawn from the List of Subscribers for Shares of £2000 and Upwards to the Railway Subscription Contracts deposited in the Private Bill Office in Session 1845–46. Also Chatsworth, Paxton Group S-P, 13 April 1845.

Paxton experimented with hydraulics and pneumatics: Paxton's article on the Emperor Fountain is found in *MB* 11 (1844), pp. 223–7. Here he stated that, with over 2,500 feet of new piping laid from the fountain to the lake, he saw no reason not to install a further 3,500 feet of piping to generally improve all the waterworks in the pleasure grounds and gardens over the next few months. The sea-horse fountain was given nine new jets and smaller fountains were installed either side of the Emperor.

Paxton's obituary of Loudon: *MB* 10 (19 Dec. 1843), p. 273.

Debt . . . ran rife in nineteenth-century aristocracy: I have relied on Cannadine, *Aspects of Aristocracy*, for much of this chapter; also Proudfoot, *Urban Patronage and Social Authority*, p. 256.

'A sensible fellow': Chatsworth, 6th Duke's Group, George Cavendish to the 6th Duke, Aug. 1843, also a copy in the Paxton Group, numbered 239.

'The goodwill and praise of the highest and lowest': Cavendish, *Handbook*, pp. 110–11.

He 'has the command of every railway influence in England': quoted by Tudor Edwards in 'Sir Joseph Paxton the Versatile Gardener'.

Hornblower's entrance to Birkenhead Park: Chadwick, *Works*, believes it was, in fact, designed by Gillespie Graham, the architect of the city of Edinburgh at this time. It is clear from material in the Wirral Archive, however, that Hornblower was the architect. He later, temporarily, worked with Paxton in his office at Chatsworth.

'The greater number of our readers will have never heard of this place': *Edinburgh Journal*, 17 May 1845.

'In democratic America there is nothing to be thought of as comparable with this people's garden': Olmstead, *Walks and Talks of an American Farmer in England*, pp. 79–83.

At the request of the commissioners, Paxton made a new plan for the sale of land: in fact, only some 40 houses were ever built, and the original conception of terraces was abandoned.

The Duke of Devonshire was overjoyed at the prospect of the railway . . . and subscribed: Lees-Milne, *The Bachelor Duke*, p. 70. The MBMMJR brought together many of Paxton's friends; George Cavendish was the chairman, George Hudson and John Ellis of the Midland Railway and William Jackson were his co-directors, and old George Stephenson was engineer to the line

Dickens . . . found a gifted, energetic and ingenious man: Ackroyd, *Dickens*, p. 477.

CHAPTER 14

A very useful piece on the **financial basis of the *Daily News*** is Tillotson, 'New Light on Dickens and the *Daily News*'.

The paper's guiding liberal philosophy: *Forster's Life of Dickens*, ed. Gissing, p. 152. For Dickens' resignations see p. 479.

The description of the *Daily News* offices: is from Crowe, *Reminiscences*, p. 69.

There was a clamour at the stands: Sir William Howard Russell, quoted in Markham, *Paxton and the Bachelor Duke*, p. 173.

Paxton on trees in cemeteries: *GM* 11 (1835), pp. 284 and 435. A review of Coventry Cemetery is printed in *The Builder*, 24 May 1862, p. 362. Loudon's early ideas on the design of cemeteries as romantic settings are found in *GM* 11 (1835), pp. 667ff.

Marples . . . was to be the foreman builder: he became a well-known building contractor in the area, later erecting the Royal Hotel in Buxton.

The Wellington Rock, named after the venerable duke: a national

NOTES   271

institution in his own right, Wellington now recognised Paxton on sight.
In January 1848, at a dinner with the Duke at Lord Palmerston's house,
he shook Paxton's hand cordially.

George Hudson operated over 1,500 miles of British track: by 1849
committees of inquiry into Hudson's business practices multiplied and
he found himself attacked on all sides. The sale of Londesborough in
1849 marked the beginning of the loss of his entire capital and rank.
(For more on Hudson see Beaumont, *The Railway King*.) Paxton
continued to defend him, against Sarah's sharp tongue – he considered
him a friend badly treated who had done much through his advice to
build the Paxtons' own fortune. There was no doubt, however, that
Hudson employed shady practices in the paying of dividends from
company capital.

The account of Paxton's triumphant return to Chatsworth is reported
in Harley, *A Gardener at Chatsworth*, diary entry for 10 Aug. 1848.

CHAPTER 15

Sportingly, the Duke wrote to Mrs Lawrence: Chatsworth, 2nd Series
ref. 61.18, undated letter.

The day was not entirely free from worry for Paxton: see Harley, *A
Gardener at Chatsworth*, diary entries for 4 June 1849 and similar entries
for descriptions of the day trippers following the opening of Rowsley
station.

Dickens described as 'an extraordinary object . . . a titanic water
plant': 'A Private History of the Palace of Glass', *Household Words*, no.
43, 18 Jan. 1851, p. 385.

Paxton wrote immediately that he would start to build a large tank
for the plant: Kew, Hooker Correspondence, vol. 28, Paxton's letter dated
11 July 1849.

A great poppy head or a large peach placed in a cup: Chatsworth,
6th Duke's Group, Paxton to Duke, 2 Nov. 1849.

Paxton revived it by pouring warm water into the stalk: Henry
Silver's unpublished diary, Punch Cartoon Library and Archive, April
1863 note.

The *Illustrated London News* printed a long report: *ILN* 17 Nov.
1849.

Louisa Lawrence declined the Duke's invitation: this and following quotation, Chatsworth, 2nd Series, Mrs Lawrence to the Duke, 21 Nov. 1849, item 61.18c.

Paxton's own description of the lily was printed in *GC* 10 (31 Aug. 1850), p. 548.

'A leaf . . . suggesting some strange fabric of cast iron': Hooker and Fitch, *Victoria Regia*, p. 9.

'Freemasonry of gardening': Harley, *A Gardener at Chatsworth*, Introduction.

CHAPTER 16

The history of the Great Exhibition has been widely told and there are more books and papers, in more languages, on the several details of its story than on almost any other Victorian subject. Latterly there has been an outpouring of books of great detail and quality. Most of the detail of this chapter has been taken from the two archives held at the 1851 Commission at Imperial College, a goldmine of primary source material.

'The Exhibition of 1851 is to give us a true test and a living picture of the point of development': Prince Albert's speech at the Mansion House, 21 March 1850, quoted in Sir Theodore Martin, *The Life of the Prince Consort*, vol. 2, 1876, p. 248.

Turner and the Palm House at Kew: unlike Paxton's Great Stove at Chatsworth, the palm house was constructed primarily of iron rather than wood. Initially the glass was infused with copper oxide said to mitigate the scorching effects of the sun, but Paxton's own experiments with light were borne out when the plants in the Palm House failed to thrive and the glass was replaced.

'Had great hopes the cost of Mr P.'s plan': Cole's hopes were reported in a letter to Col. Grey, 10 July 1850. 1851 Win., vol. 4, item 60.

He advised Fox, Henderson as, separately, did Brunel: reported by Paxton in his speech to the Derby Mechanics Institute in October 1850 (Paxton's draft speech forms part of the Paxton Group, item no. 624; it was also published in the *ILN* 17, p. 322). See also his speech at the Derby Dinner of June 1851, reported in *Morning Chronicle*, 22 June 1851 (1851 Win., vol. 7, item 94). The Brunel Archive, Bristol University, Letterbook 7, p. 253, letter from Brunel to Charles Fox dated 3 July 1851 also substantiates this.

Patent for his ridge and furrow roof: Patent Number 13186, 22 July 1850, Roofs etc. – British Library.

'When we consider the manner of supporting a vast glass roof': *ILN*, 6 July 1850, published a full report on the building as well as Paxton's designs.

£88,000, against £141,000: 1851 Win., vol. 4, item 60, letter Cole to Grey, 10 July 1850.

Peto was fiercely in favour of Paxton: 1851 Win., vol. 4, item 61, Peto to Grey, 12 July 1850.

Brunel . . . arrived at Devonshire House: Derby Mechanics Institute speech, *ILN*, 10 Nov. 1850.

'It was to your fostering hand . . . kindness and liberality': Chatsworth, 2nd Series, Paxton to Duke, 13 Oct. 1850.

CHAPTER 17

'No one thought that before the nineteenth century was half out': *The Times*, 26 Oct. 1850, also called it the 'blazing arch of lucid glass'.

Genius may have dashed off the design: reported by the *Morning Chronicle*, 25 April 1851.

He had only to clap on 'his considering cap': *Punch*, quoted in Markham, *Paxton and the Bachelor Duke*, p. 209.

Fixed . . . within 18 hours: *The Times*, 27? Nov. 1850 – see 1851 Win., vol. 5, item 63.

The influence of the Palace would be far-reaching: Paxton laid out this belief in his lecture to the Society of Arts, *ILN*, 10 Nov. 1850.

The glaziers swarmed over the pellucid roof: Digby Wyatt gave a paper to the Institute of Civil Engineers published in their *Minutes of Proceedings* 10 (1850–51), which is packed with the technological detail of the building. He said that the average amount of panes fixed by each man each day was 58 squares. The largest amount of work in a week was by 80 men who put in over 18,000 squares between them. Wyatt also mentions that the glazing wagon was the invention of Mr Fox, though it is clear that Paxton had used an earlier prototype on the Great Stove.

Urinals for the men and 'monkey closets' for the ladies: the Metropolitan Sewers Act of 1848 authorised commissioners of sewers to install public lavatories, but none had yet been opened. The assumption was that the waste would be sold on for general agricultural use, and it was calculated that based on an average deposit of half a pint per person, each lavatory might make a profit of £48 a year, or about 10 per cent of the estimated construction cost. (See Leapman, *The World for a Shilling* p. 92.) The George Jennings flushing loos at the exhibition encouraged far more widespread purchase of domestic models, adding to the strain on the metropolitan sewerage system.

'Mathematicians have calculated': Prince Albert's letter to his relation, quoted in Leapman, *The World for a Shilling*, p. 76.

'Prove to demonstrate that all our houses and large buildings are liable to be blown': 1851 Win., vol. 5, item 117, Granville to Grey, 31 Jan. 1851.

Paxton's 'head has been turned by the events': ibid., vol. 5, item 110, Granville to Grey, 24 Jan. 1851.

Leaks in over a thousand places: ibid., vol. 6, item 34, Reid to Grey, 19 March 1851.

A workaholic 'whose very leisure would kill a man of fashion': Dickens, 'The Private History of the Palace of Glass'.

Metal bird feeders should be charged with an electric current: *The Times*, 10 April 1851, anonymous letter from YMH to the editor.

'He rose from being a common gardener's boy': Queen Victoria's diary, 1 May 1851, quoted in Markham, *Paxton and the Bachelor Duke*, p. 216.

Parade Paxton around wearing 'his dress and his cocked hat': Leveson-Gower, *Bygone Years*. The Duke did not keep a regular diary throughout the period of the Great Exhibition but he wrote a special journal for his nephew Freddie Leveson-Gower, which appears to have been lost. The following quotation is from the same source.

'Exquisite lightness and tone of colour . . . a visual feast': Mayhew and Cruikshank, *1851 or the Adventures of Mr & Mrs Sandboys and Family*.

'A wonder of beauty that seemed to realise the fiction of fairy-land': 'Shall the Crystal Palace Stand?', *Punch*, 1851.

A very admirable conception from an active and intelligent brain: Ruskin, *The Stones of Venice*, appendix 17.

Paddington Railway Terminus building: Brunel had worked previously with Wyatt (see Buchanan, *Brunel*). He now persuaded him to work at night on the exquisite floral iron work detailing of the new building, while continuing to fulfil his duties for the Royal Commissioners at the Crystal Palace during the day.

'When Paxton is got safe out of his court dress': Chatsworth Archive,

Scrapbook of the Guild of Literature and Art, kept by the 6th Duke, Dickens to the Duke, 1 May 1851.

The Derby dinner gave the Duke a public forum: it was reported extensively in the *ILN*, 9 Aug. 1851.

Plans for Mayer de Rothschild's grand romantic mansion: Paxton's designs were drawn as plans by Stokes for presentation to the Royal Academy exhibition in 1854.

Myers' contract with the Baron forms part of the Rosebery Archives at Dalmeny House, Scotland.

The people themselves had now become the exhibition: *The Times* report, *c.* 27 Sept. 1851, 1851 Win., vol. 8, undated item 77.

CHAPTER 18

Possible applications for factories, circuses and theatres: Derby Mechanics Institute speech, *ILN*, 10 Nov. 1850.

Glass roof over the Royal Exchange: see *Civil Engineer and Architects Journal,* vol. 14, 8 Feb. and 29 March 1851.

Paxton's New York Crystal Palace designs were ultimately lost. The building was destroyed by fire in 1858.

A 'Crystal Sanatorium': see *ILN* 18 (1851), p. 621.

'Free circulation of air without direct currents': letter to the editor of *ILN*, 5 July 1851.

The likely cost of fitting-out and maintaining the building: Paxton wrote several letters to *The Times* on this subject, including 15 and 28 July 1851.

The Prince himself . . . against the building's retention: 1851 Win., vol. 7, item 128.

'Mr Paxton's answer is try it': *The Times* (1851 Win., vol. 7, item 124). *The Times* leader as early as 27 June 1851, p. 5, shows its support for the retention of the building only two months after its opening. It continued to press its suit with leading articles throughout the year.

Fox and Henderson's position: their responsibility in taking on the contract for the Crystal Palace for a fixed amount became a financial trap. The company had outlayed almost £180,000 in the construction, almost £70,000 more than Parliament were contracted to pay. In addition, final small sums were withheld until the grounds were reinstated. After auditing of their accounts, Cubitt and Granville arranged for a further £50,000 to be paid to them. They tried to charge for admittance to the empty structure to make up some of their shortfall, bringing them into a battle with the Commissioners for Woods and Forests who forbade it. They fought the pig headedness of the Treasury for months, despite the enormous profit of the Exhibition in general. The losses they sustained as a result sowed the seeds of the company's demise a decade later.

Paxton's honorarium: in the many honoraria given to those involved with the Great Exhibition, only John Scott Russell was omitted; although much of his time had been taken up with private contracts throughout those years, this was undoubtedly unfair given his impetus at an early stage of the planning and he was embittered by the decision.

The committee reported in mid-February: House of Commons Sessional Papers, Report of the Commissioners Appointed to Inquire into the Cost and Applicability of the Exhibition Building.

Made to murder his own child: Paxton's speech at a meeting in the Crystal Palace, 31 March 1852, was reported widely. See the clippings scrapbooks in the possession of the 1851 Royal Commission for the Great Exhibition, at Imperial College, London.

The Crystal Palace had been bought for £70,000: 1851 Win., vol. 10, Grey to the Prince, 13 May 1852.

Barbrook alterations paid for by the Duke: Chatsworth, The Duke's Private Account Books, show March–Dec. 1851 £1,753 and May 1852 £1,282 paid to Paxton.

Salary rises to £650 a year: Chatsworth, Green Vellum Account Books. To put this in perspective, the head gardener at Chiswick was still paid £150 a year at this time, the housekeeper £60 a year and the footman £35 a year.

CHAPTER 19

'A place of perfect solitude': *ILN* quoted by Alan Warwick, *The Phoenix Suburb: A South London Social History,* pp. 101–2.

The most extraordinary structure in the world: *The Builder* 10 (7 Aug. 1852), p. 504.

The grand hall: Barry had also used the idea of a covered central court at an earlier date for the Reform Club – completed 1838 – of which Paxton was a member, though this was unglazed.

Derided this Jacobethan mansion: *The Builder*, vol. 12 (4 May 1854). Revised its criticism vol. 15 (19 Dec. 1857), pp. 738–41.

'I don't believe the Medici were so lodged': Allibone, *'Not Just Grand Mansions'*.

The accident at the central transept: reported in *The Times*, 17 Aug. 1853, p. 8. Twenty tons of woodwork crashed on to the floor, killing two wagon horses instantly.

He drew up plans for four large hotels: *The Builder*, vol. 11 (1853), p. 530.

Tanks of wrought and not cast iron: Brunel Archive, op. cit. Letterbook 9, p. 201. Buchanan, *Brunel*, supplies a useful summary of Brunel's work on the towers in chapter nine. All original documents relating to the work are contained in Brunel's Letterbooks, vols. 7–11.

Wild's dismissal: ibid., vol. 9, p. 266, 2 Nov. 1853, letter to Wild.

CHAPTER 20

'Hextinct hanimals': Packenham, *Victoria RI*, p. 238.

Dinosaurs: the best report of Owen's work is found in Cadbury, *The Dinosaur Hunters*.

The Alhambra court featured running water and a large basin in which Paxton planted a *Victoria regia* lily, the size and structure of whose leaves echoed the structure of the building which housed it.

The Loddiges palm: details in *Cockney Ancestor*, no. 72 (Autumn 1996), p. 5.

The opening ceremony: *ILN*, 17 June 1854, p. 580.

Ruskin's pamphlet: *The Opening of the Crystal Palace, Considered in Some of its Relations to the Prospects of Art*.

Sunday opening: Paxton's advocacy of Sunday opening is made clear in a letter to the 7th Earl of Carlisle, part of the Castle Howard Collection, dated 21 April 1853.

No English architect had . . . constructed a large private mansion in France: according to Marcilhacy, *Les Rothschilds*, p. 93.

'Les plans de Paxton ont enlevé tous les suffrages': ibid., p. 93.

Had been invited to stand as Liberal candidate for Nottingham: un-catalogued letter in Chatsworth, Paxton to William Taylor, 11 March 1852.

CHAPTER 21

Russian cottage at Chatsworth: Chatsworth Accounts show the cottage cost £346 in 1855. Sarah wrote to Paxton on 22 April 1857 that the cottage would be completed that week (Chatsworth, Paxton Group).

200,000 people entered the city on foot: House of Commons Sessional Papers, Report of the Select Committee Appointed to Inquire into the State and Conditions of the Several Communications to and in the Metropolis Including Bridges over the Thames and the Approaches Thereto, Report of 23 July 1855.

Peto, Betts and Brassey in the Crimea: see Walker, *Thomas Brassey*.

Army Works Corps: a folder of all correspondence between Paxton and Panmure, with draft regulations and details of the exercise in all its parts, forms part of the Chatsworth, Paxton Group.

Paxton's Crimea huts: see Herbert, *Pioneers of Prefabrication* pp. 82ff.

Great Victorian Way: Paxton's evidence, given on 23 July 1855, is found in the House of Commons Sessional Papers, Report of the Select Committee into Communications in the Metropolis.

Radical, modern town planning: following the route of London's circle line on the underground, a similar plan had been proposed by William Moseley in 1855, called the 'Crystal Way'. Moseley's plan was less sophisticated but it showed a prevailing appreciation not only for the most obvious route for any such design, but for the materials made popular by the original Crystal Palace.

An impractical visionary: Chadwick, *The Works of Sir J. Paxton*, p. 210.

'I should enormously impress upon you': Brunel Archive, op. cit. Letterbook 10, p. 164, Brunel to Paxton, 30 June 1855.

CHAPTER 22

Brunel's testimonial for George Wythes can be found in Brunel Archive, op. cit. Letterbook 7, p. 269.

Paxton's report on the Queen's Park proposal is quoted in Chadwick, *Works*, p. 65.

The project in Scarborough: designs lost. Paxton's report of 18 July 1862 is contained in the Scarborough Town Council Resolution Minutes.

The Duke appeared to be gazing at him: statements taken after the Duke's death, Chatsworth, item 1298.1–9.

'It is so pleasant to be loved and to know one is': Letters to Paxton on the death of the 6th Duke, ibid., item 1299.1–83.

'You will readily believe that it is not without a feeling of great sorrow': Paxton's resignation letter, Chatsworth, 2nd Series, item 100.44, 27 Jan. 1858.

CHAPTER 23

£500 a year on Paxton for life: the 7th Duke's private account books at Chatsworth show that this was paid in two instalments a year from February 1859 until July 1865.

Hothouses for the Millions: British Library, Patent no. 1420 for Manufacture of Horticultural Buildings or Glazed Structures for Horticultural and Other Purposes (Agricultural Buildings).

More information about Paxton's railway interests in Spain and India is found in Walker, *Thomas Brassey*, and Vignoles, *Charles Blacker Vignoles, Romantic Engineer*, pp. 857–63. An interesting aside to the Bilbao railway project is that the 10,000 local labourers that they hired refused to be paid in paper money – over a ton of cash had to be sent up the mountain in a large coach each fortnight for pay day.

CHAPTER 24

Description of Rockhills: *Norwood News*, 29 June 1956, plus inventory of the house after Paxton's death, Chatsworth, Paxton Group, item no. 1726.

Descriptions of the gardens at Rockhills are taken from the *Journal of Horticulture and Cottage Gardener*, 29 July 1862, p. 325, and *The Cottage Gardener and Country Gentleman*, 4 Sept. 1860, pp. 337–40.

Impossible to succeed without a good wife: Punch Cartoon Library and Archive, Silver Diaries, 9 May 1860.

'One of his happiest efforts': review of Battlesden in obituary of George Stokes, *Building News*, vol. 19, (10 July 1874), p. 57. Sadly, the house was never lived in by Edward Turner but leased. It was bought by the Woburn Estate on his death and demolished soon after, in 1885.

Shepperton Park: see Chadwick, *Works*, p. 68. Details of this scheme have not survived.

CHAPTER 25

An avant-garde and yet eminently sensible solution: House of Commons Sessional Papers, 2nd Report of the Select Committee on the Sewerage of Towns, July 1862.

'The most marvellous Crystal Palace ever beheld': the Rothschild Archive, London, Charlotte de Rothschild correspondence, letter to her sons, 17 Oct. 1863, reference 000/84.

The Crystal Palace Paris: for Paxton's designs, see Chadwick, *Works*, p. 158, and also Hix, *The Glasshouse*.

'More fatal overwork!': Punch Cartoon Library and Archive, Silver diary, 14 June 1865.

'The Prince of Gardeners': *GC* 24 (1865), p. 544.

'The greatest gardener of his time': *The Times*, 9 June 1865.

PAXTON'S LEGACIES

Paxton's design philosophy led, in the twentieth century to those embraced by Le Corbusier in the 1930s and by Richard Buckminster Fuller in the 1950s. Interviewed about the US Pavilion at the Montreal Expo of 1967, Buckminster Fuller said 'from the inside there will be uninterrupted visual contact with the exterior world . . . but the unpleasant effects of climate, heat, dust, bugs, glare . . . will all be modulated by the skin to provide a garden of Eden interior'. He might have been Paxton discussing the Great Victorian Way.

Paxton's greenhouses at Chatsworth were, during the early years of the twentieth century, destroyed. There are some small, early ridge and furrow greenhouses which have managed to survive, including one in the kitchen garden at Lismore Castle. The paradise of curious beauty that was the Great Stove stood firm until 27 May 1920 when, too expensive to heat and maintain, it was blown up. It was so well built that it took several attempts and only when Paxton's grandson, Charlie Markham, arrived with 200 pounds of explosives did it finally fall. Now the vast plastic-skinned greenhouses of the Eden Project are the Great Stoves of the twenty-first century.

Amherstia nobilis flowers gloriously each spring in the Palm House at Kew.

Barbrook was demolished in 1963. Edensor thrives. Mentmore is in the process of being converted into a luxury hotel. Ferrières stands empty, owned by the University of Paris.

Paxton's other additions to the gardens at Chatsworth have all survived. Birkenhead Park is the only landscape in England to be originally designed as a public park to have been given grade one listing. It is the recipient of a Heritage Fund Lottery grant, is undergoing restoration. Several of Paxton's other parks, in Liverpool and Scotland, are also subject to restoration plans.

The *Daily News* continued as a truly radical newspaper until 1930 when it became the *News Chronicle*. It finally declined in the late 1950s. *The Gardener's Chronicle* ran to three series – the last one ended at vol. 179 in 1976 when it became *GC and Horticultural Trade Journal*. In 1985 it became *Horticulture Week*. It continues to this day.

After the fire in 1936 the Crystal Palace site was never redeveloped. It remains desolate.

Paxton's only son George disappeared, possibly to America. Some reports suggest that Paxton's grandson, little George, pursued his father's feckless habits. Their descendants have not been traced by genealogists. Blanche and her husband left Ireland and moved to America with their children, from where their second son, Alwyn, the eldest surviving male in the Paxton line, returned to England, changed his surname to Paxton and inherited the substantial capital built up by his grandfather. Emily soon moved to Darley House with George Stokes, who died within a decade. She re-married Joseph Dalton, a vicar. They had no children. Victoria had a second daughter five years after Paxton's death. Rosa had three further children. Annie divorced Wayte after bearing him four children. She remarried a vicar.

A Paxton family tree can be found at
        http//www.apvm51.dsl.pipex.com/SirJosephPaxton1.htm.

A NOTE ON CURRENCY

The current approximate value of each pound in Paxton's pocket:

1830 = £37.76
1835 = £48.98
1840 = £39.40
1845 = £46.47
1851 = £53.30
1855 = £41.19
1860 = £46.47
1865 = £47.69

Source: Bank of England Enquiries Service

ACKNOWLEDGEMENTS

This book is no different from the thousands of others that could not have been written without the support of an enormous number of people. I owe a great deal to those whose serious generosity and kindness have made the writing of it not only pleasurable, but possible, and my wholehearted thanks go to: The Trustees of the Chatsworth Settlement who graciously allowed me months of access to their glorious archives. I would particularly like to thank Her Grace the Duchess of Devonshire, the archivists Peter Day and Charles Noble, Dianne Naylor, Andrew Peppit and Stuart Band, the head gardener Ian Webster, Simon Seligman, Helen Marchant, David Robinson, John Oliver, who was particularly helpful on the origin of the rocks for the rockery at Chatsworth, Gerard Coleman and Sandra Elliott, Fran Beardsley and Pauline Vardy.

Elsewhere, I received help from all the following and to them I am similarly grateful: Carol Anderson; James F. Anderson, from Paxton, Illinois; Melanie Aspey and Elaine Penn at the Rothschild Archive in London; Bob Aspinall at the Museum of London; Ivon Asquith; Stephen Ball at the National Library of Ireland; Roger Beaton at the Bank of England; Susan Bennett; Dennis Bidwell; Trevor Brighton; Marie Thérèse de Brignac, archivist at the Château de Prégny; Mrs G. H. Briscoe – an extraordinary plantswoman – the staff at the British Library St Pancras and at Colindale and to Edmund King at Colindale; John Kenworthy Browne; Geraldine Burdis; Jeremy Carey at Tavistock Communications; Emma Challiner and her colleagues at the Wirral Archive and Library; Patricia Cifrian Ruiz de Alda; Pam Clark at the Royal Archives Windsor; Gillian Clegg; Gill Coleridge; Lord Dalmeny; Spencer De Gray at Norman Foster Associates; Ray Desmond; Mrs Desseine; Derek Dottie and his colleagues Stephen Vose, Steve Perkins and Nigel Sharp at Liverpool County Council Parks and Heritage departments; Nigel Farndale; Moureen Fearn and Vince Gwilym; Sister Aileen Fenton; Judith Flanders; Jill Furlong, Head of Special Collections at University College London; Mike Garbutt at Wirral County Council; Elizabeth Gilbert and staff at the Lindley Library of the Royal Horticultural Society; Jennifer Gill, archivist at Durham

County Records Office; John Glasse; Ruth Gordon; Hervé Grandsart, Chargé de Mission au Château de Ferrières; Anthony Grayling; Gill Green at Woburn Heritage Centre; Mr Simon Halabi; Carolyn Hammond, Reference Librarian at Chiswick Public Library; Eddie and Ann Hanley at Lismore Presentation Convent; Melvyn Harrison and the Crystal Palace Foundation; Mary Houlihan at Lismore Heritage Centre; Lady Inglewood, descendant of Rosa; Ken Kiss at the Crystal Palace Museum; Angela Knox; Mike Langham; Patrick Leary at the University of Indiana for information about Henry Silver's diaries; Professor Robert Lee; Andrew Lewis at the National Register of Archives Historic Manuscripts Commission; Mark Leyton at Mentmore House; the wonderful staff of the London Library and at the House of Lords Record Office; Hannah Lowrey at University of Bristol Special Collections; Ann Marshall and the staff at the library of the Royal Botanical Gardens Kew, Kate Pickard, archivist at RBG Kew, Emma Fox, the keeper of the Palm House at RBG Kew, Dr Jeffrey Wood at the RBG Kew herbarium and Professor Peter Crane, the director of RBG Kew; Jock and June Miller; Ravi Mirchandani; Alfred Mueller at Yale University Library; Keith Oliver and Stephen Guy at the Conservation Department of the National Museums and Galleries on Merseyside; Susan Orlean who unwittingly started it all; Michael Penruddock at Lismore Castle; Valerie Phillips, archivist to the Royal Commission for the Exhibition of 1851; the staff of the Public Record Office Kew; Eddie Richardson, my mainline to the Paxton family tree; John Richomme; Dr Christopher Ridgway and Alison Brisby at Castle Howard Archives; Jim Rieuwerts; Deborah Rogers; the Earl and Countess of Rosebery; Baron Guy de Rothschild; Lord Rothschild; Joanne Rothwell at Dungarvon Library; Bernadette Ruzsa; Gerry Savage at Upper Norwood Library; Clare Sawyer, James Collett White and Nigel Lutt, archivists at the Bedfordshire and Luton Archives and Record Service; the late Fritz Spiegl; Peter Straus; Tessa at *Country Life*; Julie Thornhill at the Burton Closes Care Centre; Mr and Mrs Tyacke, descendants of Victoria; Christiane Viedma at L'Art du Texte, Geneva; Theo Wayte, Annie's great grandaughter; Terry Wilson and Susan Worrall at Coventry City Council.

I gratefully acknowledge the Harold Hyam Wingate Foundation without whose generous assistance it would have been far harder to research Paxton's life.

Thank you to my extraordinary agent, Stephanie Cabot, to Eugenie Furniss, Hamish Crombie and Doug Davis, all at William Morris. And in particular to the most visionary of all editors, Nicholas Pearson, whose work on this book makes it at least in part his own. Also to Rachel Skerry, Zoe Mayne, Nick Davies, Julian Humphries, Nicky Eaton, Sarah White and Kate Hyde of Fourth Estate.

My parents Iain and Sally Colquhoun deserve my love and thanks for all their encouragement and help. Freddie was the sweetest of boys, whose smile made the worst bits better and the best bits great. But it would have been impossible to finish this book without the support and love of my husband David Miller, who shouldered the pressures that it brought with his innate grace, patience and humour. This book is for him.

For permission to quote from manuscript sources, I am indebted to:

Her Majesty the Queen
The Duke of Devonshire and the Chatsworth Settlement Trustees
    for permission to quote extensively from the papers in their
    collection, including: the 6th Duke's Diaries, the 6th Duke's
    Group of Correspondence, the 2nd Series of Correspondence, the
    Paxton Group of Correspondence including the Indian
    Correspondence, the 6th Duke's Album of the Guild of
    Literature and Art, the Green Vellum Account Books, the 6th
    Duke's Scrapbook for the Queen's Visit of 1843, collected maps
    and plans and uncatalogued material.
The Architectural Review.
The Director of Information Services, University of Bristol, for
    permission to quote from the correspondence of I. K. Brunel.
Cambridge University Press for permission to quote from *The
    Correspondence of Charles Darwin*, ed. F. Burkhardt and S. Smith.
Faber and Faber Ltd for permission to quote from Peter Carey's
    Oscar & Lucinda [in Australia: University of Queensland Press,
    St. Lucia (1998)]
The Punch Cartoon Library and Archive for permission to quote
    from the unpublished Diary of Henry Silver, © Punch Ltd.
The Rothschild Archive, London.
The Royal Commission for the Exhibition of 1851. Quotations are
    made from the 1851 Archive and the Windsor Archive, on
    permanent loan.
The Royal Horticultural Society, Lindley Library for permission to
    quote from Transactions and Reports.

The Smithsonian Institution Libraries, The Dibner Library of the History of Science and Technology, Washington, DC, for permission to quote from the Charles Darwin papers.

All reasonable efforts have been made by the author and the publisher to trace the copyright holders of the material quoted in this book. In the event that the author or the publisher are contacted by any of the untraceable copyright holders after the publication of this book, the author and the publisher will endeavour to rectify the position accordingly.

SELECT BIBLIOGRAPHY

1. MANUSCRIPT SOURCES

The 1851 Commission:
    Correspondence of the Commissioners
    The Windsor Archive, on loan from the Royal Archive
Bedfordshire County Records Office:
    Russell Papers
Bristol University Library, Special Collections:
    The Brunel Archive
The British Library:
    Correspondence of Paxton and the 6th Duke of Devonshire
    Specification of Patents: Agriculture etc. 1661–1858, vol. 81, Greenhouses
The Chatsworth Settlement Trust:
    Paxton Group of Correspondence
    6th Duke's Diaries
    6th Duke's Group of Correspondence
    The 2nd Series of Correspondence
    6th Duke's Scrapbook of the Guild of Literature and Art
    6th Duke's Scrapbook of the Queen's Visit
    Indian Correspondence
    7th Duke's Diaries
    Green Vellum Account Books
    Collected maps, plans and uncatalogued material
House of Commons Reports:
    1852 Report of the Commissioners Appointed to Inquire into the Cost and
        Applicability of the Exhibition Building in Hyde Park
    1855 Report of the Select Committee on Metropolitan Communications
    1860 Report of the Select Committee on the Serpentine
    1860 Report of the Select Committee on the Thames Embankment
    1862 Report of the Select Committee on the Thames Embankment Bill
    1862 Second Report on the Best Means of Utilising the Sewage of Cities
        and Towns of England
    1864 Report of the Select Committee on Sewage (Metropolis)
Imperial College, London:
    Edwin Chadwick Correspondence
Presentation Convent, Lismore:
    Annals

Public Record Office, Kew:
    1838 Royal Gardens Inquiry
Punch Cartoon Library and Archive:
    Unpublished Diary of Henry Silver
The Rothschild Archive, London:
    Correspondence of Charlotte de Rothschild
The Royal Archive, Windsor:
    Paxton Correspondence
The Royal Botanic Society, Kew:
    The Directors' Correspondence
    Lindley Correspondence
The Royal Horticultural Society, Lindley Library:
    The Book of Handwriting of Undergardeners
    Minute Books
University College London:
    Chadwick Correspondence
Wirral Archive:
    Papers of the Birkenhead Commission

2. PUBLISHED MATERIAL

Ackroyd, Peter. *Dickens.* London: Sinclair Stephenson, 1990

Adams. *Gem of the Peak.* London, 1850

Aiton, William T. *Hortus Kewensis.* London, 1789

Aldrich, Megan. 'The Furniture of J G Crace and Son'. *The Magazine of Antiques.* New York, (June 1991)

Allibone, J. 'Not Just Grand Mansions. The Rothschilds in the Vale of Aylesbury'. *Country Life,* 183 (16 and 23 Feb. 1989)

Altick, Richard D. *Victorian People and Ideas.* London: Dent, 1973

Amherst, The Hon. A. M. T. *A History of Gardening in England.* London, 1895

Anthony, John. *An Illustrated Life of Sir Joseph Paxton.* Aylesbury: Shire Publications, 1973

Bazalgette, J. W. 'On the Metropolitan System of Drainage etc.'. *Minutes and Proceedings, Institution of Civil Engineers,* 24 (1865), p. 38

Beaumont, Robert. *The Railway King: A Biography of George Hudson.* London: Headline, 2002

Beaver, Patrick. *The Crystal Palace 1851–1936: A Portrait of Victorian Enterprise.* London: Hugh Evelyn, 1970

Beckett, Derrick. *Brunel's Britain.* Newton Abbot, Devon: David and Charles, 1980

Bird, Anthony. *Paxton's Palace.* London: Cassell, 1976

Bourne, J. M. *Patronage and Society in Nineteenth Century England.* London: Edward Arnold, 1986

Brooks, John Thomas. *Diary of a Bedfordshire Squire 1794–1858*. Ed. Richard Morgan. Bedfordshire Historical Records Society, 1987

Buchanan, Angus. *Brunel: The Life and Times of Isambard Kingdom Brunel*. London: Hambledon, 2002

Buchanan, Angus, Kiss, Ken and Jones, Stephen. 'Brunel and the Crystal Palace'. *Industrial Archaeology Review*, (1994)

Burkhardt, Frederick and Smith, Sydney. *The Correspondence of Charles Darwin, vol. 3, 1844–6*. Cambridge: Cambridge University Press, 1985

Cadbury, Deborah. *The Dinosaur Hunters*. London: 4th Estate, 2000

Campbell, Susan. 'The Genesis of Queen Victoria's New Kitchen Garden'. *Garden History Journal*, (1984), pp. 100–19

Campbell-Culver, Maggie. *The Origin of Plants*. London: Headline, 2002

Cannadine, David. *Aspects of Aristocracy*. London: Yale University Press, 1994

Carre, Jacques. 'Lord Burlington's Gardens at Chiswick'. *Garden History Journal*, 1(3) (Summer 1973)

Cavendish, W., 6th Duke of Devonshire. *Handbook to Chatsworth*. London: Privately printed, 1845

Chadwick, Edwin. *Report on the Sanitary Condition of the Labouring Population of Great Britain*. Poor Law Commission (1834–47), 1842

Chadwick, George F. *The Works of Sir J. Paxton 1803–1865*. London: Architectural Press, 1961

— 'Paxton and Sydenham Park'. *Architectural Review* (Feb. 1961)

— 'The Great Stove at Chatsworth'. *Architectural History*, 4 (1961), p. 129

— 'The Genius of Sir Joseph Paxton'. *Country Life*, 9 Dec. 1965, pp. 1806–8

Chapman, Caroline and Dormer, Jane. *Elizabeth and Georgiana: The Duke of Devonshire and His Two Duchesses*. London: John Murray, 2002

Chapple, E. C. and Pollard, A. *The Letters of Mrs Gaskell*. Manchester University Press, 1966

Clark, George S. R. Kitson. *The Making of Victorian England*. The Ford Lectures. London: Methuen, 1962

Clifford, Augustus. *Sketch of the Life of the 6th Duke of Devonshire*. London: privately printed, 1864

Cole, Sir Henry. *Fifty Years of Public Work*. 2 vols. London: George Bell & Sons, 1884

Conway, Hazel. *Public Parks*. Princes Risborough, Bucks.: Shire Publications, 1996

Cook, Thomas & Son. *The Business of Travel: A Fifty Year Record of Progress*. London: Thomas Cook & Son, 1891

— *The Story of Thomas Cook*. London: Cook, Thomas & Son, 1966

Cornforth, John. 'Devonshire House', Parts 1 and 2. *Country Life*, 151 (13 and 20 Nov. 1980)

— 'Chiswick House, London'. *Country Life*, 166 (16 Feb. 1995)

Craven, Maxwell and Stanley, Michael. *The Derbyshire Country House*. 2 vols. Derbyshire Museum Service, 1982

Crowe, Sir Joseph. *Reminiscences of Thirty-Five Years of My Life.* London: John Murray, 1895

Darby, M. F. 'Joseph Paxton's Waterlily'. In *Bourgeois and Aristocratic Cultural Encounters in Garden Art 1550–1850.* Michael Conan (ed.). Washington, DC: Dumbarton Oaks, 2002

Davis, John R. *The Great Exhibition.* Stroud, Glos.: Sutton, 1999

Desmond, R. G. C. 'Victorian Gardening Magazines'. *Garden History Journal,* 5(3) (1977), pp. 47–66

Devonshire, Deborah. *The Garden at Chatsworth.* London: Frances Lincoln, 1999
— *Chatsworth – The House.* London: Frances Lincoln, 2002

Dickens, Charles. 'The Private History of the Palace of Glass'. *Household Words,* 43 (18 Jan. 1851), pp. 385–91

Dodd, Stephen. *An Account of the Town of Woburn.* 1818

Edwards, Tudor. 'Sir Joseph Paxton: The Versatile Gardener'. *History Today,* (Dec. 1965), pp. 855–64

Elliott, Brent. *Flora: An Illustrated History of the Garden Flower.* London: Scriptum Editions, 2001

Emmerson, George. *J. Scott Russell: A Great Victorian Engineer and Naval Architect.* London: John Murray, 1977

Ffrench, Yvonne. *The Great Exhibition, 1851.* London: Harvill, 1950

Fletcher, H. R. *The Story of the Royal Horticultural Society, 1804–1968.* London: Oxford University Press, 1969

Forster, J. *Forster's Life of Dickens.* Abridged and revised by G. Gissing. London: Chapman and Hall, 1903

Fox, Francis. *River, Road and Rail – Some Engineering Reminiscences.* London: John Murray, 1904

Girouard, Mark. 'Lismore Castle'. *Country Life,* 135 (6 and 13 Aug. 1964), pp. 336–40 and 389–93
— 'The Genius of Sir Joseph Paxton'. *Country Life,* 138 (1967), pp. 1606–8
— *Life in the English Country House: A Social and Architectural History.* London: Yale University Press, 1978
— *The Victorian Country House.* London: Yale University Press, 1979

Gloag, John. *Victorian Taste – Some Social Aspects of Architectural and Industrial Design 1820–1900.* London: Adam and Charles Black, 1962
— *Mr Loudon's England.* Newcastle-upon-Tyne: Oriel Press, 1970

Glover, Stephen. *The Peak Guide.* Derby, 1830

Godber, Joyce. *The History of Bedfordshire.* Bedfordshire County Council, 1984

Gower, H., Countess Granville. *Letters of Harriet, Countess Granville 1810–1845.* 2 vols. Ed. F. Leveson-Gower. London: Longman, 1894

Granville, A. B. *The Spas of England & Principal Sea Bathing Places,* vol. 2. London, 1841

Hadfield, M. *Pioneers in Gardening.* London: Routledge & Kegan Paul, 1955

Hall, Michael. 'Village Eden'. *Country Life,* 160 (10 Aug. 1989)

— 'Crace in Favour'. *Country Life*, 162 (11 Oct. 1990), pp. 74–7

Halliday, Stephen. *The Great Stink of London: Bazalgette and the Cleansing of the Victorian Capital*. Stroud, Glos.: Sutton, 1999

Hammond, J. L. and B. *The Village Labourer 1760–1832*. London: Longman, 1911

Hanley, Ann (ed.). *Lismore Convent and Gardens*. Lismore: Blackhall Publishing, 1999

Hansard's Parliamentary Debates. Third Series, vols 137–176 (1855–64)

Harley, Basil and Jessie (eds). *A Gardener at Chatsworth: Three Years in the Life of Robert Aughtie, 1848–1850*. Self-Publishing Association, 1992

Harvey, J. *Early Nurserymen*. London: Phillimore, 1974

Henricus. *The Matlock Tourist and Guide Through the Peak*. Matlock: Bath, 1838

Herbert, Gilbert. *Pioneers of Prefabrication: The British Contribution in the Nineteenth Century*. Baltimore: Johns Hopkins University Press, 1978

Hix, John. *The Glasshouse*. London: Phaidon, 1996

Hobhouse, Christopher. *1851 and the Crystal Palace: An Account of the Great Exhibition and its Contents*. London: John Murray, 1937

Hobhouse, Hermione. *The Crystal Palace and the Great Exhibition – A History of the Royal Commission for the Exhibition of 1851*. London: Athlone Press, 2002

Hooker, W. and Fitch, W. *Victoria Regia, Or Illustrations of the Royal Water Lily*. London: Reeve & Benham, 1851

Houfe, Simon. *Bedfordshire*. London: Pimlico, 1995

Houghton, Walter Edwards. *The Victorian Frame of Mind 1830–1870*. New Haven, CT: Yale University Press, 1957

Johnson, George William. *A History of English Gardening, Chronological, Biographical, Literary*. London, 1829

Jones, Owen. 'An Attempt to Define the Principles Which Should Regulate the Employment of Colour in the Decorative Arts'. *Lectures on the Great Exhibition of 1851, Series 2*. Delivered to the Society of Arts, Manufactures and Commerce. London: David Bogue, 1853

Jordan, Harriet. 'Public Parks'. *Garden History Journal*, 22(1), (1994), p. 85

Kemp, Edward. *How to Lay Out a Small Garden*. London, 1850

Kilby, Charles. *Sketch of the Life of Sir Hugh Inglis, Bart*. Bedfordshire County Records Office, n.d.

Knight, T. A. 'Curvilinear Iron Roofs to Hothouses'. *Transactions of the Horticultural Society*, 5 (1811), art. 26

Koppelkamm, Stefan. *Glasshouses and Wintergardens of the Nineteenth Century*. Trans. Kathrine Talbot. London: Granada, 1981

Langham, Mike. *Buxton: A People's History*. Lancaster: Carnegie Publishing, 2001

Leapman, Michael. *The World for a Shilling: How the Great Exhibition of 1851 Shaped a Nation*. London: Headline, 2001

Le Corbusier. 'The Crystal Palace: A Tribute'. *Architectural Review*, 81 (1937), p. 72

Lees-Milne, J. *The Bachelor Duke: The Life of William Spencer Cavendish*. London: John Murray, 1991

Lemmon, Kenneth. *The Golden Age of Plant Hunters*. London: Phoenix House, 1968

Leveson-Gower, E. F. L. *Bygone Years*. London: John Murray, 1905

Lightman, Bernard (ed.). *Victorian Science in Context*. London: University of Chicago Press, 1997

Lindley, John. *Instructions for Collecting and Packing Seeds Coming from Foreign Countries*. London, 1825

— *The Theory of Horticulture*. London, 1840

Linstrum, David. *Sir Jeffry Wyatville: Architect to the King*. Oxford: Clarendon Press, 1972

Loudon, John Claudius. *A Short Treatise on the Several Improvements Recently Made in Hot Houses*. Edinburgh, 1805

— *Hints on the Formation of Gardens & Pleasure Grounds*. London, 1812

— *Remarks on the Construction of Hot Houses*. London, 1817

— *Comparative View of the Curvilinear & Common Mode of Roofing Hot Houses*. London, 1818

— *The Encyclopaedia of Gardening*. London, 1822

— *The Greenhouse Companion*. London, 1824

— *Gardener's Magazine*. 19 vols. London, 1826–43

— *Encyclopaedia of Cottage, Farm and Villa Architecture*. London: Longman, 1835

— *Encyclopedia of Plants*, London, 1829

— *Arboretum et Fructum Britannicum*. 8 vols. London, 1838

— *Hortus Britannicus*. London, 1839

— *The Landscape Gardening and Architecture of the Late H. Repton*. London, 1840

— *On the Laying Out, Planting and Managing of Cemeteries*. London, 1843

— *Self Instruction for Young Gardeners, Foresters, Bailiffs, Land Stewards*. London, 1845

Macintosh, C. *The Greenhouse Hothouse and Stove*. London, 1838

Malchow, H. I. *Gentleman Capitalists – The Social and Political World of Victorian Businessmen*. London: Macmillan, 1991

Mandler, Peter. *The Fall and Rise of the Stately Home*. London: Yale University Press, 1997

Marcilhacy, Pauline Prevost. *Les Rothschilds: Bâtisseurs et Mécènes*. Paris: Flammarion, 1995

Markham, Violet R. *Paxton and the Bachelor Duke*. London: Hodder & Stoughton, 1935

Massingham, B. *A Century of Gardeners*. London: Faber & Faber, 1982

Mawer, A. and Stenton, F. M. *Place Names in Bedfordshire and Huntingdonshire*. Cambridge, 1926

Mayhew, H. and Cruikshank, G. *1851 or the Adventures of Mr & Mrs Sandboys and Family*. London: George Newbold, 1851

McKean, John. *The Crystal Palace, Joseph Paxton and Charles Fox*. London: Phaidon, 1994

Morton, A. G. *The History of Botanical Science*. London: Academic Press, 1981

Mundy, Harriet (ed.). *The Journal of Mary Frampton 1799–1846*. London: Sampson Low, 1885

Olmstead, Frederick Law. *Walks and Talks of an American Farmer in England*. New York, 1852

Orlean, Susan. *The Orchid Thief*. London: William Heinemann, 1998

Packenham, E. *Victoria RI*. London: Weidenfeld & Nicolson, 1964

Page, W. (ed.). *The Victoria History of the County of Bedford*, vol 2. London: 1908

Paxton, J. *The Horticultural Register and General Magazine*. 5 vols. Sheffield: London, 1831–6

— *Paxton's Magazine of Botany and Register of Flowering Plants*. 16 vols. London, 1834–49

— *Practical Treatise on the Culture of the Dahlia*. London, 1838

— *A Pocket Botanical Dictionary*. London, 1840

— *The Cottager's Calendar of Gardening Operations*. London: The Gardener's Chronicle, 1859

— *The Gardener's Chronicle*, 1841–

Paxton, J. and Lindley, J. *Paxton's Flower Garden*. 3 vols. London, 1850–53

Pearce, David. *London's Mansions*. London: Batsford, 1986

Pevsner, Nikolaus. *The Buildings of England – Derbyshire*. Revised Elizabeth Williamson. London: Penguin, 1979

Phillips, Henry. *Sylva Florifera*, 1823

Power, Patrick. *Waterford and Lismore*. Cork University Press, 1937

Proudfoot, Lindsay. 'The Duke of Devonshire's Irish Property'. *Irish Economic History*, 13 (1986)

— *Urban Patronage and Social Authority: The Management of the Duke of Devonshire's Towns in Ireland 1764 to 1891*. Catholic University of America Press, 1995

Pugin, A. W. N. *Contrasts*. London, 1836

Quest-Ritson, Charles. *The English Garden: A Social History*. London: Viking, 2001

Reed, H. S. *A Short History of the Plant Sciences*. Waltham, MA: Chronica Botanica Co., 1942

Reinikka, Merle A. *A History of the Orchid*. Portland, OR: Timber Press, 1995

Rennison, William H. *Succession List of the . . . Clergy of the Dioceses of Waterford and Lismore*. Waterford: Croker and Co., 1920

Rhodes, Ebenezer. *Modern Chatsworth or the Palace of the Peak*. Sheffield, 1837

Rolt, L. C. T. *Victorian Engineering*. London: Allen Lane, 1970

Royal Horticultural Society. *Transactions*, 1st and 2nd Series, 1812–30 and 1835–48

Ruskin, John. *The Stones of Venice*. London: Smith Elder & Co., 1851

— *The Opening of the Crystal Palace Considered in Some of its Relations to the Prospects of Art*. London: Smith Elder & Co., 1854

Sala, George Augustus. *The House that Paxton Built*. London: Ironbrace, Woodenhead & Co., 1851

Shand, P. Morton. 'The Crystal Palace as Structure and Precedent'. *Architectural Review*, 81 (1937), p. 65

Sigaux, Gilbert. *History of Tourism*. Trans. Joan White. London: Leisure Arts, 1966

Slater, Michael. *Douglas Jerrold*. London: Duckworth, 2002

Smit, Tim. *Eden*. London: Bantam, 2001

Society of Arts. *Transactions* 57, 1850–51. London

Spavins, Kenneth and Applin, A. *The Book of Woburn*. Buckingham: Barracuda, 1983

Spencer Silver, Patricia. 'George Myers 1803–75'. *Journal of the Construction History Society*, 5 (1989), pp. 47–55

Spielmann, M. H. *The History of Punch*. London: Cassell, 1895

Stearn, William T. (ed.). *John Lindley 1799–1865: Gardener, Botanist and Pioneer Orchidologist*. Woodbridge: Antique Collectors' Club, 1998

Taylor, G. *Some Nineteenth Century Gardeners*. London: Skeffington, 1951

Thomas, F. M. (ed.). *Fifty Years in Fleet Street: Recollections of Sir John R. Robinson*. London: Macmillan, 1904

Thomas, Keith. *Man and the Natural World: Changing Attitudes in England 1500–1800*. London: Allen Lane, 1983

Thompson, Francis. *English Landed Society in the Nineteenth Century*. London: Routledge & Kegan Paul, 1971

Thorne, Robert. 'Paxton and Prefabrication'. In *Engineering and Architecture*. Ed. D. Walker, T. Happold and J. Kunz. Architectural Design, 1987

Thornton, Clifford E. *The People's Garden: A History of Birkenhead Park*. Metropolitan Borough of Wirral

Tillotson, K. 'New Light on Dickens and the *Daily News*'. *The Dickensian*, 78(2) (summer 1982), pp. 89–92

Vaughan, Adrian. *I. K. Brunel: Engineering Knight Errant*. London: John Murray, 1991

Verrill, A. H. *Wonder Plants & Plant Wonders*. New York: Appleton-Century Co., 1939

Vignoles, K. H. *Charles Blacker Vignoles: Romantic Engineer*. Cambridge University Press, 1982

Walker, Charles. *Thomas Brassey: Railway Builder*. London: Frederick Muller, 1969

Walpole, Horace. *Anecdotes of Painting in England*, vol. 4. Strawberry Hill, London, 1771

Walton, John K. *The English Seaside Resort, A Social History 1750–1914*. Leicester University Press, 1983

Ward, Nathaniel Bagshaw. *On the Growth of Plants in Closely Glazed Cases*. London, 1842

Warner, Tim. 'The Railway that Never Was'. *Derbyshire Life*, 54 (Jan. 1989), p. 32

Warwick, Alan. *The Phoenix Suburb: A South London Social History*. Richmond, Surrey: Blue Boar Press, 1972

Waterhouse-Hawkins, Benjamin. *Crystal Palace: Guide to the Palace and the Park*. London: Dickens & Evans, 1877

Wayte, George H. *Prospecting: 18 Months in Australia and New Zealand*. London: Simpkin, Marshall & Co., 1879

Whitley, T. W. *The Parliamentary Representation of the City of Coventry*. Coventry: Curtis & Beamish, 1894

Whittle, Michael Tyler. *The Plant Hunters*. London: Pan, 1975

Wigley, John. *The Rise & Fall of the Victorian Sunday*. Manchester University Press, 1980

Wyncoll, Keith. 'The Crystal Palace Is on Fire'. *Crystal Palace Foundation News*, (1986)

3. PAMPHLETS

The Crystal Palace: A Dialogue [Against Sunday Opening]. Oxford and London, 1854

The Crystal Palace: Why Should it Not be Open on the Afternoon of Sundays Etc.? London: Simpkin, Marshall & Co., 1855

The Crystal Palace and the Christian Sabbath, A Solemn Protest. Liverpool, 1852

Paxton, J. *What is to Become of the Crystal Palace?* London: Bradbury and Evans, 1851

Medical Man, A. *The Parson & The Palace – Reply to the Letter of Rev. J. Cumming to Sir J. Paxton on the Opening of the Crystal Place on Sundays*. Pamphlet. W. Horsell, 1853

4. PERIODICALS

Reference is made to several newspapers and periodicals including, most notably, the *Illustrated London News*, *The Times*, *Punch*, *The Builder* and both Paxton's and Loudon's horticultural magazines. Specific sources will be found in the endnotes.

PICTURE CREDITS

Chapter 12
'The Queen Arriving at Chatsworth' from the *Illustrated London News*
(December 9th 1843) (© ILN Picture Library)
'The Great Stove' from the *Magazine of Botany* (© Royal Botanic Gardens Kew)

Chapter 14
'Conservative Wall' (© The Devonshire Collection, Chatsworth. Reproduced
by permission of the Duke of Devonshire and the Chatsworth Settlement
Trustees)

Chapter 15
'Annie on Lily Leaf' and 'Interior of the Lily House' both from the
Illustrated London News (November 17th 1849, and November 16th 1850)
(© ILN Picture Library)

Chapter 16
'Paxton's Blotting Paper Sketch for the Great Exhibition' (© The Victoria
& Albert Museum, London)

Chapter 17
'The Great Exhibition of 1851 General View of the Works Looking East';
and 'Glazing Wagon' both from *Illustrated London News* (November 16th
1850 and December 7th 1850) (© ILN Picture Library)

Chapter 18
'Colonel Sibthorpe' from *Punch* (© Punch Cartoon Library)

'Barbrook House' (© The Devonshire Collection, Chatsworth. Reproduced by
permission of the Duke of Devonshire and the Chatsworth Settlement
Trustees)

Chapter 20
'The Iguandodon Dinner' from the *Illustrated London News* (© ILN Picture
Library)

Chapter 23
'Hothouses for the Millions' from *Gardener's Chronicle* (February 4th 1860)
(© Royal Botanic Gardens Kew)

Chapter 25
'The Crystal Palace at St Cloud, Paris' (© The Victoria & Albert Museum,
London)

Plate 1

'Battlesden Park: Gardens and Family' by George Shepherd (1818) (© Bedford County Records Office)

'Paxton's Signature' from the *Book of Handwriting of Under Gardeners and Labourers* (© RHS Lindley)

'The Sixth Duke of Devonshire' by Sir Thomas Lawrence (© The Devonshire Collection, Chatsworth. Reproduced by permission of the Duke of Devonshire and the Chatsworth Settlement Trustees)

'Amherstia nobilis' from the *Magazine of Botany* (© Royal Botanic Gardens Kew)

'Plan of the Great Stove' and photograph of the 'Great Stove' both (© The Devonshire Collection, Chatsworth. Reproduced by permission of the Duke of Devonshire and the Chatsworth Settlement Trustees)

'The Lily Leaf' from *Victoria Regia* by John Fiske Allen, and lithograph of 'The Emperor's Fountain, Chatsworth' by J. C. Bourne, both (© Royal Botanic Gardens Kew)

'Musi Cavendishii', 'Paxton's Letter from Constantinople' and 'Portrait of Sir Joseph Paxton 1836 by Henry P Briggs (© The Devonshire Collection, Chatsworth. Reproduced by permission of the Duke of Devonshire and the Chatsworth Settlement Trustees)

Plate 2

'Sir John Lindley' (1862) (© RHS Lindley)

'William Jackson Hooker' (© Royal Botanic Gardens Kew)

'The Royal Commissioners of The Great Exhibition of 1851' by Henry Wyndham Phillips; 'The Opening of the Great Exhibition by Queen Victoria' by Henry Courtney Selous, 'Aeronautic view of the Palace of Industry For All Nations, from Kensington Palace' by Charles Burton; photograph of 'Crystal Palace Transept in Hyde Park' in 1852 by Benjamin Brecknell Turner; and print of 'Crystal Palace & Park, Sydenham' all (© The Victoria & Albert Museum, London)

'Mentmore: The Meeting of the Baron's Staghounds' by H W Brewer; and 'Baron Meyer de Rothschild' by Joshua Dighton, both (by permission of The Earl of Rosebery)

'Vue du château de Ferrières' by Felix Thorigny (Reproduced with the permission of The Rothschild Archive)

'Lismore Castle' (©RIBA)

'The Great Victorian Way' by Sir Joseph Paxton (© The Victoria & Albert Museum, London)

'Rockhills' (circa 1860) (© The Devonshire Collection, Chatsworth. Reproduced by permission of the Duke of Devonshire and the Chatsworth Settlement Trustees)

INDEX